The Animal Rights/Environmental Ethics Debate

**SUNY Series in
Philosophy and Biology**

David Edward Shaner, Editor

The Animal Rights/ Environmental Ethics Debate
The Environmental Perspective

Edited
Eugene C. Hargrove

STATE UNIVERSITY OF NEW YORK PRESS

Production by Ruth Fisher
Marketing by Dana E. Yanulavich

Published by
State University of New York Press, Albany

For information, address State University of New York Press,
State University Plaza, Albany, NY, 12246

Library of Congress Cataloging-in-Publication Data

The Animal rights, environmental ethics debate : the environmental
    perspective / edited by Eugene C. Hargrove.
        p.   cm.—(SUNY series in philosophy and biology)
    Includes bibliographical references and index.
    ISBN 0-7914-0933-3 (acid-free).—ISBN 0-7914-0934-1 (acid free : pbk.)
    1. Animal rights.   2. Animal rights—Environmental aspects.
3. Human ecology—Moral and ethical aspects.   I. Hargrove, Eugene C., 1944-
II. Series.
HV4711.A575 1992
179′.3—dc20   91-3431
                                                                    CIP

10   9   8   7   6   5   4   3   2

To My Father

Contents

Preface
Animal Welfare Ethics "versus" Environmental Ethics: The Problem of Sentient Life

This book is about the relationship of environmental ethics to animal welfare ethics, especially, the animal liberation position represented by Peter Singer and the animal rights position represented by Tom Regan.[1] The approach of this book is historical. It covers in succession a series of articles and chapters in books that present the evolution of an environmental ethics stance on animal welfare matters as it developed in the last decade. Because this book does not include any author specifically advocating the animal liberation or animal rights perspectives, some readers may erroneously conclude that the book is intentionally biased in favor of environmental ethics literature. The animal welfare positions are not directly defended in this book for two reasons. First, a very large number of books already present those perspectives in great detail. A book that tried to incorporate that literature adequately would be very large and expensive and extensively duplicate selections of readings commonly available. This book has a more modest purpose: to present a series of positions from the standpoint of environmental ethics that has not found its way, in any consistent manner, into the animal welfare ethics literature. In this sense, the book is supposed to complement that literature, not present an alternative. Second, the papers presented in this book are concerned more with clarifying the environmental position than with trying to supplant animal welfare positions. The question at issue in this book is not whether we should adopt an environmental ethic or an animal welfare ethic, but whether an animal welfare ethic

can be an adequate foundation for an environmental ethic; for example, whether our ethical intuitions about the treatment of wild animals in natural exosystems can be justified in terms of animal welfare
ethics. The answers to such questions do not necessarily challenge the
value of animal welfare ethics positions in those areas on which most
of that literature primarily focuses: the treatment of domestic
animals with regard specifically to scientific experimentation and
factory farming.

The animal liberation position of Singer arises directly out of
nineteenth-century utilitarianism as presented by Bentham, in which
good is defined as pleasure and *bad* or *evil* as pain. When *good* and *evil*
are defined in this way, the class of morally considerable entities includes all creatures that are sentient, capable of feeling pain and
pleasure. In his book *Animal Liberation*, Singer makes the division
between animals and "vegetables" somewhere between the oyster and
the shrimp.[2] Regan's animal position, as he presents it in *The Case for
Animal Rights*, is a rejection of Singer's position that is more narrowly
focused on protecting the rights of those nonhuman entities with inherent value—those capable of being the subject of a life—which turn
out to be mammals and no other forms of life.[3]

Neither of these ethics has dealt very effectively with wild animals and natural systems. Singer suggests in his book that humans
have done enough if they stop inflicting unnecessary suffering on wild
animals, and that it is none of our business what animals do to each
other among themselves. We should not become Big Brother after
giving up the role of tyrant, he writes, and we should recognize that
attempts to manipulate ecosystems for the benefit of wild animals (for
example, the elimination of all predators), based on past history, will
likely cause more harm than good, increasing suffering rather than
decreasing it. Singer specifically refuses to consider the possibility that
plants may deserve moral consideration as well, arguing that even if
plants do feel pain, eating them directly rather than eating animals
that have been fed plants will still reduce suffering enough.[4]

Regan, in turn, argues against any direct moral concern for
plants, animals other than mammals, or ecosystems; and he criticizes
environmentalists for protecting species and systems instead of individual mammals, an approach he calles *environmental facism*.[5] According to Regan, environmentalists have their priorities mixed up, showing too little concern for mammals and too much concern for other
biological and botanical forms of life, which he argues are not morally
considerable. He does not totally abandon nonmammals and plants,
however, for he argues that the protection of the habitats of mammals

will also incidentally benefit them. Regan's disapproval of the environmental perspective is especially clear with regard to endangered species. He holds that the individual members of endangered species are no more or less worthy of moral concern than individuals representing nonendangered species.[6] Like Singer, Regan ultimately recommends a policy of noninterference, letting animals be, although he does come close to suggesting the removal of predators from natural systems, a policy that, as already noted, Singer rejects.[7]

The relationship of environmental ethics literature to the animal liberation position of Singer (which is not a rights position) and the animal rights position of Regan (which is not a utilitarian position) is inexact and sometimes confusing, not only because the differences between these two positions were not always clearly understood, but also because environmental ethics relates to and is troubled by each position in very different ways. Because the pain and suffering of wild animals is a difficult theoretical and practical issue in environmental ethics, there always has been a close relationship between environmental ethics and animal liberation literature. Nevertheless, because environmental ethicists are nearly unanimous in rejecting utilitarianism as the foundation of environmental ethics, on the grounds that the anthropocentric instrumentalism explicit in utilitarianism is one of the primary causes of the environmental crisis, it is difficult, if not impossible, for animal liberationists and environmental ethicists to find a common starting point for debate. Because environmentalists often speak as if nature has or ought to have rights, rights theory has also been an important topic in environmental ethics, inviting comparative debate with animal rights theorists. Nevertheless, because environmentalists are nearly unaminous in rejecting rights for nature, debate between environmental ethicists and animal rights theorists has not been very fruitful. Of the two positions, the animal liberation position of Singer has been discussed more fully in environmental ethics literature because the position was already fully developed before environmental ethics emerged as a distinct subject area.

Environmental ethicists have not been especially concerned with defending environmental ethics against animal welfare ethics. Environmental ethics as a professional field can trace its origins to the first Earth Day in 1970, when environmentalists began seeking out philosophers and asking them to deal with the ethical issues in environmental affairs. The field developed slowly during the 1970s and did not have a commonly agreed upon name until the philosophy journal *Environmental Ethics* began publication in 1979, thereby providing an appropriate label. During that first decade, environmental ethicists

did little more than tentatively look into the possibility of creating a
field. At that time they were interested primarily in determining
whether (and how) environmentalist attitudes could be morally justified. Animal liberation, which developed as a field much more quickly,
because of the impact of Singer's *Animal Liberation,* was an important issue at that time, but not the primary one, for much more attention was usually focused on the Lynn White debate, which concerned
the philosophical and religious origins of the environmental crisis.
Animal liberation was not viewed as an alternative or competing
theory, but as a position that ought to be taken into consideration and
that might be usefully incorporated into the environmental ethics of
the future, however it developed.

The formal debate about rights for nature officially began in
1974, the year before the publication of Singer's *Animal Liberation,*
with the publication of three books: William Blackstone's *Philosophy
and Environmental Crisis,* Christopher Stone's *Should Trees Have
Standing? Toward Legal Rights for Natural Objects,* and John Passmore's *Man's Responsibility for Nature: Ecological Problems and
Western Traditions.*[8] The Blackstone book, which was based on a con-
ference held at the University of Georgia in 1971, contained a paper by
Joel Feinberg, "The Rights of Animals and Unborn Generations." In
this paper, Feinberg argues that rights can apply only to entities
capable of having interests and that interests are based on desires and
aims, which in turn presuppose some kind of belief or cognitive awareness.[9] Feinberg concludes that it is meaningful to speak of animals
having rights, but he finds vegetables, species, dead persons, human
vegetables, fetuses, and future generations to be more problematic.
Stone, in an extended version of an essay that originally was published
in a special issue of the *Southern California Law Review* in 1972,
takes the matter of rights in a different direction, toward legal rights
for animals, plants, and ecosystems. Using the legal precedents of
rights for corporations and human vegetables, neither of which have
minds, he argues that any entity capable of being harmed and benefited can acquire legal rights by legislation or by the extension of legal
precedent through court action. Although Stone's discussion is primarily legal, he suggests that legal rights for nature, once they are
recognized by a court system, could gradually translate into moral
rights for nature as well.[10] Finally, Passmore, in the first full-length
book on environmental ethics by a philosopher, argues against rights
for nature on the grounds that rights are not applicable to nonhumans and that extending rights to nonhuman entities will bring about
the end of Western civilization.[11] Passmore argues that changes in

behavior toward animals in the nineteenth century should not be interpreted as an extension of moral rights to animals, but rather as the restriction of human rights over animals.[12] Although he concedes that humans do have moral responsibilities with regard to nature, these are anthropocentric: they are not responsible *to* nature, but rather *for* nature *to* other human beings, the point of the title of his book. (Passmore's belief that environmental ethics requires a rights theory is apparently based on two passages in Aldo Leopold's essay, "The Land Ethic," where he speaks of the right of nature to exist and of the biotic rights of songbirds, and perhaps on the fact that environmentalists frequently talk in terms of rights, even though they have no idea what they are saying.[13])

Taken together, these positions staked out a lot of territory—the extension of rights to animals, the extension of rights to nature generally, and the restriction of rights that humans had previously possessed by default—and provided the context within which Singer's *Animal Liberation* would be read by proto-environmental ethicists in the following year. Passmore, who is actually arguing that environmental ethics is not needed, takes a very conservative position, accepting that our behavior toward animals has changed, but denying that the change has any conceptual significance. The connecting thread between the other two positions is their discussion of marginal persons: human vegetables. Although Feinberg finds human vegetables problematic, he accepts rights for animals as a workable possibility. Stone, in contrast, embraces human vegetables, along with corporate entities, as noncontroversial rights holders. Singer's position falls into natural opposition to the conservative view of Passmore and the radical view of Stone. It is, however, at least on the surface, similar to Feinberg's position, because it elevates healthy animals to the moral status of defective humans and denies the further extention of rights to plants and other (nonliving) elements of nature.

When Singer's book appeared in 1975, it was viewed as an alternative rights theory and placed alongside the theoretical speculations of Stone and Feinberg in opposition to the conservative view of Passmore. For example, John Rodman's influential review discussion, "The Liberation of Nature?" which appeared in *Inquiry* in 1977, stresses the similarities between the positions of Singer and Stone, criticizing both for developing rights theories that although elevating the status of animals in some respects also degrades them by assigning them a status comparable to that of disfunctional humans.[14] There are several reasons why this "error" was made. First, as noted earlier, a rights debate had already begun, and it was natural to incorporate Singer's views into that debate. Second, because Singer was coeditor with Tom Regan of a historical anthology called *Animal Rights and Human Obligations*, the term *animal liberation* was taken uncritically to be a synonym for *animal rights*. [15] Third, Singer discusses the possibility of rights for animals in the preface of his book and continues this discussion in the first two pages of the first chapter, where he shows that speculations about rights for animals arose directly and immediately out of the debate over the rights of women in the nineteenth century. Although Singer does not explicitly claim to have developed a rights theory, he does not speak against rights for animals or indicate explicitly anywhere in the book that his view is not a rights theory. Furthermore, the index directs readers to various parts of the book that are supposed to be discussing rights (although the word *right* frequently does not appear in those discussions). It seems likely that Singer, from his standpoint, though not actually arguing for a rights theory as such, did not want to speak against such theories and further wanted to make his own views appear more reasonable by tying them to the historical debate in the nineteenth century, which though developing out of Bentham's utilitarianism was focused on animal rights. It is even possible that Singer may have been undecided about the relationship of his position to rights theory at the time he wrote his book. In any event, the distinction between animal liberation and animal rights was not fully clarified until the mid-1980s, after Singer and Regan began debating each other and Regan's own book, *The Case for Animal Rights*, was published. Singer first acknowledged that his discussion of rights in *Animal Liberation* was inessential in an article published in *Ethics* in 1978, "The Fable of the Fox and the Unliberated Animals." [16]

This book does not follow up on all aspects of the animal liberation/animal rights debate as it developed in the late 1970s. For example, it makes no mention of (1) the argument that animals do not have rights because they do not speak a language and therefore are not able to make claims, or (2) the debate over the limits of moral considerability. The former is omitted because those discussions did not help clarify the relationship of animal welfare ethics and environmental ethics. [17] The latter is omitted because it focuses on a boundary that is not contested within the animal welfare/environmental ethics debate, although many environmental ethicists do extend their conception of moral considerability to include nonliving components of natural systems. In environmental ethics literature, the argument that animals are unable to make claims because they cannot speak is undermined by Stone's legal rights position. The primary impact of the debate over moral considerability has been the establishment of a term that allows ethicists to speak in general terms about the moral status of nonhumans without commitment to a specific theory or position.

This book begins with an essay by Richard A. Watson, "Self-Consciousness and the Rights of Nonhuman Animals and Nature," published in the second issue of *Environmental Ethics* in 1979. The paper is an attempt to develop and apply a historically accurate account of rights to the debate over animal rights and rights for nature. Although the paper has received little attention, it carefully maps out the limits of a traditional approach to the issues with some surprising results. Because Watson is a Cartesian scholar, the paper can be read as an example of the degree to which Cartesianism, believed by many to be the cause of the environmental crisis and the mistreatment of animals, can be stretched to accommodate the animal rights and environmental ethics perspectives. In the end, Watson concedes that many animals may qualify as rights holders intrinsically, and he also condones the assignment of rights to entities that do not qualify, if necessary, for behavioral convenience (the approach we take with regard to human children). Although Watson "falsely" attributes a rights position to Singer, his discussion, nevertheless, insightfully shows that key elements of Singer's view ultimately are based not simply on sentience, but on self-awareness, another name for the self-consciousness that Watson finds in traditional rights theory. His analysis of Stone's proposal also reveals moral problems that would develop if it were incorporated into current law, and he shows that Stone does not really manage to develop a theory that eliminates reference to higher mental functions. Watson, in my view, is less successful in his treatment of Leopold's discussion of biotic rights, which, as I have argued elsewhere, is not an important feature of Leopold's overall position and can easily be removed without any noticeable impact.[18] Readers should bear in mind when evaluating Watson's position that, though he is a Cartesian, his position is not anthropocentric, because he acknowledges that some animals other than humans may qualify as rights holders. The pool of creatures eligible for rights-holder status is only slightly more restrictive than Regan's in *The Case for Animal Rights*, primarily because Watson insists that individual animals not be recognized as having rights unless they intend to act with or against moral principles; that is, are consciously trying to act as moral agents within a moral community.

The second paper in this collection, J. Baird Callicott's "Animal Liberation: A Triangular Affair," is the single most influential paper written by an environmental ethicist on the subject of animal welfare ethics. Callicott argues that animal liberation and environmental ethics require distinct and incompatible foundations. In particular, he argues that pain, a key element in the utilitarian calculus, is morally irrelevant in terms of the land ethic. Curiously, however, Callicott, who is the chief defender of and apologist for Leopold's land ethic, leaves open the possibility that a rights theory could be developed within the framework of the Leopold's position, although he does not elaborate on how one might go about it. With the publication of this paper, most animal welfare ethicists abandoned their efforts to create an environmental ethic based on animal liberation or animal rights foundations. Although Callicott now regrets his stridency in this particular paper and some overstatement, and is now trying to mend fences with the animal welfare movement, he does not seem to have rejected any part of his basic argument.

Bryan Norton's paper, "Environmental Ethics and Nonhuman Rights," is a third major attempt to clarify the relationship between animal welfare ethics and environmental ethics. In this case, however, it is not intended as part of a dialogue with animal liberationists, but rather as a guide to these matters for environmentalists who wish to argue for the preservation of nature in terms of rights. In a note, Norton speaks favorably of Watson's analysis, but points out that Watson's necessary conditions for rights holding have been viewed by rights advocates as being too restrictive to be taken seriously. To produce a more persuasive argument, he substitutes a more general set of conditions, which he argues would apply to any utilitarian or deontological rights theory. Although Norton is aware that Singer has abandoned rights as an essential element of his utilitarian position, he treats Singer's animal liberation position as a rights position, taking the word *right* in a broader sense in which it means something similar to Goodpaster's term *moral considerability*. Norton makes two critically important points in this paper. First, rights talk is of little help in efforts to preserve natural systems because rights are tied to the specific interests of individuals, and what is good for the individuals within a system most likely will bear little or no direct relationship to the good of the system as a whole. Although it is not in the personal interest of plants and animals be killed and eaten, it is essential for the continuation of the system in a natural state that many of them suffer this fate. Second, attempts to assign rights to natural collectives on the model of corporate entities in law, following out Stone's suggestion, is completely arbitrary, because any particular collective is also part of many other collectives. For example, a particular area could just as easily be assigned rights as a mountain or a forest, and the assignment would depend not on the interests of the natural areas, but on the interests of the humans pushing for the designation; that is, whether they are mountain climbers, bird watchers, or representatives of a paper mill or a mining company.

Although Paul W. Taylor's paper, "The Ethics of Respect for Nature," was published approximately six months before Norton's essay, I have placed it after Norton's because it represents a new direction in the debate. Rather than simply evaluating and rejecting rights theory, Taylor develops an alternative position. This position takes a biocentric perspective, calling for respect for the inherent worth of plants and animals; that is, the value a living organism has because it has a good of its own. Taylor speaks in terms of an organism having a good of its own rather than in terms of interests to avoid the Feinbergian claim that interests require self-awareness. This position is not an animal rights position because Taylor calls for equal respect not only for humans and other animals, but for plants as well. Unlike the previous three authors, who are trying to find a way to account for and justify the environmental perspective, Taylor recommends a new perspective, biocentric egalitarianism, that would require significant new changes in our behavior toward plants and animals, if it were put into practice, comparable to the changes in moral practice toward animals and nature that occurred in the nineteenth century. Significant changes are required because Taylor's moral concern is placed on individuals rather than systems, creating the practical problems discussed by Norton in the previous paper. Despite these problems, however, Taylor's position, which he has expanded into a book-length treatise, proved to be influential in the theoretical debate in both the animal welfare and environmental ethics camps.[19] Regan's position in *The Case for Animal Rights* is a variant that restricts inherent value or worth to those organisms that not only have goods of their own, but also, as noted earlier, have subjective, experiential (mental) lives. Moving in a completely different direction, Holmes Rolston, III has developed a similar position in his new book, *Environmental Ethics*, in which organisms are said not only to have goods of their own, but also goods of their kind.[20] One unfortunate confusion that has arisen out of this approach to environmental ethics and animal liberation has been Taylor and Regan's use of the word *inherent*, which is contrary to traditional usage. Traditionally, entities with inherent value or worth have been things that are valuable because contemplation of them has been good or rewarding intrinsically (noninstrumentally) from a human or anthropocentric perspective; for example, art objects.[21] In accordance with the new definition, entities with inherent value or worth are valuable because they are teleological centers of purpose that are valued intrinsically (for their own sake) from a non-anthropocentric perspective.

The next essay is the first of two chapters from Mary Midgley's *Animals and Why They Matter*, the second of which is placed out of chronological but nevertheless in proper thematic order. Midgley's book is a valuable contribution to the animal rights/environmental ethics debate because she approaches the issues from a completely nonideological perspective; that is, she approaches each issue without preconceptions and does not try to develop an analysis in terms of a predetermined set of environmental or animal welfare principles. In this chapter, she challenges the claim made by Singer and others that speciesism is analogous to racism, pointing out, among other things, that species differences, unlike racial differences, must be carefully noted and taken into consideration if the needs and welfare of particular animals are to be properly attended to and that concern for one's own kind is natural part of species bonding, which must take place for an individual member of any species to be able to function normally.

"Moral Considerability and Extraterrestrial Life," an essay that I commissioned from J. Baird Callicott for *Beyond Spaceship Earth: Environmental Ethics and the Solar System*, an edited book of essays applying environmental ethics to the space program, is included in this volume because it reveals some unexpected limitations of Leopold's land ethic, at least as Callicott interprets it, and hints at his eventual shift to reconcilliation with animal welfare ethics. Callicott insists that the land ethic has nothing at all to say about the treatment of extraterrestrial life, should it ever be discovered. In other words, species of life are morally irrelevant from the perspective of the land ethic unless they are part of our biotic community on Earth. Conceding that there ought to be some kind of theory available to provide them some moral consideration, Callicott goes on to suggest that reverence-for-life ethics, in terms of the writings of Feinberg, Goodpaster, and Albert Scheweitzer, though a dismal failure on this planet, would be a "serviceable" extraterrestrial environmental ethic. Nevertheless, claiming that having a land ethic for Earth and a reverence-for-life ethic for off-planet would make ethics too complicated, Callicott concludes his paper, perhaps tongue in cheek, by recommending a weak anthropocentric position[22] that could provide guidance for both kinds of life and would "elevate the human spirit and the human mind."

My paper, "Foundations of Wildlife Protection Attitudes," is intended primarily as a examination of the history of ideas behind the environmental ethics/animal liberation debate, but it includes a criticism of Callicott's views on extraterrestrial life. I show that the histories of ideas out of which animal liberation and environmental ethics evolved are distinct, involving completely different concerns and completely different animals. Environmental ethics developed out of the biological classification activities of naturalists while animal liberation developed out of concern about domesticated animals. The key phrase with regard to the former was *wanton destruction* and the key phrase with regard to the latter was *unnecessary suffering*. In the final section of the paper, I argue that the same historical influences that produced the land ethic would also guide humans to similar ethical concern for extraterrestrial life if it were ever discovered. Further, I argue that the change in moral behavior in the nineteenth century on which Callicott claims the land ethic is based took place before evolution and ecology found their place in science and that, although evolution and ecology play a role in environmental ethics, our attitudes and behavior today toward wildlife would be little different without them. For the themes of this book, these discussions show that the history of ideas supports Callicott's radical separation of animal welfare ethics and environmental ethics in "Animal Liberation: A Triangular Affair," but does not support the (terracentric or Earth-chauvinist) limitations of the land ethic that he describes in "Moral Considerability and Extraterrestrial Life."

The next two selections, Mary Anne Warren's "Rights of the Nonhuman World" and Mary Midgley's "The Mixed Community," though published in 1983, are introduced at this point so that they can be read in the context of Callicott's admission that the land ethic may need to be supplemented by one or more other moral theories and my treatment of animal liberation and environmental ethics as distinct positions that deal with different animals, domestic and wild, respectively, and that have distinct and largely unrelated historical origins. Warren, in response to Callicott's "Animal Liberation: A Triangular Affair," argues that animal liberation and environmental ethics, rather than being incompatible positions, are really complementary, dealing with different aspects of our moral intuitions and with different animals. In addition, she suggests ways in which separate (and complementary) rights theories might be developed for humans, animals, and, to a very limited degree, for plants and nonliving natural objects (though she does not encourage this view). Animals need not be regarded as having the same rights as humans, she says, merely some rights. Moreover, she adds, the term *right* is not really essential, because we could speak equally well in terms of the *intrinsic value* of humans and animals. The details of Warren's position are not particularly new. Singer, for example, on the second page of *Animal Liberation* points out that we need not give animals rights that they do not need, noting that a dog does not need the right to vote. In addition, because she is not absolutely committed to a rights view, her approach toward rights for animals is similar to Watson's conception of rights assigned for human behavioral convenience. Nevertheless, her suggestion that animal liberation and environmental ethics be treated as complementary rather than incompatible positions provides an easy way to ameliorate the radical break between theorists in the two camps brought about by Callicott's analysis in "Animal Liberation: A Triangular Affair."

In "The Mixed Community," Mary Midgley takes a more general and long-term look at the historical relationships of humans and animals than I do in "Foundations of Wildlife Protection Attitudes," pointing out that it is simply is not true that human (moral) communities until very recently have excluded animals. Rather, she argues, animals have had a place throughout human history and probably for tens of thousands of years in prehistory. Moreover, the relationship to most of these animals has been as persons. Treating them as persons has not been so much a reflection of a high moral view as a matter of expediency. As Midgley notes, if there was a better way to get work out of elephants than by taking into account that they have minds of their own and have good and bad, grumpy and happy days, it would have been found long (centuries) ago. In conjunction with her earlier paper in this book (the preceding chapter in *Animals and Why They Matter*), Midgley goes on to suggest that, though humans and other animals focus primarily on their own species, most animals have little difficulty crossing the species barrier; and the route is not specifically by way of concern for unnecessary suffering, but natural sympathy, which is most apparent in the special tolerance most animals show for the young of other species. Midgley's position in this paper, though focused on the relationship of humans and domestic animals, on the one hand, goes a long way toward undercutting the idea that animals have no part in the moral communities of humans, found in traditional philosophy and reinforced by Callicott's "Animal Liberation: A Triangular Affair," and, on the other hand, parallels changes (specifically with regard to the role of sympathy) in Callicott's own views as he moves toward reconciliation with animal welfare ethics.[23]

John Fisher's "Taking Sympathy Seriously" is included at this point in the book because it develops in some detail Midgley's suggestion that humans and animals are tied together morally through sympathy. This paper, though perhaps little known in the animal rights/environmental ethics debate, has had considerable impact on my own thinking on the subject. At the time that I considered this paper for publication in *Environmental Ethics* I (naively) informed the author that he had failed to note the differences in treatment that we accord wild and domestic animals, as explained, for example, in Callicott's "Animal Liberation: A Triangular Affair," to which he replied that the point of his paper was that this distinction was illegitimate in terms of the moral psychology of humans. On reflection, I found that I had to agree. The paper not only is a good answer to Callicott's excessive disregard of animal suffering in "Animal Liberation," a position he no longer holds, but is also an answer to the charges sometimes made by environmentalists (and particularly hunters) that those concerned about animal suffering in the wild are victims of the "Bambi syndrome." Nevertheless, because sympathy, as developed by Fisher, though natural, is selective—permitting us to have sympathy both for the wildebeest and the lion who kills it—it may not alter our attitudes and behavior toward wild animals in any significant way.

This book concludes with a third essay by J. Baird Callicott, "Animal Liberation and Environmental Ethics: Back Together Again." In this essay, Callicott repents his extremism in "Animal Liberation: A Triangular Affair" and begins looking for a way to reconcile animal liberation and environmental ethics. Dismayed that Warren's position, that the two ethical positions are complementary rather than incompatible, might win the day (the view I personally support, independent of the particular details of her full position), Callicott calls for an attempt to find a common position that will account for our moral behavior toward animals in both the human and biotic communities. He finds the foundation for this common position in Midgley's account of sympathy in "The Mixed Community," which he joins with his own account, based on links between Hume, Darwin, and Leopold.[24] Interestingly, Callicott, who previously argued that Singer's concern about suffering went too far, now argues that Singer failed to go far enough. As Callicott notes, Singer pointedly refused to speak on behalf of sympathy on the grounds that to do so would be too much of a concession to the emotions. (It is possible that Singer was himself trying to avoid the equivalent of the Bambi syndrome in animal welfare ethics.)

Will animal liberation and animal rights unite harmoniously with environmental ethics and live happily ever after as Callicott now hopes? To be honest, it does not seem to be very likely. As I see it, environmental ethics will continue to be an unpleasant thorn in the side of animal welfare ethicists, even though they themselves have no plausible solutions to the problem of what to do, and not do, with sentient wild animals. As the chapters in this book demonstrate, from the perspective of environmental ethics, a rights approach focused exclusively on animals is too narrow to cover all the entities living and nonliving that members of the environmental movement feel ought to be considered morally, and a rights approach that encompasses both living and nonliving entities stretches the traditional concept of rights too far, producing rights that are so watered down that they are hardly recognizable as rights at all. It is possible that animal welfare ethicists may succeed eventually in establishing moral rights for domestic animals with regard, in particular, to scientific research and factory farming. Because legal rights do not require the development of elaborate theoretical foundations, merely the act of an authoritative body, legal rights could be established that might prepare the way for the eventual acceptance of some kind of moral rights. Such legal and moral rights, nevertheless, seem unlikely to form the foundations of environmental ethics and at best would be complementary to an environmental ethic, established on some other basis.

Criticism of rights in environmental ethics is usually directed at the use of the concept by environmentalists, not animal welfare advocates. When environmentalists call for rights for nature, they are borrowing the legal concept of rights to express their belief that nature should be protected for its own sake, not simply because it is instrumentally valuable to humans. Because environmental ethicists have been unable to construct a theory to support the rights statements of environmentalists, these statements can appropriately be dismissed, in accordance with the emotivist critique of ethics, as developed by logical positivists in the early twentieth century, as arbitrary and subjective expressions of emotion. Having abandoned efforts to develop a rights theory for environmentalists, most environmental ethicists, following Warren's suggestion in the "Rights of the Nonhuman World," are looking into the development of a theory of intrinsic value as a way to establish an objective sake for nature. Whether environmentalists, environmental professionals, and ordinary people will accept intrinsic value terminology in place of their emotivist rights talk is a question that will not be answered for some time to come.

In speculating about the future of the animal rights/environmental ethics debate, it is important to recognize that ultimately the controversy will not be resolved by philosophers at the theoretical level, but by environmental professionals and concerned citizens at the practical level. The resolution of the controversy is not simply a matter of finding a winning argument, but of finding a position that all those concerned about the environment can understand, feel comfortable with, and apply in their professional work and their daily lives. This position could be the actual position of a particular philosopher, but it need not be, for it could just as easily be a generalized position—or group of positions in accordance with moral pluralism—that borrows from the views of various theorists from both camps.

Whether the solution to the debate will be a single position that covers both environmental ethics and animal welfare ethics (moral monism) or several positions (moral pluralism) that are complementary, covering distinct areas, is an open question. Even if environmental ethics and animal welfare ethics remain distinct fields theoretically, in practice some areas will overlap. For example, when tourists find injured wild animals, they almost always seek out park and nature center officials expecting them to render immediate medical acid. If the animals are small enough, they are rushed to park interpretation centers by car. Although the naturalists or interpreters frequently accept the animals, they do so with misgivings, for usually they believe such aid to be pointless and counterproductive. Most are convinced that helping injured animals is an inappropriate interference in natural systems. They hold that there is little likelihood that such animals will recover adequately to continue their lives in the wild and that, even if they do, they will take up space and food that could more appropriately be used by healthy animals able to contribute to their species' gene pool through reproduction. Sometimes naturalists accept these animals but make no real effort to save them, performing mercy killings or simply using them as food for captured animals after the tourists have left. When they do attempt to save the animals, they do so without any conviction that they are doing the right thing. Their motivation for rendering assistance is a response to the feelings of the tourists, not any real concern for the injured animals. Some merely respond to these feelings, wishing not to cause offense. Others respond because they hope that the feelings of the tourists, which they regard as being inappropriate, can eventually be redirected away from concern for individual animals to concern for habitat preservation.

Although animal liberationists, following Singer, frequently insist that feelings and emotions are not the issue, if one attends to the matter closely, it is difficult to conclude that there is any other issue. Animal liberationists apparently deny that they are emotionally concerned about the suffering of sentient animals because they are afraid that they will be accused of not being rational and objective.[25] In denying the emotional basis of their concern, however, they paradoxically become appropriate targets for the ecofeminist criticism that they have improperly divorced themselves from the emotional side of their natures. The animal liberationist approach is basically an extensionist approach. On the basis of some characteristic that humans and animals hold in common, the ability to suffer or to be the subject of a life, some moral concern is extended to some animals (but not to nonsentient animals, plants, and other lower organisms). As I indicated earlier, neither Regan nor Singer, nor any other animal liberationist, has offered a realistic plan to manage natural systems; nor have they expressed any inclination to try. According to Singer, for example, humans have done enough if they do not contribute further to natural suffering in the wild.[26] Viewed in this way, the problem is not determining appropriate ethical action, but simply coming to grips with our emotions, our natural expressions of sympathy as they cross species boundaries. And this problem is one that also plagues environmentalists, who frequently also deny the relevance of their natural sympathies when they invoke the Bambi syndrome in defense of hunting or natural regulation. Resolution of this emotional discomfort about the natural and human-induced suffering of sentient wild animals, if and when it comes, will likely eliminate most of the conflict (the incompatibility) between animal welfare and environmental ethics, leaving proponents of each perspective to focus on matters that are truly complementary: the problem of unnecessary suffering among domestic animals (those living in the mixed community), which is not a major concern of environmental ethics; and the problem of ecosystemic health, which because it includes nonsentient animals, nonanimal organisms, and nonliving entities, is not a concern of animal liberation and animal rights.

Notes

1. Peter Singer, *Animal Liberation: A New Ethics for Our Treatment of Animals* (New York: New York Review, 1975); Tom Regan, *The Case for Animal Rights* (Berkeley: University of California, 1983). Page numbers for *Animal Liberation* refer to the commonly available Avon edition, first published in 1977.

2. Singer, *Animal Liberation*, pp. 178-79.

3. Regan, *The Case for Animal Rights*, p. 78.

4. Singer, *Animal Liberation*, pp. 238-39; 248-49.

5. Regan, *The Case for Animal Rights*, p. 362.

6. Ibid., p. 359.

7. Ibid., p. 361.

8. William T. Blackstone, ed., *Philosophy and Environmental Crisis* (Athens: University of Georgia Press, 1974); Christopher D. Stone, *Should Trees Have Standing? Toward Legal Rights for Natural Objects* (Los Altos, Calif.: William Kaufmann, 1974); and John Passmore, *Man's Responsibility for Nature: Ecological Problems and Western Traditions* (London: Duckworth, 1974).

9. Joel Feinberg, "The Rights of Animals and Unborn Generations," in Blackstone, *Philosophy and Environmental Crisis*, p. 52.

10. Stone, *Should Trees Have Standing?*

11. Passmore, *Man's Responsibility for Nature*, pp. 116-17; 178-79.

12. Ibid., p. 115.

13. Aldo Leopold, *A Sand County Almanac: With Essays on Conservation from Round River* (New York: Ballantine Books, 1970), pp. 240, 247. The book was originally published by Oxford University Press in 1949.

14. John Rodman, "The Liberation of Nature?" *Inquiry* 20 (1977): 83-145.

15. Peter Singer and Tom Regan, eds., *Animal Rights and Human Obligations* (Englewood Cliffs, N.J.: Prentice-Hall, 1976).

16. Peter Singer, "The Fable of the Fox and the Unliberated Animals," *Ethics* 88 (1978): 122; see also Tom Regan, "Animal Rights, Human Wrongs," *Enviornmental Ethics* 2 (1980): 99-120; Peter Singer, "Animals and the Value of Life," in Tom Regan, ed., *Matters of Life and Death: New Introductory Essays in Moral Philosophy* (New York: Random House, 1980), pp. 338-80; and Tom Regan, *The Case for Animal Rights* (Berkeley: University of California Press, 1985).

17. See R.G. Frey, *Interests and Rights: The Case Against Animals* (Oxford: Clarendon Press, 1980) and Kenneth E. Goodpaster, "On Being Morally Considerable," *Journal of Philosophy* 75 (1978): 308-25.

18. Eugene C. Hargrove, *Foundations of Environmental Ethics* (Englewood Cliffs, N.J.: Prentice-Hall, 1989), pp. 177-78.

19. Paul W. Taylor, *Respect for Nature* (Princeton, N.J.: Princeton University Press, 1986).

20. Holmes Rolston, III, *Environmental Ethics: Duties to and Values in the Natural World* (Philadelphia: Temple University Press, 1988).

21. See William Frankena, *Ethics*, 2d ed. (Englewood Cliffs, N.J.: Prentice-Hall, 1973), p. 82.

22. Bryan G. Norton, "Environmental Ethics and Weak Anthropocentrism," *Environmental Ethics* 6 (1984): 131-48.

23. Callicott first introduced sympathy as a key element in the

intellectual foundations of the land ethic in "Hume's *Is/Ought* Dichotomy and the Relationship of Ecology to Leopold's Land Ethic," *Environmental Ethics* 4 (1982): 163-74, a year before the publication of Midgley's book.

24. Ibid.

25. Singer, *Animal Liberation*, p. 255.

26. Ibid., p. 239.

Acknowledgments

I thank the individual authors, Environmental Philosophy, Inc., publisher of *Environmental Ethics*, Sierra Club Books, Universitetsforlaget, publisher of *Inquiry*, the University of Georgia Press, and the University of Queensland Press for permission to reprint the following articles and chapters: J. Baird Callicott, "Animal Liberation: A Triangular Affair," *Environmental Ethics* 2 (1980): 311–338; "Moral Considerability and Extraterrestrial Life," in Eugene C. Hargrove, ed., *Beyond Spaceship Earth: Environmental Ethics and the Solar System* (San Francisco: Sierra Club Books, 1986), pp. 238–259; "Animal Liberation and Environmental Ethics: Back Together Again," *Between the Species* 5 (1988): 163–69, and in J. Baird Callicott, *In Defense of the Land Ethic* (Albany: State University of New York Press, 1989), pp. 49–59; John A. Fisher, "Taking Sympathy Seriously: A Defense of Our Moral Psychology Toward Animals," *Environmental Ethics* 9 (1987): 197–215; Eugene C. Hargrove, "The Foundations of Wildlife Protection Attitudes," *Inquiry* 30 (1987): 3–31; Mary Midgley, "The Significance of Species" and "The Mixed Community," in Mary Midgley, *Animals and Why They Matter* (Athens: University of Georgia Press, 1983), chaps. 9–10; Bryan G. Norton, "Environmental Ethics and Nonhuman Rights," *Environmental Ethics* 4 (1984): 17–36; Paul W. Taylor, "The Ethics of Respect for Nature," *Environmental Ethics* (1981): 197–218; Mary Anne Warren, "The Rights of the Nonhuman World," in Robert Elliot and Arran Gare, eds., *Environmental Philosophy: A Collection of Readings* (St. Lucia: University of Queensland Press, 1983), pp. 109–134; Richard A. Watson, "Self-Consciousness and the Rights of Nonhuman Animals and Nature," *Environmental Ethics* 1 (1979): 99–129.

All royalties from this book have been donated to the Environmental Ethics Endowment Fund of the Center for Environmental Philosophy at the University of North Texas.

Self-Consciousness and the Rights of Nonhuman Animals and Nature

Richard A. Watson

Introduction

> Unless men are held to possess some attribute over and above those which they have in common with other natural objects—animals, plants, things, etc.—(whether this difference is itself called natural or not), the moral command not to treat men as animals or things has no rational foundation[1]

The central question in this paper is: do nonhuman animals and nature have rights? I approach this question by analyzing the human moral milieu to provide a reciprocity framework for explaining and justifying the attribution of moral rights and duties, by examining the justification for distinguishing humans morally from nonhumans, by giving critical expositions of four standard arguments for attributing rights on bases other than reciprocity, and finally by arguing that some nonhuman animals are sometimes moral agents and thus merit rights. I conclude that individuals belonging to a very wide range of animal species should at least have assigned to them basic rights to life and relief from suffering caused unnecessarily by humans because they are capable of self-conscious communication.

1. The Reciprocity of Rights and Duties

A specific set of six natural characteristics seems to me to be the best (and perhaps the only) ground on which the intrinsic possession of moral rights—those having to do with good and bad, right and wrong —can be explained and justified. This framework is one in which to say that an entity has rights makes sense only if that entity can fulfill reciprocal duties. This means that only moral agents—those who act according to duties—merit rights.

The reciprocity of rights and duties is suggested both by the Golden Rule and by Kant's categorical imperative. Consider the admonition to do unto others as you would have them do unto you. Even if it is only a hope, this implies that if you assume a right of behavior toward others, then they have the same right of behavior toward you, and that they should accept as a duty to behave toward you as you behave toward them. Similarly, the admonition to act only in ways, the general description of which can be proposed as universal moral principles, is to imply that, by assuming rights, you accede that all others have the same rights, and that it is the duty of all to abide by the embodied universal principles. Reciprocity of rights and duties here may be merely implied, but this interpretation of the Golden Rule and the categorical imperative is clearly plausible. When most people assume or accept a right, they do expect others in similar circumstances to have the same right, and they expect everyone including themselves to fulfill the duty of honoring this right in others. And, in this rendering, it is apparent that rights are based on duties, that one is worthy of or earns rights only by fulfilling reciprocal duties.

Accordingly, if the primary way to gain moral worth is to act according to moral duties, then any entities that cannot act according to moral duties—such as stones, crickets, and trees—cannot perforce earn moral rights. And, because they cannot act according to moral duties, neither does it make sense to say that they have moral duties. Thus, one must be a moral agent—a being who relates morally to others—in order to earn rights. I outline below the six necessary and (in combination) sufficient characteristics for being a moral agent.

The primary characteristic required of a moral agent is *self-consciousness*. To act at all, and particularly to get credit for acting morally, an agent must, first of all, act from within its own self. Further, the action must be *free* (the agent could have acted otherwise), and it must be *intentional.* Both of these characteristics depend further on the ability of the agent to *understand moral principles*, and on his *understanding in the instant* the principle according to which he is freely and intentionally acting. It seems fairly obvious that an entity cannot be said to have a duty unless he is capable of understanding that duty. It is less obvious that an entity cannot be said to have a right unless he is capable of understanding that right, but I agree that this is both plausible and true because both duty-bearing and right-bearing behavior—according to or opposed to duties and rights—depend on understanding them. In short, to behave with reference to moral principles, one must understand them. The Greek maxim that action merely in accord with proper behavior does not merit moral praise, but only action done with the intent to behave properly, implies that one must understand both one's duties *and* rights in order to have them. Otherwise, one does not behave in a moral milieu and one's behavior cannot be evaluated morally (but see below, sections III and IV). Finally, it is generally assumed that the agent is *physically capable*, at least potentially, of carrying out the action. Thus, someone who is constrained, or paralyzed, or ill, and thus cannot act freely, may be accorded moral worth if he knows his duty and would intentionally do it if he could. Good intentions—intent to act according to duty—also often give moral worth even if they fail, and, in some cases, even when the results (that the agent could not have anticipated) are bad.

The explanatory analysis I am advocating, then, is that to have moral worth, to have moral rights, or to be a primary part of a moral milieu, an entity must be a *moral agent*, which requires that it have:

1. self-consciousness,

2. capability of understanding moral principles about rights and duties,

3. freedom to act either according to or opposed to given principles of duty,

4. understanding of given principles of duty,

5. physical capability (or potentiality) of acting according to duty, and

6. intention to act according to or opposed to given principles of duty.

This *reciprocity framework* provides a justification for intrinsic possession of moral rights. If an agent does or intends to do, his duty, then he is a moral agent acting in a moral milieu and is worthy of moral rights. *Morality*, on this view, is a milieu in which self-conscious moral agents earn rights by behaving according to duties.

All six of these characteristics are necessary for an entity to be a moral agent. Note that one can remain in the *moral milieu* even if one freely acts opposed to duty (3), in which case one loses or foregoes certain rights. Also, one may still be a moral agent if one does not understand given moral principles (4), but does have the general capability of understanding (2). If one intentionally acts (6) according to a misunderstood principle (5), one may be forgiven or blamed depending on whether or not it was an avoidable mistake, but in either case one remains a moral agent. But, if one is not self-conscious (1), one can do none of these things, which is why self-consciousness is basic to all the other characteristics. However, mere self-consciousness (1), or intelligence and rationality (2), or free will (3), or comprehension of given principles pertinent to a situation (4), or ability to act (5), does not, nor does any combination of these first five characteristics qualify one as a moral agent. Only the intent to act according to or opposed to a moral principle (6) is sufficient to qualify an entity as a moral agent, but (again), an entity must have the first five characteristics if the attribution of such an intent to that entity is to make sense. The first five characteristics alone may be sufficient to qualify one as a *moral entity*, but such attribution raises a very difficult problem. Because mere moral entities do not earn rights through intentional action, do they have any rights? Do they have any duties? What is their status in the moral milieu?

The problem that arises, if one accepts the view that to be a moral entity—in the moral milieu but not as a moral agent—one need have only the first five characteristics (the additional of the sixth making one a moral agent), can be approached by examining the related problem of what counts as amoral behavior. There are at least two possible kinds of amoral behavior, one outside, the other inside, the moral milieu.

First, an entity—e.g., a cricket—may be said to behave amorally because it lacks the sixth plus some or all of the first five characteristics listed above. Such an entity would not be a moral entity, and would not be a part of the moral milieu. Whether or not nonhuman animals and nature are amoral in this sense is one of the questions toward which this present discussion is leading.

The second kind of amoral behavior is undertaken by an entity that has the first five characteristics, but not the sixth. He does not intend to act either according to or opposed to moral pinciples. He is an agent, but not—at least not in intent—a moral agent. His is a difficult case, as Camus makes abundantly clear in his novel, *The Stranger*. The stranger's intent is amoral, for he intends to act not within, but outside the moral milieu (to the extent that he has intentions at all). Most people's inclinations are to say that this strange being is a moral *agent* because he *could* act morally, and to punish of him—deprive him rights—because he does not act according to the duties he under-stands. People suspect that his profession of amoral intent is a ruse to cover intent to behave immorally. People would punish him because they say he knows better. But just as the Greek view, that he who knows the right thing to do will do it, is simplistic, probably so also is the view that he who understands moral principles will intend to behave either in accord with or in opposition to them. On this view, he is accused of being a moral agent, and his intent to act outside the moral milieu is taken to be immoral. It is apparently difficult to accept the view that an agent who has the first five characteristics can avoid having the sixth. Is it the case that anyone who has the first five characteristics is then driven to be a moral agent, even if his doing or not doing his duty is not a result of his intent to act by or against moral principles? Can one not act outside the moral milieu? This involve-ment of an agent in the moral milieu against his intent makes some people uneasy for the same reasons that the view that pagans or agnostics will go to hell, despite their lack of intent to be a part of the religious milieu, makes them uneasy.

Those who do grant that one can intend to act amorally, outside the moral milieu, may attribute this ability to an agent's lack of moral sense. Perhaps just as there are some people who understand reli-gious principles but who have no religious "feelings," so also there may be some people who understand moral principles but who have no moral "feelings." And as the one sort is not "religious," so is the other not "moral." But just as many people say that the areligious will go to hell despite their lack of "religious sense," so, also, even if it is agreed that an agent lacks the intent or sense to act with respect to moral principles, his actions are usually evaluated morally anyway. And, as Pascal suggests, that those without "religious sense" behave as though they feel it to save their souls, one might suggest that those who lack "moral sense" behave as though they have it to save themselves from punishment.

This talk of "feelings" suggests that possession of a "moral sense" might be a seventh characteristic necessary for one to be a moral agent. I have not added this characteristic because its actuality is even more suspect than the one highly debated characteristic (free will) that I do list. It seems to me that a moral milieu is possible even if there is no such thing as moral sense, but not if there is no free will. Also, the inclusion of moral sense might bring up problems about merit not un-related to problems of determinism that might arise if free will were deleted. Possession of a moral sense might (though not necessarily) incline one so far toward doing his duty that we might question whether or not he is doing it because it is his duty. Is the "naturally" well-intentioned agent of the same moral worth as one who does his duty despite strong disinclination? I would like to avoid such questions here. And perhaps moral sense is redundant, or irrelevant, if one does possess the intent to act with respect to moral principles. In any event, this second kind of amoral behavior comes up on section IV, for it is conceivable that just as a cricket is amoral in the first sense (say, because it cannot understand moral principles), a chimpanzee may be amoral in the second sense (understanding but not intending to act as a moral agent). The cricket would be outside, the chimpanzee inside, the moral milieu. That is, most people would probably say that the cricket is not, while the chimpanzee is, an intrinisic moral entity (neither being a moral agent). The question that would arise with such a chimpanzee (as it does with Camus' stranger) is: given that possession of the first five characteristics qualifies it as a moral entity, do we punish it for not intending to behave as a moral agent? (Camus' stranger was guillotined.) I consider this question in section IV.

To conclude this section (1), I present this framework both as an analysis of the concepts of moral rights and duties that shows their reciprocity, and also as an argument for this position. The operative or explanatory value of the framework is that it provides a way of answering the question: why does or should a given entity have these rights? The answer is: because this entity does or intends to fulfill these related duties. I know of no better way to explain or justify the intrinsic possession of moral rights.

2. The Moral Division between the Human and the Nonhuman

Let us see how this framework helps explain two humanistic moral positions.

Most notions of moral, legal, divinely ordained, natural, and "ordinary" rights and duties apply primarily to relations among human beings, their institutions, and their gods. Ordinarily or naturally (in the West) human beings are thought to have rights to life, liberty, and property or the pursuit of interests, and duties to behave fairly or equitably. There is, however, enough world-wide cultural variation to suggest that rights and duties may be human conceptual artifacts. Because I want to contrast two extreme positions, I assume for one of them that natural and ordinary rights and duties are informal human inventions, just as legal rights and duties are formal inventions. Also, at this extreme, gods and divinely ordained rights and duties, as well as moral rights and duties, are assumed to be human inventions, as suggested by the immense variety of gods, religions, and moral codes that proliferate in human history. This stance is anti-supernatural. It is the position that human beings and all their works—including rights and duties—are natural in the sense of being a part of nature. However, those who hold this position have not generally found that entities other than humans inhabit the moral milieu. Morality, while natural, is apparently a cultural artifact unique to human beings. I call this the *empirical* position.

The contrasting position is that human beings are not part of nature. Also, human works and conceptual inventions—such as rights and duties as described above—are not part of nature. The position has variants in which moral codes are innate in human beings, and/or are intuited by means of a human moral sense, and/or are divinely ordained and revealed by supernatural gods. But whether innate, intuitional, or divinely ordained, rights and duties on this view are uniquely human and thus do not apply to nonhuman animals and nature. I call this the *supernatural* position.

Both the empirical and the supernatural positions are *humanistic* in that according to them rights and duties apply intrinsically or primarily only to human beings. Human beings may decide to take on nonreciprocally certain unsanctioned duties to nonhuman nature, and to accord to nature certain unearned rights or claims on human beings. But relationships between human beings and nonhuman nature with respect to rights and duties are held on both these views to differ drastically from reciprocal moral relations among human beings. I believe that the reciprocity framework of section 1 provides the explanation for this claim that only humans populate the moral milieu, a claim shared by advocates of these two radically different positions.

According to the reciprocity framework, the radical division between human beings and nonhuman animals and nature is justified and explained by the fact that among human beings, reciprocal rights and duties are *intrinsic* or *primary* in the sense of being earned or sanctioned by possession of natural characteristics. Any purported rights of and duties to entities that cannot reciprocate are *extrinsic* or *secondary* in the sense that they are unearned and unsanctioned by possession of any natural characteristics, but are assigned by human beings. This assignment on both the empirical and supernatural positions is made as a convenience to human interests, and does not result in "real" rights and duties. If reciprocity is taken as central to the general concepts of rights and duties, then the moral milieu is populated only by human beings because—it is usually claimed—only human beings are moral agents. The framework further explains why both empiricists and supernaturalists come to this conclusion. They find that nonhuman animals and nonhuman nature, say, in the form of ecological communities, are not self-conscious.

There is a third position according to which human beings are a part of nature (or of supernature), but do not uniquely populate the moral milieu. Advocates of this position claim that either their moral intuitions or their gods inform them that all of nonhuman nature has rights (and some say duties) as do humans. I call this the *mystical* position. This is a variety of the supernatural position in which all the world (and not just humankind and gods) is supernatural, with no moral division between human beings and nonhuman nature. All the world *is* the moral milieu. This mystical, panmoralistic position contrasts sharply with the humanistic empirical and supernatural positions that distinguish the moral milieu as exclusively human.

Obviously, advocates of the mystical position must hold either that nonhuman animals and nature are self-conscious moral agents (an extreme version of panpsychism), or justify the ascription of rights to them on some other grounds. Apparently some mystics do hold that all of nature is self-conscious and morally active, but others hold merely that it is alive or minimally spiritual or psychic. This *is* to offer an explanation for why nature purportedly has primary rights, but, since this general panpsychism is not obvious to empirical observation, many people reject it. Advocates then usually claim that their mystical intuitions or gods inform them that all of nature has the right to existence or to life, and that this intuition or revelation is evidence enough. One notorious problem with this claim is that not everyone enjoys mystical knowledge. My general reservations about a "mystical sense" are the same as those about the "religious sense" and "moral sense" discussed in section 1. Perhaps it is not necessary to remark that I do not possess any of these three special senses. (Are they like "mathematical sense"? Perhaps, but, like most human beings, I do have some sense for mathematics—can "see," for example, that 2 plus 2 equals 4—and so the fact that I cannot comprehend esoteric mathematical insights does not lead me to disbelieve those who assure me that they can.)

To conclude this section (2), I remind you that the central question in this paper is: do nonhuman animals and nature have rights? Of course human beings can *assign* legal, secondary, extrinsic rights to them, but these make them secondary (even merely honorific or expedient) citizens in the moral world. I am concerned to discover whether or not they are intrinsically primary moral entities or agents. I present a framework of moral reciprocity which I believe best explains and justifies the intrinsic possession of moral rights. In the ideal case, to merit moral rights, an entity must be a self-conscious moral agent who intends to act according to duty. Because according to the reciprocity framework self-consciousness is the primary characteristic—the ultimate *sine qua non*—for being a moral agent, it is reasonable to begin by asking whether or not nonhuman animals and nature are self-conscious, if they are, then we can check to see if they have the other characteristics. (2) through (5), required to be a moral entity, and then the sixth (intent) necessary and sufficient to be a moral agent.

3. Standard Arguments for the Rights of Nonhuman Animals and Nature

Before pursuing the question of the self-consciousness of nonhuman animals and nature, I want to strengthen my argument for the reciprocity framework by utilizing it to examine and criticize the four main arguments that have been advanced to explain and justify the attribution of rights to animals and nature on the basis of natural characteristics other than those specific to moral agents. Like the reciprocity framework, each of these arguments is "naturalistic" in the sense that none of them rests on supernatural claims. The arguments, in order of decreasing strength, are the *ecological*, the *prudential*, the *sentimental*, and the *contractual*. In none of these arguments is it assumed that nonhuman animals or nature are self-conscious.

The Ecological Argument

The strongest argument for the view that nonhuman animals and nature have rights is based on the facts of ecology. All living things on Earth are interdependent parts of ecological communities. The Earth as a whole, including its atmosphere, its waters, and its soil and rocks, is essential to the existence of these communities. For this reason, Aldo Leopold refers to living things in their habitat as "the land," and argues that we ought to have an "ecological conscience," i.e., that we ought to recognize that "the land" has rights.[2]

A very serious problem with this proposal is that it may be a claim that whatever *is* thereby has a right to exist. This is to derive value from fact, which is a procedure generally rejected by philosophers. The mere existence of "the land" is neither an explanation of nor a justification for its having rights. Consider the entirely natural possibility that these entities do not exist. If they do not exist, they do not (on his ground) have a right to exist. Furthermore, if their right to exist depends on their existence, then, if they are destroyed, their rights are destroyed. And once they no longer exist, there are no longer any rights anyone could appeal to to blame the destroyers or to deplore the destruction. The paradoxical situation would be that they have a right to existence only until they are deprived of existence. But it is usual that moral systems be general or universal in the sense that their attributions do not depend on the mere existence of the entities evaluated. As Kant argued, existence itself is not a characteristic useful for designating the character or essence of a thing. Further, a primary use of moral systems is to distinguish good from bad, right from wrong, among existing entities. Existence and nonexistence are obviously useless for making such a distinction. Note that *mutaits mutandis* the same objection holds if it is proposed that whatever is living has a right to life. Now some ecological moralists may in fact mean to assert that all that exists or is alive thereby has the right to existence or to life. Even if this is true, one awaits an argument for it.

Mere existence is not adequate to explain or to justify possession of rights. The next step, then, is to suggest that an ecological system gains its right to existence because of its function. "The land" might be said to earn its right to existence because it makes possible the existence of all the individual elements in it. If the argument were no more than this, it would revert to the view that mere existence is a value, for in effect all that is claimed is that whatever makes existence possible itself has a right to be. The argument also swallows it own tail, for the entity whose existence it makes possible is itself. And I disallow the supernatural claim that it creates itself to avoid the question of why. (The answer would be: because existence is of value. But the only evidence of this would be that it was created.) In any event, the function of making existence possible would make an ecological system worthy of the right to exist only if it is the case that whatever exists is valuable, but so far we have no reason for believing that this is the case (or, as far as that goes, that it is not the case).

There is another, more subtle, but related difficulty that has to do with given ecological systems themselves. In relatively regular and stable conditions an ecological system reaches an *optimal* or *climax* state of dynamic equilibrium. Often ecological moralists attach some premium to such states. They have the most right to exist. However, if all the frogs in a pond in optimal equilibrium were to be destroyed, or sewage from a small town were to be pumped into the pond, then after a while a new state of equilibrium would be established at an optimum for the new conditions. While the first existed, it had a right to be, but after it was destroyed and the second established, then the second has a right to be to the exclusion of the first. Rain forests are nice, but if they are destroyed and deserts take their places, deserts are nice, too. And if everything is destroyed, then nothing exists, so nothing has any rights, and it doesn't matter. Again, no reason is given for the preference of one ecological system over another, nor, indeed, any reason for preferring the existence of something to nothing.

However—and now the strength of the ecological argument shows itself—most prominently, "the land" makes possible (is indeed essential to) the existence of human beings. "The land" is thus a foundation for the human moral milieu. Unwittingly, to be sure, "the land" nevertheless provides essential conditions for human life, and thus (most importantly) for morality. Thus it has a right to be.

This is a stronger foundation than mere existence, and it also explains the predilection of most ecological moralists for communities in optimal dynamic equilibrium, for these communities—by providing great genetic variety so as to make possible adjustment to a great variety of changing conditions—best provide the conditions for the long-range survival of the human species. Thus the basic characteristic proffered to explain and to justify the possession of rights by "the land" is that it makes possible the existence and survival of the human species, and thus of morality.

This is a fairly strong argument. "The land" is related to general morality by being an essential condition for a particular exemplification of morality by an existing human species. Of course the argument suffers from the same problem that taking mere existence to be of value does, namely, that if all moral beings were destroyed, there would remain no existing morality. Still, one might argue that "the land" would continue to provide the conditions for a moral milieu, even if no moral agents existed to populate it, and thereby would continue to earn its right to existence.

I would like to stress my inclination at this point to say that there would be no purpose to the provision of conditions for moral agents if none existed (not necessarily assuming that all moral agents are human, or even living beings, but imagining a world consisting only of entities that are not moral agents). I believe this inclination stems from the implicit or explicit recognition that (as argued above and below) the purpose in question is rooted only in human interests (or only in the interests of moral agents). Consider: what would it matter whether or not "the land" had the right to exist if there were no moral agents existing to act according to or in opposition to this right? (In the ecological argument "the land" itself is not a moral agent.) In a world without moral agents, there would be no existing morality, no rights and duties, no danger of being deprived of rights. Thus the strength of the argument from function rests on its relating ecological systems to the milieu of existing human moral agents. By providing conditions for morality, "the land" is said to earn the right to be.

In fact, however, ecological moralists recognize that "the land" is "morally blind." It does not know what it is doing, and cannot be said to have the duty to provide livable conditions for moral agents. It cannot reciprocate. Because of this, the "rights" accorded to "the land" are secondary. They are related to moral issues, but are unearned because unintended.

In view of this, the argument can be taken a step further, as a transition to the prudential argument. Many ecologists argue not on the basis of the rights of "the land," but on the brute facts of necessity. Whether or not "the land" has rights, we had better treat it as though it does, for our own survival. This strikes me as a vivid and conclusive argument. I am not convinced that ecological moralists adequately explain or justify the claim that "the land" has rights in the moral milieu, but ecologists certainly do show why it would be prudent to treat "the land" as though it does.

The Prudential Argument

Decartes said that nonhuman animals are insentient machines, and the Cartesian, Malebranche, is said to have kicked a pregnant dog in the stomach in the presence of Fontenelle to demonstrate the case. This viewpoint made the advancement of physiology possible by providing a justification for vivisection. Nevertheless, literally hundreds of books were written attacking the Cartesian claim that animals are machines.[3] A very common suggestion is that if we treat animals as machines, then very soon we will be treating humans the same way. In all prudence, then, a strong argument goes, whether or not animals are machines, we should treat them as though they are not. We should act as though animals have rights to comfortable lives, very like human rights, to avoid the possibility that some people will treat humans as Cartesians propose we treat animals.

I say that this is strong argument for treating animals *as though* they have rights. In their single-minded concentration on protecting human beings from being treated like beasts, its proponents need not argue that animals actually do have rights. Animals certainly *seem* to resent being treated as machines, and, whether or not they are machines, most people think they are not. So, those who treat them as machines become calloused to this seeming, and then may very well (the argument goes) find it easy to treat humans the same way.

I think the argument is worth considering, because, although it does not show that animals have primary rights, it does suggest that by treating animals as though they do, some humans might be conditioned to treat other human beings *as though humans have rights.* This may be no more than a hope, but Nazi doctors did practice vivisection on Slavs partly on the theory that they were like animals, so every possibility of avoiding such inhumanity ought to be pursued.

The argument might be further strengthened by suggesting that animals unconsciously and unintentionally earn their right to existence by providing the opportunity for us to be kind to them, as practice and conditioning for being kind to other humans. This seems rather strained, and the comparison may merely show that there actually isn't much to the notion of earning rights unintentionally. (It also breathes of the air in which noses are provided for eyeglasses to rest upon.)

This is, of course, a backhanded way of ameliorating the lot of animals. The prudential argument does provide some ground for attributing rights to animals, that is, they do have the characteristic of *appearing* to enjoy life as human beings do. This alone is not enough to explain or justify their having intrinsic right to a comfortable life, but it is at least related to concern for the human moral milieu that we do know exists. And it overlaps the sentimental argument whose advocates do claim that animals have rights in their own right.

The Sentimental Argument

The primary argument from sentiment is that whatever is sentient has a right to life. It is weaker than the prudential argument in that it does depend on animals not being machines (and many people are not convinced of this in the sense that they doubt the behavioral evidence that animals have conscious feelings). It is also weak because there is no explanation why the characteristic of sentience should entitle an entity to rights, minimally to the right to life, or as in the argument below, to the right not to be made to suffer unnecessarily. The appeal to sentience is, however, better than the appeal to mere existence, for a least there is a generally accepted way of distinguishing between sentient and insentient existence (for the same reason the appeal to life is better than the appeal to mere existence). Nevertheless, all these appeals suffer from the same problem. Why, one must ask, does the mere possession of sentience (or in some versions, merely of life) endow an entity with the right to life or to relief from unnecessary suffering, let alone a right to a comfortable habitat in order to live out its natural life?

I treat the ecological and prudential arguments in general outline, partly because it is easy to see their strengths and weaknesses, and partly because they are ubiquitous. However, since the sentimental and contractual arguments have recently had strong advocates, I examine these arguments with reference to named proponents.

In his book, *Animal Liberation: A New Ethics for Our Treatment of Animals,*[4] Peter Singer argues that all sentient beings have a right to life free from needless suffering, and that they are the moral equals of humans. Singer's basic assertion is that it is "wrong to inflict needless suffering on another being" and that animals should be "treated as the independent sentient beings that they are, and not as means to human ends."[5] This last, at least in theory (but not in practice), rules out for Singer the appeal made to human interests that leads to the assignment of secondary rights in the ecological and prudential arguments. However, note that only humans can cause animals needless suffering. Needless suffering is a human moral concept. The use of *needless* implies that the suffering is from no animal need, but from unnecessary or needless needs ("human ends") of humans. I prefer the term *unnecessary* as being somewhat more general than *needless*, but, still, only humans can cause "unnecessary suffering." Thus from the outset, animal rights are generated only by the action of moral agents (which in the argument nonhuman animals are not). Animal sufferings in nature are natural, and as such are neither morally necessary nor unnecessary.

Animals are thus said to have the rights to live unsubjected to needless suffering, and independently of human interference. Singer claims that this "is to appeal to the basic moral principles that we all accept,"[6] and insists that "there can be no reason—except the selfish desire to preserve the privileges of the exploiting group—for refusing to extend the basic principle of equality to members of other species."[7] He defines this principle of "moral equality" as follows:

> Each to count for one and none for more than one.... In other words, the interests of every being affected by an action are to be

taken into account and given the same weight as the like interests of another being.[8]

Most people would accept Singer's assertion that humans and nonhuman animals are alike in having sentience (again note that this *is* a moot point, and the prudential argument is stronger for not having to assume it). I accept this assumption, pausing only to remark that the philosophical level of this discussion is high above the primary problems of philosophy. A serious and difficult problem at the primary level is how one knows or establishes that *humans* are sentient beings. To assume that animals are sentient is to rise above a lot of philosophical underbrush. However, I have done the same in assuming that other humans are self-conscious. More precisely, both Singer and I depend on an argument from analogy. Animals (and other humans) appear to us to be sentient (or self-conscious) because they behave the way we do in similar circumstances, and *we* are sentient (and self-conscious). The argument in each case is invalid, for, although one can observe one's own behavior, one's own sentiments and thoughts, and the other's behavior, one constitutionally cannot observe the other's sentiments and thoughts, and so has no independent way to check to see if the other has them. (Even if one could "plug in" to the other, there would be problems as to whose sentiments and thoughts were being observed, one's own, or the other's.)

Even after accepting that (many) nonhuman animals are sentient, however, the question of whether or not they have interests as humans do still remains. In section IV I conclude, not unlike Singer, that some do. Singer's argument that they do, nevertheless, must be considered in detail because it is often offered in a form that is fallacious. Briefly, Singer (and many others) jumps from statements about the differing interests of different classes of humans to claims about rights of animals based on their "interests." The argument is fallacious because nonhuman animals are not shown by it to have interests in the relevant sense that humans do.

Singer puts the argument in the context of women's liberation. He begins:

> Women have the right to vote, for instance, because they are just as capable of making rational decisions about the future as men are; dogs, on the other hand, are incapable of understanding the significance of voting, so they cannot have the right to vote.[9]

Here women and men, but not dogs, are said to have the right to vote because the former understand the significance (implicitly, the principles) involved—characteristics (2) and (4) of the reciprocity framework—and dogs do not. But Singer goes on:

> Many feminists hold that women have the right to an abortion on request. It does not follow that since these same feminists are campaigning for equality between men and women they must support the right of men to have abortions too. Since a man cannot have an abortion, it is meaningless to talk of his right to have one. Since a dog can't vote, it is meaningless to talk of his right to vote.... The basic principle of equality does not require equal or identical *treatment;* it requires equal *consideration.* Equal consideration for different beings may lead to a different treatment and different rights.[10]

Singer thinks this argument establishes that dogs can have rights which are different from men's rights. But this does not follow. Obviously women need not campaign for the right of men to have abortions, but it would be appropriate under the equal consideration clause for them to campaign for men's right of self-determination over their bodies (e.g., against military conscription). But the reason for this is not because male and female bodies are different, but because they understand the principles involved. They possess rational self-determination in a moral milieu, characteristics (3) and (5) of the reciprocity framework. The dog also has a bodily configuration different from that of a woman, but the reason a dog cannot vote is not, e.g., because it cannot pull the lever in a voting booth. The dog differs from both women and men in not being capable of understanding the relevant moral principles, characteristic (4). Women and men are shown to have moral interests and rights here because they are moral agents as defined by the reciprocity framework. Singer's talk of women's and men's ability to vote implies that they (1) are self-conscious, (2) can understand general principles, (3) have free will, (4) understand the given principles, (5) are physically capable, and (6) intend to act. Singer's argument that the dog deserves equal consideration is fallacious because he does not show that the dog shares any of these relevant characteristics. All his example explicitly shows is that humans have interests and rights.

It might seem fairer if I presented Singer as implicitly arguing here (as I do below) from the dog's possession of characteristic (2) to his having interests as humans do. But Singer emphatically wants to *deny* here the relevance or necessity of reason or understanding to the generation of either interests or the right to relief from needless suffering. (Later he admits their relevance to the right to life.) All he has shown (or assumed) *here* is that the dog is sentient, and he insists that this is all that is necessary to establish intrinsic rights. My critique is so precise because I deny that sentience is enough. Sentience is not even relevant in the particular case of voting, and is probably irrelevant to a very wide range of moral actions. That is, Singer takes sentience to be the capability for physical suffering and enjoyment, but someone who had the relevant characteristics listed above but who could not suffer or enjoy physical pain or pleasure (who was self-conscious but insentient) would surely have the right to vote, and also the duty to behave according to moral principles. (Consider Thomas Aquinas on angels for a corroborating viewpoint.) What Singer must do is show what sort of consideration an entity is entitled to by the mere possession of sentience. Right to relief from needless suffering is his basic claim, but his excursion into the human moral milieu does not establish this for nonhuman animals. He has not yet shown that mere sentience entitles an entity to any rights at all.

Parenthetically, I should remark that many advocates of animal rights simply "feel" that possession of sentience entitles an entity to the right to relief from unnecessary suffering, and are very impatient with those who ask for an argument to establish this claim. I've already said my piece on such special senses. Some people may in fact have them, but they are not going to convert the heathen without argument.

Singer now goes on to deny that a level of intelligence permitting the understanding of rights is required to have them (although he says above that lack of understanding debars the dog from voting). In arguing that the principle of equality must "be extended to all beings, black or white, masculine or feminine, human or nonhuman,"[11] Singer says that "If possessing a higher degree of intelligence does not entitle one human to use another for his own ends, how can it entitle humans to exploit nonhumans for the same purpose?"[12] But it is not the degree of intelligence *per se* that is significant to the possession of rights here, but rather what is understood. The relevant difference is that humans have a general capacity to understand moral principles such as those involved in voting, or concerning rights and duties, whereas many nonhumans do not.

Singer continues to try to establish rights on the basis of sentience alone, going on to say in his major pronouncement:

The question is not, Can they *reason?* nor Can they talk? but, *Can they suffer?* ... The capacity for suffering and enjoyment is *a pre-requisite for having interests at all,* a condition that must be satisfied before we can speak of interests in a meaningful way. ... A stone does not have interests because it cannot suffer.[13]

Sentience, or the ability to suffer and to enjoy physical sensations, may be a necessary condition for having some kinds of interests, but it is not necessary for all (cf. the insentient voter). Moreover, Singer presents it also as a sufficient condition, which it is not. Again it might seem fairer if I presented Singer as implying that sentience is neces-sarily related to self-consciousness (as I argue in section IV), but he insists on resting his case on sentience alone.

I have shown that "The capacity for [physical] suffering is" *not* "*a prerequisite for having interests at all.* "But what about mental pain and pleasure? Cases from fiction suggest both alternatives. Camus' unfeeling stranger finds himself without interests. However, *Star Trek's* unemotional Mr. Spock is a very stern moralist with firm interests. I suggest that most people would go with Mr. Spock. There would seem to be no reason why lack of either physical or mental pain or pleasure would deprive one of all interests, or in particular of moral rights and duties. One might still know what is right and have an interest in doing it, not for pleasure, but as Kant asks, out of duty.

Singer's criterion for moral equality remains mere physical senti-ence:

> If a being suffers there can be no moral justification for refusing to take that suffering into consideration. No matter what the nature of the being, the principle of equality requires that its suffering be counted equally with the like suffering—in so far as rough comparisions can be made—of any other being. If a being is not capable of suffering, or of experiencing enjoyment or happiness, there is nothing to be taken into account. So the limit of sentience (using the term as a convenient if not strictly accu-rate shorthand for the capacity to suffer and/or experience enjoyment) is the only defensible boundary of concern for the interests of others. To mark this boundary by some other characteristic like intelligence or rationality would be to mark it in an arbitrary manner. Why not choose some other characteris-tic, like skin color?[14]

Singer here again combines selective special pleading with cross-categorial comparisons. By implying that skin color and sex are characteristics no different in moral importance from "intelligence and rationality," Singer belittles the importance of the characteristics on which the liberation of blacks and women is actually based. It *is* because blacks, women, and white men have intelligence and reason in common that they can be compared as moral equals. Obviously skin color, sex, sharpness of reason, and level of intelligence make no difference to their moral equality, for this is based on their general capability to interact morally. Many sentient animals cannot be so compared because they have no understanding of moral principles. Singer does not meet this argument at all.

Singer goes on to attack the view that possession of language is a criterion for distinguishing humans morally from other animals. He dismisses out of hand the Wittgensteinian view that "we cannot meaningfully attribute states of consciousness to beings without language,"[15] which, incidentally, is a very Cartesian point. However, the strongest confirmation we have that other beings are sentient or self-conscious is their telling us that they are, and it may well be that only through language can one recognize even in oneself that one is sentient or self-conscious.

Despite his insistence that mere sentience is enough to establish the right to relief from needless suffering, Singer uses self-consciousness (he uses the phrase self-awarness) and rational self-determination as criteria for determining the value of a being's life:

> To avoid speciesism we must allow that beings which are similar in all relevant respects have a similar right to live—and mere membership in our own biological species cannot be a morally relevant criterion for this right [Note that the reciprocity framework is applicable to any moral agent, not just to human beings.] Within these limits we could still hold that, for instance, it is worse to kill *a normal adult human, with a capacity for self-awareness, and the ability to plan for the future and have meaningful* [surely meaningful here implies reciprocal] *relations with others* [my italics], than it is to kill a mouse, which presumably does not share all of these characteristics....We may legitimately hold that there are some features of certain beings which make their lives more valuable than those of other beings; but there will surely be some nonhuman animals whose lives, by any standards, are more valuable than the lives of some humans. A chimpanzee, dog, or pig, for instance, will have a higher degree of self-awareness and a greater capacity for meaningful relations with others than a severely retarded infant or

someone in a state of advanced senility. So if we base the right to life on these characteristics we must grant these animals a right to life as good as, or better than, such retarded or senile humans.[16]

Singer goes on to say that on these grounds we might also claim that "the severely retarded and hopelessly senile have no [he means very low] right to live and may be killed for quite trivial reasons, as we now kill animals."[17] I do not intend here to get into the questions of the rights of human infants who have the potential of being moral agents, nor of senile adults who once were, but it certainly does not follow that whatever has a right to life of low (or even of no) value can be killed for trivial reasons. We can accept (e.g., as in the prudential argument) the duty not to kill or to be cruel unnecessarily. Singer evidently means to argue that such criteria should not be used to determine whether a being has a right to life *per se*, but because he agrees that they can be used to determine the values of lives on an hierarchical scale, his argument backfires.

There is also an important confusion in Singer's plea: although we are more or less aware of our selves at different times, and thus might speak loosely of different degrees of self-awareness or self-consciousness, self-awareness *per se* does not admit of degrees. One either is or is not self-conscious, no matter how vaguely or clearly. (Although I do not believe that this needs argument, I consider it again in section IV.) The important criterion is surely self-awareness *per se* (the being knows something is happening to himself), and not some degree of its clarity.

Singer goes on to determine the criteria that are important for ranking one life higher than another, but tries to discount them as criteria for determining that one sentient being has any more or less right to be relieved of needless suffering than does any other:

> I conclude, then, that a rejection of speciesism does not imply that all lives are of equal worth. While self-awareness, intelligence, the capacity for meaningful relations with others, and so on are not relevant to the question of inflicting pain— since pain is pain, whatever other capacities, beyond the capacity to feel pain, the being may have—these capacities may be relevant to the question of taking life. It is not arbitrary to hold that the life of a self-aware being, capable of abstract thought, of planning for the future, of complex acts of communication, and so on, is more valuable than the life of a being without these

capacities.... The evil of pain is, in itself, unaffected by the other characteristics of the being that feels the pain; the value of life is affected by these other characteristics.

Normally, this will mean that if we have to choose between the life of a human being and the life of another animal we should choose to save the life of the human; but there may be special cases in which the reverse holds true, because the human being in question does not have the capacities of a normal human being.[18]

In this last case, it would surely be prudent to give the defective human being normal rights (unless perhaps he is mad and wants his sword back to kill his wife). In any event, Singer gives away his case here. For if the characteristics listed (very much like those of the reciprocity framework) are crucial in the decision to kill a being that does not have them rather than one who does, when the choice must be made, then in a choice of inflicting pain, the being that is more valuable on these criteria should be spared at the expense of the less valuable life. It is surely false to argue that criteria appropriate for determining which of two lives is of higher or lower value are not relevent when there is a choice of causing suffering in one of two lives. One might argue that if pain must be inflicted on one of two beings, then it is necessary. But it is unnecessary for one of them, and unless Singer allows the criteria given above (or some criteria) for making the choice, we are at a loss. (To keep from starving, shall we eat the cat, or the baby? Singer's criterion for when it is permissible to experiment on an animal, only when an experimenter "would be prepared to use a retarded human at a similar mental level to the animal he is planning to use,"[19] is of no help. Does he mean this? Which experimenter?)

Thus, pain is not the same, except perhaps when two entities share exactly the same characteristics. Singer comes to the opposite conclusion, but he has no argument for claiming that only "the capacity to feel pain" is relevant, and (as I say) his argument about lives of higher and lower value undercuts his claim. In admitting that some lives are more valuable than others, he admits that they should be more protected. Singer implicitly shows that sentience is not a sufficient condition for moral equality with human beings.

Thus, despite Singer's rhetoric and explicit denial,[20] his case for treating animals humanely reduces to a plea based merely on the principle that we should not cause unnecessary suffering. I believe the prudential argument makes a stronger case for this than does Singer's argument from sentience. That we accept a duty not to treat animals cruelly does not mean that they have any other than a secondary right not to be treated cruelly. Far from proving that sentience entitles a being to intrinsic rights, Singer implicitly admits that the six characteristics of the reciprocity framework are necessary to establish rights, and that only moral agents can be moral equals. All his attempts to argue that animals have rights, because humans do, fail because none of the human rights he alludes to derive from sentience alone, but rather from the fact that humans are moral agents. Humans and animals *do* share sentience, but all that follows from this with respect to rights is that it would be prudent for humans to assign secondary rights to animals.

There is another variety of the argument from sentiment that Singer appeals to. This is the argument from empathy, identification, compassion, pathos, projection, or sentimentality. Most people wince to witness or to think of the suffering of animals. Perhaps recognizing the weakness of his direct moral claim, Singer rests his main appeal on factual reporting about the deplorable conditions in which experimental animals, battery chickens, and beef cattle spend their lives. He is struck (as everyone ought to be) by the fact that when news got out that the U. S. Air Force and U. S. Army were planning to use 600 beagle hounds to test poison gas, "the volume of mail to the Department [of Defense] received was the greatest ever for any single event, surpassing even the mail on the bombings of North Vietnam and Cambodia."[21] Singer mentions this again to stress that the cause of animal liberation "does not lack popular support,"[22] but I must say that considering what was going on in Vietnam and Cambodia at the time, this incidence of compassion for the suffering of animals gives me a sinking feeling about the hope of ordinary human beings to avoid cluster bombs and napalm.

But perhaps concern for beagles will also lead to concern for human beings (the prudential argument) for whom the gas is actually designed. And, of course, most people who argue for animal rights also staunchly support human rights, but, again, given the amount of suffering and death meted out to human beings by other humans in the world to day, I can easily sympathize with those who object to the following kind of hyperbole. Singer says:

> The tyranny of human over nonhuman animals ... has caused and today is causing an amount of pain and suffering that can only be compared with that which resulted from the centuries of tyranny by white humans over black humans. The struggle against this tyranny is a struggle as important as any of the

moral and social issues that have been fought over in recent years.[23]

Can animals actually be tyrannized? Even if one agreed to that, Singer's final sentence in the above quotation is quite unsupported. It is so insulting to past and present human victims of moral and social oppression as to be hard to believe that anyone would actually make it. At the danger of explaining the obvious so as not to be misunderstood, I say it is insulting because Singer himself gives excellent grounds for establishing that human lives are far richer and more valuable than those of nonhuman animals.

The weakness of Singer's philosophical claims thus lead him in the bulk of his book to present standard emotional appeals for prevention of cruelty to animals and for vegetarianism. As such, these emotional appeals are quite persuasive, but they are an inadequate substitute for philosophical argument. And so in the end Singer's sentimental argument (like the ecological and prudential arguments) is strongest when he builds a case for improving the lot of animals on the interests of human beings. Humans will just feel more comfortable if everyone treats animals kindly. There is no argument that supports the view that causing merely sentient beings unnecessary suffering is bad because it deprives them of their rights, for there is no argument establishing that they have any rights. But most people do agree that kindness to animals is praiseworthy, if only because it is so easy to identify with their suffering. It is vacuous to argue that we should, e.g., treat nonhuman animals as we would have them treat us, for that line of argument depends on the implication that they are moral agents, which most are not. However, in the interests of decreasing the suffering of humans who suffer when animals do, we can assign to animals secondary rights not to be caused unnecessary suffering. And, since it can be established that humans have a right not to be caused unnecessary suffering, extending this right to animals in order to decrease *human* suffering is a good thing. This links animal rights to the human moral milieu, just as do the ecological and prudential arguments. And, although this final sentimental argument is not as strong as the ecological and the prudential, it is still a fair argument, and should not be despised by those who might argue against it (and against the prudential argument) that a more calloused attitude toward animals might release emotional energy to be used to work for the relief of the suffering of a billion or more human beings on Earth today. As a matter of fact, one of the strongest arguments for vegetarianism— which Singer stresses—and which holds quite apart from any discussion of animal rights—is that this would release for starving humans immense quantities of vegetable food that is now unnecessarily fed to animals to provide meat for the rich. However, there are those who claim the right to eat meat, and this leads us naturally to the last argument I consider, the argument based on property and contract.

The Contractual Argument

Whereas the contractual argument is weakest in offering why non-human animals and nature purportedly have any primary, earned, or intrinsic rights, it probably is the strongest for effectively motivating the assignment of secondary rights to nature. Let me say at the outset (parallel to the other three arguments) that nature in the contractual argument is related to the human moral milieu, and rights are assigned to it because of the pleasure it affords to human beings. Humans have an interest in this pleasure. Thus, nature might be said to earn the right to peaceful existence because (even though unwittingly, and not out of duty) it provides pleasure for human beings. I rank this characteristic of less value than the characteristic of not-causing-humans-discomfort-by-not-suffering-unnecessary-pain, and thus rank the contractual argument lower than the sentimental argument. It seems reasonable to think that it is more valuable to relieve humans of suffering (which they have when other animals suffer) than to provide humans pleasure (which, unfortunately, is provided to some humans not just by communion with nature, but also by the suffering of animals).

   I call the argument the contractual argument because it openly treats nature as property in which human beings have an interest (which interest I refer to generally as pleasure, though of course it could also be because such property provides the bare necessities for survival without much pleasure other than that of surviving itself). The contractual relation is among human beings, who contract to treat each other's property as though it had rights of its own. These rights are, however, often transparently, extensions of the rights of the human beings who own or have an interest in the property in question.

   This argument (although not in the blunt way I present it above) is given voice most persuasively by Christopher D. Stone. In his book, *Should Trees Have Standing? Toward Legal Rights for Natural Objects,*[24] Stone proposes that natural objects such as redwood forests and mountains be given the status of legal persons such as corporations now have under the law. This would give them rights under the Fourteenth Amendment to the U.S. Constitution. It would make nature, or parts of it, into institutions, which are human artifacts.[25] In effect, the proposal is to incorporate nature into human moral and legal affairs, and to treat it as we now treat corporations. Because these abstract corporate entities cannot in fact speak for themselves (they are not rationally self-determined), they would have legal guardians to speak in their names.

Something like this approach was taken by Sierra Club representatives trying to save Mineral King Valley from commercial development by Walt Disney Enterprises. In this case the courts specifically required the testimony of individual human beings who could show that it was to their interest that Mineral King Valley remain undeveloped. In effect, then, this move is to treat nature as something in which individual human beings have a proprietary interest. In itself, nature has no right, say, to noninterference by humans. But, if individual human beings can show that noninterference in some part of nature is to their benefit and pleasure, then they can appropriate enough of a property right to that part of nature to claim that it is incorporated in their interests, and thus has the rights of a legal person as do other corporations under the Fourteenth Amendment.

From a philosophical viewpoint, there are grave difficulties with this approach that extend far beyond the question of the rights of nature. They have to do with the fact that corporations are not real persons in the self-conscious independent way humans are, and thus cannot have reciprocal rights and duties. Further, some believe that there is ideological danger in promoting the concept of a legal person having rights just as human persons do under the Fourteenth Amendment. As I indicate below, this fiction fascinates, and may take on an aura (or be given it by unscrupulous or misguided human beings) of importance and value that seems higher than that of individual human beings. Some even worry, harking back to the Cartesian animal-machine, that if we begin to treat things like corporations as persons, this may harden us so that we begin to treat persons as things.

The concept of a legal person has often been criticized. Adolf O. Berle points out that Justice Hugo Black argued in *Connecticut General Life Insurance Company v. Johnson* that the Fourteenth Amendment applies only to natural, not to artificial persons,[26] and that Justice William O. Douglas in *Wheeling Steel Company v. Glander* and in *Bell v. Maryland* "powerfully reaffirmed his position that corporations were *not* 'persons' entitled to the protection of the Fourteenth Amendment."[27] Berle also quotes Woodrow Wilson as saying:

> I regard the corporation as indispensible to modern business enterprises. I am not jealous of its size and might, if you will but abandon at the right points the fatuous, antiquated, and quite unnecessary fiction which treats it as a legal person; if you will but cease to deal with it by means of your law as if it were a single individual not only, but also—what every child may perceive *it is not—a responsible individual* [my italics].[28]

Stone himself points out that when it was first proposed, many jurists, including Chief Justice Marshall, found it "unthinkable" that corporations could have rights as persons do.[29] And, besides those mentioned above, such diverse thinkers as George Orwell, Karl Popper, Henry Miller, and Isaiah Berlin, etc. (their number is legend) continually warn against personifying abstract entities such as corporations. The point is that it is just false (contrary to what Stone says) that corporate entities such as institutions

> have wills, minds, purposes, and inertias that are in very important ways their own, i.e., that can transcend and survive changes in the consciousness of the individuals who supposedly comprise them, and whom they supposedly serve.[30]

Stone probably means merely that they appear in some ways to have wills, etc. of their own, but his way of putting it illustrates the danger of personifying abstract entities. Institutional inertia does affect the decisions of human beings, but if corporate persons actually did have "wills, minds, and purposes" of their own, presumably they could speak for themselves.

Stone goes on to show the result that Isiah Berlin *et al.* find so disconcerting. After commenting in an aside that "it is more and more the individual human being, with his consciousness, that is the legal fiction," Stone adds in a note:

> The legal system does the best it can to maintain the illusion of the reality of the individual human being. Consider, for example, how many constitutional cases, brought in the name of some handy individual, represent a power struggle between institutions—the NAACP and a school board, the Catholic Church and a school board, the ACLU and the Army, and so forth. Are the individual human plaintiffs the real moving causes of these cases —or an afterthought?[31]

Note how insidious the device is: Stone does not say that lawyers or legislators or judges do the best they can, etc., but instead personifies an abstract entity, *the* legal system. No one can totally avoid this mode of expression, but in cases like this it is not, I insist, innocuous, for it does contribute to thinking as though corporations, e.g., actually do have wills, etc., and—as we all know—it can be a means of avoiding individual responsibility.

Corporations are not responsible moral agents. They cannot reciprocate. They can have no primary rights because they cannot fulfill any duties. It is suspected that the concept of legal personhood for corporations is a device to allow actually responsible persons to escape punishment. This has certainly been the result in many corporation scandals. Also, those who speak in the name of abstract corporate entities, asking you, e.g., not to think what your nation-state can do for you (although it was designed to serve you), but what you can do for it (such as fight in an illegal war), may be in fact merely using the corporate device to do something that is in their (and not necessarily in your, or, for that matter, in the nation-state's) interests.

This is enough to show that corporations are not really persons, and to present some of the reasons why many people think it dangerous to assign rights to them as though they were, even when the concept of legal personhood is clearly labeled as a fiction. Stone, however, in no way argues that natural objects should have rights on the ground that they are real persons. His is a lawyer's proposal to assign rights to nature or natural objects under the Fourteenth Amendment by having individual human beings show enough interest in them to justify their designation as legal persons. As I said above, this is to view nature as property, and to link any rights assigned to it to the moral milieu of human interests. If nature earns its rights, it is through providing pleasure for humans. And once the status of natural objects as legal persons is established, their treatment (or their rights) is then established through contractual agreements among human beings.

To the end of concurring with Stone's recommendation, Justice Douglas swallows his former reservations about corporate persons, clearly stating that "the voice of the existing beneficiaries of these environmental wonders should be heard."[32]

This legal move is proposed to protect the "natural" state of parts of nature. However, as I show in my comments on the ecological argument, any state is as natural as any other. Representatives of Walt Disney Enterprises might argue, for example, that they and their works are just as natural as beaver dams.[33] And they certainly have interests that are more quantifiable and familiar in corporation law than the qualitative interests of environmentalists. In short, the incorporation of nature does provide human voices speaking *about* it, but they can speak for either side. Nevertheless, since it is better to have some voice in a dispute than none, Stone's recommendation is to be applauded. And the incorporation of nature is, in any event, a natural outcome of its increasing value to human beings. Whoever wins—e.g., representatives of either the Sierra Club or Walt Disney Enterprises— then gets to dispose of the natural object according to their interests (but not according to the interests of Mineral King Valley—the voices do not speak *for it*—for in fact it has no interests).

This, then, is not, as Stone claims throughout, a great "advancement" in morality. It is merely an extension of corporation law, which, while being one of man's more clever inventions for furthering business interests, is probably not a jewel in anyone's moral crown. And, like Singer (with even less attempt at argument), Stone lumps nature with oppressed human beings, claiming that

> we are cultivating the personal capacities *within us* to recognize more and more the ways in which nature—like the woman, the Black, the Indian and the Alien—is like us (and we will also become more able realistically to define, confront, live with and admire the ways in which we are all different).[34]

(In this passage Stone even makes abstract entities out of women, Blacks, Indians, and Aliens.) This self-congratulatory sort of conclusion about moral progress supported by environmentalist rhetoric is, as I argue above, a *non sequitur*. The difference between Mineral King Valley and, e.g., *a* woman are extensive. On this note, I close my discussion of these four arguments.

4. Self-Consciousness

In section 1, I present a reciprocity framework as an analysis of morality, and to explain and justify the attribution of moral rights and duties. I propose that rights derive from the fulfillment of duties, which can be accomplished only by rationally self-determined individuals who intend to abide by moral principles. Such moral agency is grounded in self-consciousness and crowned with intent.

In section 2, I outline an empirical position according to which human beings are a part of nature, and a supernatural position according to which they are not. My intent is to show that in either case human beings are classed apart from nonhuman animals and the rest of nature on the basis of the reciprocity characteristics that make them moral agents. This division between a human milieu which is moral and a nonhuman milieu which is not is justified by reference to natural characteristics humans have which many nonhumans (but not all, I argue below) lack. I put aside the mystical position, according to which all of nature belongs to the moral milieu, because this view (though perhaps true) is unsupported by any natural (non-supernatural) evidence.

In section 3, I provide a justification of the reciprocity framework by using it to illuminate and criticize four standard arguments for attributing rights on other than reciprocity grounds. I argue that the attributions made on the basis of these arguments are in fact implicitly or explicitly based on reciprocal human interest.

In this section (4), I now expand and answer two questions that arise from consideration of the reciprocity framework. The primary characteristic necessary for being a moral entity is self-consciousness. For determining whether or not an entity is part of the moral milieu, then, the primary question is: is it self-conscious? The sufficient condition for being a moral agent is intent to act according to or opposed to moral principles. The crucial question, then, is: does it intend to act with reference to moral principles?

To determine whether or not an entity is self-conscious, one must know what self-consciousness is. My answer is to appeal to introspection. If you understand what Descartes means when he says, "I think, therefore I am," then you have experience of your self which is self-consciousness. Beyond this, one knows that others are self-conscious by observing that their behavior is similar to one's own behavior. Most important is their verbal or other communicative behavior. I have already criticized the fallacious analogical argument that others have self-consciousness because their behavior is like one's own self-conscious behavior, but as Hume says, our natural inclinations lead us to accept it anyway.

This makes self-consciousness sound very much like one of the special senses I criticize above. A being who has no sense of self might say of my claim what I say of the mystic's claim to special knowledge. And there is a parallel here. A non-conscious being cannot understand or accept my talk of self-consciousness because it has no experience of any such thing as a self and cannot imagine it. I have the same problem with the mystic's ineffable experience.

Such speculation is droll, but in fact the criticism attributed above to a non-self-conscious being could be made only by one who is self-conscious. Consider a being who is sentient but not self-conscious. Such a being presumably experiences sensations of pain and pleasure, but has no experience of self. Without any sense of self, this being would also have no sense of continuity, no notion or memory of past experience as its own, and no anticipation of future experience. Some people have thus suggested that non-self-conscious animals live only in the present. They experience pain and pleasure only in the moment. Now I think that merely spelling this out is enough to show its inadequacy. Even if sensations are experienced only in the moment, to be experienced they must be experienced as one's own by a temporally restricted self-consciousness. Even Hume's atomic impression and ideas have a character of awareness. It seems obvious that self-awareness is essential to sentience, or to experience of any kind.

Note that I leave open the question as to whether or not life is necessary to the possession of self-consciousness, sentience, etc. I see no reason why it should be necessary to be alive to be a moral agent.

My position is very similar to that of John Locke on persons. Following a marvelous passage on a talking parrot, Locke says that

> to find wherein personal identity consists, we must consider what *person* stands for;—which, I think, is a thinking intelligent being, that has reason and reflection, and can consider itself as itself, the same thinking thing, in different times and places; which it does only by that consciousness which is inseparable from thinking, and, as it seems to me, essential to it: it being impossible for any one to perceive without *perceiving* that he does perceive.[35]

Locke concludes that if an entity has self-consciousness, then it is a person, whether it is in the form of a man, parrot, cat, or whatever. I believe that this view is correct, and that no one has said it better. Strikingly, the claims of mystics seem to confirm the view that to perceive, one must perceive that one perceives. Mystics often say that their experience is beyond self-consciousness, that they lose themselves to merge in a nonindividual whole. Some people claim to have such experiences under the influence of drugs. However, usually this is reported as an experience of both being and not being one's self. I do not think it is merely to be trapped in bimodal logic to respond to this by saying that as long as one can report what happened, to that extent one was self-conscious in the experience.

Some people also talk of degrees of self-consciousness. I have already said that self-consciousness is surely an all-or-nothing phenomenon, like pregnancy. People who talk about degrees of self-consciousness are probably thinking rather of degrees of clarity or vagueness of self-consciousness. But, however vaguely, if you know you are self-conscious, you are self-conscious; if you don't know it, you aren't. This probably means that we are sometimes awake but not self-conscious. My position requires me to say that if you remember, then you were still vaguely self-conscious, no matter how abstracted. If you don't remember at all—as sometimes happens to people driving cars—then you were not self-conscious during the blank interval. When one is truly bereft of self-consciousness as in a dreamless sleep or a coma, then one has nothing to report. My conclusion is that for having sentience or any experience at all, self-consciousness is necessary.

Thus, the drollery of imagining a conversation between non-self-conscious and self-conscious beings is that it depends on the contradictory assumption that the non-self-conscious being is aware of its own continuing self. The pathos or inarticulateness of the mystic stems from the fact that he himself does not have the mystical experience.

The conclusion that is relevant to the primary question at issue is that if we accept the behavioral evidence that other human beings are self-conscious, then we ought to accept the behavioral evidence that individuals of a very wide range of other animal species are self-conscious. In the present context (putting aside philosophical scepticism), I do accept this conclusion. Sentient animals are also (necessarily) self-conscious. I think failure to be explicit about this is the reason some advocates of the argument from sentience have trouble classifying some animals, e.g., oysters. Oysters, and even some plants, react instantly to being stuck, say, with a pin. If we were so stuck, we would feel pain. But does an oyster or plant really feel pain? The question arises, I believe, because, though their reaction suggests sentience, it is hard for us to imagine that they are self-conscious, that they perceive or know in themselves that they feel pain. On the other hand, it is difficult *not* to believe that mammals and birds (and probably reptiles and fish) are self-conscious. Witness how often we are warned not to anthropomorphize. There is even danger of attributing self-consciousness to corporations, and what is "unthinkable" to some jurists about treating corporations as persons is the same failure of imagination that some people have with respect to oysters: it is hard to imagine oysters feeling pain or corporations having interests because it is hard to imagine them being self-conscious.

But many animals show every sign of remembering past events and of anticipating future ones, as anyone's dog does, and they actively communicate their needs and desires to us through behavior that certainly appears to be intentional. Clearly these animals must be accepted as self-conscious on the same grounds that we accept the self-consciousness of other human beings. They have some rationality and intelligence, they communicate through sign systems that are much less versatile than is human language but is nevertheless as adequate for expressing many personal wants and desires as in human speech (particularly from a purely behavioral standpoint), and they give every indication of knowing when they are hurt. They understand general principles of various sorts, and dogs and chimpanzees, for example, apparently understand some moral principles (which would make them moral entities according to the reciprocity framework), and even seem on occasion to try sincerely and intentionally to live up to moral principles (which would occasionally make them moral agents).

Perhaps this is to anthropomorphize, but merely to attribute self-consciousness to an entity on the basis of its behavior—particularly its apparently intentionally communicative behavior about what one must infer are its own interests and desires—is *not* in fact to anthropomorphize the entity. My guess is that the worry about anthropomorphizing animals often stems from a desire to keep them out of the moral milieu, much as Descartes refuses them self-consciousness in part because he does not think they have Christian souls. But mere possession of sentience and self-consciousness, intelligence and rationality, interests and desires, and the ability to communicate about one's self, none or all of these makes an entity a moral agent in a moral milieu. Self-consciousness is indeed the foundational necessary condition for moral agency, but like the sentience which is linked to it, is far from being a sufficient condition.

But do some animals intend to act with reference to moral principles? I believe that the answer to this question—on behavioral evidence—is yes. Some chimpanzees, gorillas (probably orangutans and perhaps gibbons), dolphins, (probably whales), elephants, dogs, pigs, and maybe cats and some other animals are sometimes moral agents. That is, there is adequate behavioral evidence that they have self-consciousness, capability of understanding moral principles, free will, understanding of specific duties, physical capability, and sometimes the intent to act with respect to moral principles.

There are four main objections to this conclusion. The first is that animals without a language as complex as human language cannot understand general principles. I think that the problem-solving behavior of many animals is enough to infer that they understand general (including some moral) principles.

Second, it might be objected that animals cannot or need not understand moral principles because moral principles are human artifacts. One answer is that humans and their works are a part of nature, so moral principles are as much a part of the animals' natural environment as any other. As to why they should bother with moral principles, I'm reduced to suggesting that maybe they want to, and obviously humans sometimes want them to.

Third, some people say that they will believe that chimpanzees, for example, are self-conscious when they tell us they are. A few chimpanzees in their use of signs of self-reference come very close to doing just this. However, behaviorists consider verbal as just another form of publicity observable communicative behavior (without countenancing introspective accompaniments), and, on this basis, some nonhuman animals exhibit behavior which is as adequate (admittedly on the criticized argument from analogy) for concluding that they have the six reciprocity framework characteristics (behaviorally defined) as is human behavior for the same conclusion.

Finally, there is a very difficult problem about how to treat an animal that is only sometimes a moral agent. These animals would be moral entities in having the first five characteristics of the reciprocity framework, but, as anyone knows who has much to do with, say, dogs or chimpanzees, they sometimes seem to lose the ability to intend to act with respect to moral principles which at other times they have. Such a loss affected Camus' stranger.

I'm not sure how to solve this problem, but I have a prudent suggestion. If such animals in their amoral behavior harm other moral entities, then—just as Camus' stranger was—they should be punished as though they were moral agents. I view this punishment as restraining them from doing harm to others. Conceivably (though, as with humans, perhaps erratically), it might make them remember their duties in the future. Animals are so punished in many cultures, and were in medieval Christendom. In some cases, this may not be wrong. The crux of the matter is to determine whether they are amoral in that they understand but do not intend to act with respect to some moral principles, or amoral in the sense of not understanding moral principles at all. I can come to an agreement with a dog. I would not punish a cricket.

In conclusion, I believe that there is good behavioral evidence that many animals are moral entities, and that some are sometimes moral agents. On these recprocity grounds they merit at least intrinsic rights to life and relief from unnecessary suffering. Those incapable of understanding moral principles, but who are still self-conscious and can communicate about their interests should be assigned secondary rights at least to life and to relief from unnecessary suffering on the grounds of the prudential and sentimental arguments. Non-self-conscious nature should be assigned rights according to the ecological and contractural arguments. These appear to be the best (nonsupernatural) grounds for explaining and justifying the rights of nonhuman animals and nature.

Notes

1. Isaiah Berlin, *Four Essays on Liberty* (London: Oxford University Press, 1969), p. xxiv.

2. Aldo Leopold, *A Sand County Almanac* (New York: Oxford University Press, 1949), p. 204.

3. Leonora Cohen Rosenfield, *From Beast-Machine to Man-Machine: Animal Soul in French Letters from Descartes to La Mettre*, 2d ed. (New York: Quadrangle, 1968).

4. Peter Singer, *Animal Liberation: A New Ethics For Our Treatment of Animals* (New York: New York Review/Random House, 1975).

5. Ibid., p. viii.

6. Ibid., p. x.

7. Ibid., p. xi.

8. Ibid., p. 6.

9. Ibid., p. 2.

10. Ibid., pp. 2–3.

11. Ibid., p. 6.

12. Ibid., p. 7.

13. Ibid., pp. 8–9.

14. Ibid., p. 9.

15. Ibid., p. 15.

16. Ibid., pp. 21–22.

17. Ibid., p. 22.

18. Ibid., pp. 23–24

19. Ibid., p. 80.

20. Ibid., pp. 213ff.

21. Ibid., p. 28.

22. Ibid., p. 87.

23. Ibid., p. vii.

24. Christopher D. Stone, *Should Trees Have Standing? Toward Legal Rights for Natural Objects* (Los Altos: William Kauffman, 1972).

25. Richard A. Watson and Philip M. Smith, "Underground Wilderness," *International Journal of Environmental Studies 2* (1971): 217–20; Philip M. Smith and Richard A. Watson, "New Wilderness Boundaries," *Environmental Ethics* 1 (1979): 61–64.

26. Adolf O. Berle, *Power* (New York: Harcourt, Brace & World, 1969) pp. 368–69).

27. Ibid., pp. 369–70.

28. Woodrow Wilson, "The Lawyer and the Community," *Report of the 33rd Annual Meeting of the American Bar Association* (1910), pp. 416–31; quoted in Berle, *Power*, p. 369.

29. Stone, *Should Trees Have Standing?* p. 6.

30. Ibid., p. 47.

31. Ibid., p. 47, n. 125.

32. William O. Douglas, "Mr. Justice Douglas, Dissenting," *Living Wilderness* 36 (1972): 27.

33. Richard A. Watson and Patty Jo Watson, *Man and Nature: An Anthropological Essay in Human Ecology* (New York: Harcourt, Brace & World, 1969).

34. Stone, *Trees*, p. 51.

35. John Locke, *An Essay Concerning Human Understanding*, bk. II, chap. xxvii, par. 9, vol. I (New York: Dover, 1959), pp. 448–49.

2

Animal Liberation: A Triangular Affair

J. Baird Callicott

Environmental Ethics and Animal Liberation

Partly because it is so new to Western philosophy (or at least hereto-fore only scarcely represented) *environmental ethics* has no precisely fixed conventional definition in glossaries of philosophical terminology. Aldo Leopold, however, is universally recognized as the father or founding genius of recent environmental ethics. His "land ethic" has become a modern classic and may be treated as the standard example, the paradigm case, as it were, of what an environmental ethic is. *Environmental ethics* then can be defined ostensively by using Leopold's land ethic as the exemplary type. I do not mean to suggest that all environmental ethics should necessarily conform to Leopold's paradigm, but the extent to which an ethical system resembles Leopold's land ethic might be used, for want of anything better, as a criterion to measure the extent to which it is or is not of the environmental sort.

It is Leopold's opinion, and certainly an overall review of the prevailing traditions of Western ethics, both popular and philosophical, generally confirms it, that traditional Western systems of ethics have not accorded moral standing to nonhuman beings.[1] Animals and plants, soils and waters, which Leopold includes in his community of ethical beneficiaries, have traditionally enjoyed no moral standing, no rights, no respect, in sharp contrast to human persons whose rights and interests ideally must be fairly and equally considered if our actions are to be considered "ethical" or "moral." One fundamental and novel feature of the Leopold land ethic, therefore, is the extension

37

of *direct* ethical considerability from people to nonhuman natural entities.

At first glance, the recent ethical movement usually labeled "animal liberation" or "animal rights" seems to be squarely and centrally a kind of environmental ethics.[2] The more uncompromising among the animal liberationists have demanded equal moral consideration on behalf of cows, pigs, chickens, and other apparently enslaved and oppressed nonhuman animals.[3] The theoreticians of this new hyper-egalitarianism have coined such terms as *speciesism* (on analogy with *racism* and *sexism*) and *human chauvinism* (on analogy with *male chauvinism*), and have made animal liberation seem, perhaps not improperly, the next and most daring development of political liberalism.[4] Aldo Leopold also draws upon metaphors of political liberalism when he tells us that his land ethic "changes the role of *Homo sapiens* from conqueror of the land community to plain member and citizen of it."[5] For animal liberationists it is as if the ideological battles for equal rights and equal consideration for women and for racial minorities have been all but won, and the next and greatest challenge is to purchase equality, first theoretically and then practically, for all (actually only *some*) animals, regardless of species. This more rhetorically implied than fully articulated historical progression of moral rights from fewer to greater numbers of "persons" (allowing that animals may also be persons) as advocated by animal liberationists, also parallels Leopold's scenario in "The Land Ethic" of the historical extension of "ethical criteria" to more and more "fields of conduct" and to larger and larger groups of people during the past three thousand or so years.[6] As Leopold develops it, the land ethic is a cultural "evolutionary possibility," the next "step in a sequence."[7] For Leopold, however, the next step is much more sweeping, much more inclusive than the animal liberationists envision, since it "enlarges the boundaries of the [moral] community to include soils, waters, [and] plants . . ." as well as animals.[8] Thus, the animal liberation movement *could* be construed as partitioning Leopold's perhaps undigestable and totally inclusive environmental ethic into a series of more assimilable stages: today animal rights, tomorrow equal rights for plants, and after that full moral standing for rocks, soil, and other earthy compounds, and perhaps sometime in the still more remote future, liberty and equality for water and other elementary bodies.

Put just this way, however, there is something jarring about such a graduated progression in the exfoliation of a more inclusive environmental ethic, something that seems absurd. A more or less reasonable case might be made for rights for some animals, but when we come to

plants, soils, and waters, the frontier between plausibility and absurdity appears to have been crossed. Yet, there is no doubt that Leopold
sincerely proposes that *land* (in his inclusive sense) be ethically
regarded. The beech and chestnut, for example, have in his view as
much "biotic right" to life as the wolf and the deer, and the effects of
human actions on mountains and streams for Leopold is an ethical
concern as genuine and serious as the comfort and longevity of battery hens.[9] In fact, Leopold to all appearances never considered the
treatment of battery hens on a factory farm or steers in a feed lot to be
a pressing moral issue. He seems much more concerned about the
integrity of the farm *wood lot* and the effects of clear-cutting steep
slopes on neighboring *streams*.

Animal liberationists put their ethic into practice (and display
their devotion to it) by becoming vegetarians, and the moral complexities of vegetarianism have been thoroughly debated in the recent literature as an adjunct issue to animal rights.[10] (No one however has yet
expressed, as among Butler's Erewhonians, qualms about eating
plants, though such sentiments might be expected to be latently present, if the rights of plants are next to be defended.) Aldo Leopold, by
contrast did not even condemn hunting animals, let alone eating
them, nor did he personally abandon hunting, for which he had had
an enthusiasm since boyhood, upon becoming convinced that his
ethical responsibilities extended beyond the human sphere.[11] There
are several interpretations for this behavioral peculiarity. One is that
Leopold did not see that his land ethic actually ought to prohibit
hunting, cruelly killing, and eating animals, a corollary of this interpretation is that Lepoold was so unperspicacious as deservedly to be
though stupid—a conclusion hardly comporting with the intellectual
subtlety he usually evinces in most other respects. If not stupid, then
perhaps Leopold was hypocritical. But if a hypocrite, we should expect him to conceal his proclivity for blood sports and flesh eating and
to treat them as shameful vices to be indulged secretively. As it is,
bound together between the same covers with "The Land Ethic" are
his unabashed reminiscences of killing and consuming *game*.[12] This
term (like *stock*) when used of animals, moreover, appears to be
morally equivalent to referring to a sexually appealing young woman
as a "piece" or to a strong, young black man as a "buck"—if animal
rights, that is, are to be considered as on a par with women's rights
and the rights of formerly enslaved races. A third interpretation of
Leopold's approbation of regulated and disciplined sport hunting
(and *a fortiori* meat eating) is that it is a form of human/animal behavior not inconsistent with the land ethic as he conceived it. A corol-

lary of this intrepretation is that Leopold's land ethic and the environmental ethic of the animal liberation movement rest upon very different theoretical foundations, and that they are thus two very different forms of environmental ethics.

The urgent concern of animal liberationists for the suffering of *domestic* animals, toward which Leopold manifests an attitude which can only be described as indifference, and the urgent concern of Leopold, on the other hand, for the disappearance of *species* of plants as well as animals and for soil erosion and stream pollution, appear to be symptoms not only of very different ethical perspectives, but profoundly different cosmic visions as well. The neat similarities, noted at the beginning of this discussion, between the environmental ethic of the animal liberation movement and the classical Leopoldian land ethic appear in light of these observations to be rather superficial and to conceal substrata of thought and value which are not at all similar. The theoretical foundations of the animal liberation movement and those of the Leopoldian land ethic may even turn out not to be companionable, complementary, or mutually consistent. The animal liberationists may thus find themselves not only engaged in controversy with the many conservative philosophers upholding *apartheid* between man and "beast," but also faced with an unexpected dissent from another, very different, system of environmental ethics.[13] Animal liberation and animal rights may well prove to be a triangular rather than, as it has so far been represented in the philosophical community, a polar controversy.

Ethical Humanism and Humane Moralism

The orthodox response of "ethical humanism" (as this philosophical perspective may be styled) to the suggestion that nonhuman animals should be accorded moral standing is that such animals are not worthy of this high perquisite. Only human beings are rational, or capable of having interests, or possess *self*-awareness, or have linguistic abilities, or can represent the future, it is variously argued.[14] These essential attributes taken singly or in various combinations make people somehow exclusively deserving of moral consideration. The so-called "lower animals," it is insisted, lack the crucial qualification for ethical considerability and so may be treated (albeit humanely, according to some, so as not to brutalize man) as things or means, not as persons or as ends.[15]

The theoreticians of the animal liberation movement ("humane moralists" as they may be called) typically reply as follows.[16] Not all human beings qualify as worthy of moral regard, according to the various criteria specified. Therefore, by parity of reasoning, human persons who do not so qualify as moral patients may be treated, as animals often are, as mere things or means (e.g., used in vivisection experiments, disposed of if their existence is inconvenient, eaten, hunted, etc., etc.). But the ethical humanists would be morally outraged if irrational and inarticulate infants, for example, were used in painful or lethal medical experiments, or if severely retarded people were hunted for pleasure. Thus, the double-dealing, the hypocrisy, of ethical humanism appears to be exposed.[17] Ethical humanism, though claiming to discriminate between worthy and unworthy ethical patients on the basis of objective criteria impartially applied, turns out after all, it seems, to be *speciesism*, a philosophically indefensible prejudice (analogous to racial prejudice) against animals. The tails side of this argument is that some animals, usually the "higher" lower animals (cetaceans, other primates, etc.), as ethological studies seem to indicate, may meet the criteria specified for moral worth, although the ethical humanists, even so, are not prepared to grant them full dignity and the rights of persons. In short, the ethical humanists' various criteria for moral standing do not include all or only human beings, humane moralists argue, although in practice ethical humanism wishes to make the class of morally considerable beings coextensive with the class of human beings.

The humane moralists, for their part, insist upon *sentience* (*sensibility* would have been a more precise word choice) as the only relevant capacity a being need possess to enjoy full moral standing. If animals, they argue, are conscious entities who, though deprived of reason, speech, forethought or even *self*-awareness (however that may be judged), are capable of suffering, then their suffering should be as much a matter of ethical concern as that of our fellow human beings, or strictly speaking, as our very own. What, after all, has rationality or any of the other allegedly uniquely human capacities to do with ethical standing? Why, in other words, should beings who reason or use speech (etc.) qualify for moral status, and those who do not fail to qualify?[18] Isn't this just like saying that only persons with white skin should be free, or that only persons who beget and not those who bear should own property? The criterion seems utterly unrelated to the benefit for which it selects. On the other hand, the capacity to suffer is, it seems, a more relevant criterion for moral standing because—as Bentham and Mill, notable among modern philosophers, and Epicurus, among the ancients, aver—pain is evil, and its opposite, pleasure and freedom from pain, good. As moral agents (and this seems axiomatic), we have a duty to behave in such a way that the effect of our actions is to promote and procure good, so far as possible, and to reduce and minimize evil. That would amount to an obligation to produce pleasure and reduce pain. Now pain is pain wherever and by whomever it is suffered. As a *moral* agent, I should not consider my pleasure and pain to be of greater consequence in determining a course of action than that of other persons. Thus, by the same token, if animals suffer pain—and among philosophers only strict Cartesians would deny that they do—then we are morally obliged to consider their suffering as much an evil to be minimized by conscientious moral agents as human suffering.[19] Certainly actions of ours which contribute to the suffering of animals, such as hunting them, butchering and eating them, experimenting on them, etc., are on these assumptions morally reprehensible. Hence, a person who regards himself or herself as not aiming in life to live most selfishly, conveniently, or profitably, but rightly and in accord with practical principle, if convinced by these arguments, should, among other things, cease to eat the flesh of animals, to hunt them, to wear fur and leather clothing and bone ornaments and other articles made from the bodies of animals, to eat eggs and drink milk, if the animal producers of these commodities are retained under inhumane circumstances, and to patronize zoos (as sources of psychological if not physical torment of animals). On the other hand, since certain very simple animals are almost certainly insensible to pleasure and pain, they may and indeed should be treated as morally inconsequential. Nor is there any *moral* reason why trees should be respected or rivers or mountains or anything which is, though living or tributary to life processes, unconscious. The humane moralists, like the moral humanists, draw a firm distinction between those beings worthy of moral consideration and those not. They simply insist upon a different but quite definite cut-off point on the spectrum of natural entities, and accompany their criterion with arguments to show that it is more ethically defensible (granting certain assumptions) and more consistently applicable than that of the moral humanists.[20]

The First Principle of the Land Ethic

The fundamental principle of humane moralism, as we see, is Benthamic. Good is equivalent to pleasure and, more pertinently, evil is equivalent to pain. The presently booming controversy between moral humanists and humane moralists appears, when all the learned dust has settled, to be essentially internecine; at least, the lines of battle are drawn along familiar watersheds of the conceptual terrain.[21] A classical ethical theory, Bentham's, has been refitted and pressed into service to meet relatively new and unprecedented ethically relevant situations—the problems raised especially by factory farming and ever more exotic and frequently ill-conceived scientific research employing animal subjects. Then, those with Thomist, Kantian, Lockean, Moorean (etc.) ethical affiliation have heard the bugle and have risen to arms. It is no wonder that so many academic philosophers have been drawn into the fray. The issues have an apparent newness about them; moreover, they are socially and politically *avant garde*. But there is no serious challenge to cherished first principles.[22] Hence, without having to undertake any creative ethical reflection or exploration, or any reexamination of historical ethical theory, a fresh debate has been stirred up. The familiar historical positions have simply been retrenched, applied, and exercised.

But what about the third (and certainly minority) party to the animal liberation debate? What sort of reasonable and coherent moral theory would at once urge that animals (and plants and soils and waters) be included in the same class with people as beings to whom ethical consideration is owed and yet not object to some of them being slaughtered (whether painlessly or not) and eaten, others hunted, trapped, and in various other ways seemingly cruelly used? Aldo Leopold provides a concise statement of what might be called the categorical imperative or principal precept of the land ethic: "A thing is right when it tends to preserve the integrity, stability, and beauty of the biotic community. It is wrong when it tends otherwise."[23] What is especially noteworthy, and that to which attention should be directed in this proposition, is the idea that the good of the biotic *community* is the ultimate measure of the moral value, the rightness or wrongness, of actions. Thus, to hunt and kill a white-tailed deer in certain districts may not only be ethically permissible, it might actually be a moral requirement, necessary to protect the local environment, taken as a whole, from the disintegrating effects of a cervid population explosion. On the other hand, rare and endangered animals like the lynx should be especially nurtured and preserved. The lynx, cougar, and other wild feline predators, from the neo-Benthamite perspective (if consistently and evenhandedly applied) should be regarded as merciless, wanton, and incorrigible murderers of their fellow creatures, who not only kill, it should be added, but cruelly toy with their victims, thus increasing the measure of pain in the world. From the perspective of the land ethic, predators generally should be nurtured and preserved as critically important members of the biotic communities to which they are native. Certain plants, similarly, may be overwhelmingly important to the stability, integrity, and beauty of biotic communities, while some animals, such as domestic sheep (allowed perhaps by egalitarian and humane herdspersons to graze freely and to reproduce themselves without being harvested for lamb and mutton) could be a pestilential threat to the natural floral community of a given locale. Thus, the land ethic is logically coherent in demanding at once that moral consideration be given to plants as well as to animals and yet in permitting animals to be killed, trees felled, and so on. In every case the effect upon ecological systems is the decisive factor in the determination of the ethical quality of actions. Well-meaning actions from the point of view of neo-Benthamite ethics may be regarded as morally wanton from the point of view of land ethics, and *vice versa*. An example of the former, in addition to those already mentioned, is turning dairy cows out to pasture in a wood lot situated on a steep slope overlooking a trout stream (for the sake of the shady comfort and dietary variety of the cattle) with ruinous impact upon the floral and wildlife community native to the woods, the fish and benthic organisms of the stream, and the microbic life and the physiochemical structure of the soil itself. An example of the latter is trapping or otherwise removing beaver (to all appearances very sensitive and intelligent animals) and their dams to eliminate siltation in an otherwise free-flowing and clear-running stream (for the sake of the complex community of insects, native fish, heron, osprey, and other avian predators of aquatic life which on the anthropocentric scale of consciousness are "lower" life forms than beaver).

The Land Ethic and the Ecological Point of View

The philosophical context of the land ethic and its conceptual foundation is clearly the body of empirical experience and theory which is summed up in the term *ecology*. The specter of the naturalistic fallacy hovers around any claim to discover values in facts (and/or, probably, in scientific theories as well), but notwithstanding the naturalistic fallacy (or the fact/value lacuna), which is essentially a logical problem for formal ethics, there appears very often to be at least a strongly compelling psychological connection between the way the world is imagined or conceived and what state of things is held to be good or bad, what ways of behaving are right or wrong, and what responsibilities and obligations we, as moral agents, acknowledge.[24]

Since ecology focuses upon the relationships between and among things, it inclines its students toward a more holistic vision of the world. Before the rather recent emergence of ecology as a science the landscape appeared to be, one might say, a collection of objects, some of them alive, some conscious, but all the same, an aggregate, a plurality of separate individuals. With this "atomistic" representation of things it is no wonder that moral issues might be understood as competing and mutually contradictory clashes of the "rights" of separate individuals, each separately pursuing its "interests." Ecology has made it possible to apprehend the same landscape as an articulate unity (without the least hint of mysticism or ineffability). Ordinary organic bodies have articulated and discernible parts (limbs, various organs, myriad cells); yet, because of the character of the network of relations among those parts, they form in a perfectly familiar sense a second-order whole. Ecology makes it possible to see land, similarly, as a unified system of integrally related parts, as, so to speak, a third-order organic whole.[25]

Another analogy that has helped ecologists to convey the particular holism which their science brings to reflective attention is that land is integrated as a human community is integrated. The various parts of the "biotic community" (individual animals and plants) depend upon one another *economically* so that the system as such acquires distinct characteristics of its own. Just as it is possible to characterize and define collectively peasant societies, agrarian communities, industrial complexes, capitalist, communist, and socialist economic systems, and so on, ecology characterizes and defines various biomes as desert, savanna, wetland, tundra, wood land, etc. communities, each with its particular "professions," "roles," or "niches."

Now we may think that among the duties we as moral agents have toward ourselves is the duty of self-preservation, which may be interpreted as a duty to maintain our own organic integrity. It is not uncommon in historical moral theory, further, to find that in addition to those peculiar responsibilities we have in relation both to ourselves and to other persons severally, we also have a duty to behave in ways that do not harm the fabric of society *per se*. The land ethic, in similar fashion, calls our attention to the recently discovered integrity—in other words, the unity—of the biota and posits duties binding upon moral agents in relation to that whole. Whatever the strictly formal logical connections between the concept of a social community and moral responsibility, there appears to be a strong psychological bond between that idea and conscience. Hence, the representation of the

natural environment as, in Leopold's terms, "one humming community" (or, less consistently in his discussion, a third-order organic being)
brings into play, whether rationally or not, those stirrings of conscience which we feel in relation to delicately complex, functioning social
and organic systems.[26]
     The neo-Benthamite humane moralists have, to be sure, digested
one of the metaphysical implications of modern biology. They insist
that human beings must be understood continuously with the rest of
organic nature. People are (and are only) animals, and much of the
rhetorical energy of the animal liberation movement is spent in fighting a rear guard action for this aspect of Darwinism against those
philosophers who still cling to the dream of a special metaphysical
status for people in the order of "creation." To this extent the animal
liberation movement is biologically enlightened and argues from the
taxonomical and evolutionary continuity of man and beast to moral
standing for some nonhuman animals. Indeed, pain, in their view the
very substance of evil, is something that is conspicuously common to
people and other sensitive animals, something that we as people
experience not in virtue of our metasimian cerebral capabilities, but
because of our participation in a more generally animal, limbic-based
consciousness. *If* it is pain and suffering that is the ultimate evil beset-
ting human life, and this not in virtue of our humanity but in virtue of
our animality, then it seems only fair to promote freedom from pain
for those animals who share with us in this mode of experience and to
grant them rights similar to ours as a means to this end.
     Recent ethological studies of other primates, ceteceans, and so
on, are not infrequently cited to drive the point home, but the biological information of the animal liberation movement seems to extend
no further than this—the continuity of human with other animal life
forms. The more recent ecological perspective especially seems to be
ignored by humane moralists. The holistic outlook of ecology and the
associated value premium conferred upon the biotic community, its
beauty, integrity, and stability may simply not have penetrated the
thinking of the animal liberationists, or it could be that to include it
would involve an intolerable contradiction with the Benthamite foundations of their ethical theory. Bentham's view of the "interests of the
community" was bluntly reductive. With his characteristic bluster,
Bentham wrote, "The community is a fictitious *body* composed of the
individual persons who are considered as constituting as it were its
members. The interest of the community then is, what?—the sum of
the interests of the several members who compose it."[27]Bentham's
very simile—the community is like a body composed of members—

gives the lie to his reduction of its interests to the sum of its parts taken severally. The interests of a person are not those of his or her cells summed up and averaged out. Our organic health and well-being, for example, requires vigorous exercise and metabolic stimulation which cause stress and often pain to various parts of the body and a more rapid turnover in the life cycle of our individual cells. For the sake of the person taken as whole, some parts may be, as it were, unfairly sacrificed. On the level of social organization, the interests of society may not always coincide with the sum of the interests of its parts. Discipline, sacrifice, and individual restraint are often necessary in the social sphere to maintain social integrity as within the bodily organism. A society, indeed, is particularly vulnerable to disintegration when its members become preoccupied totally with their own particular interest, and ignore those distinct and independent interests of the community as a whole. One example, unfortunately, our own society, is altogether too close at hand to be examined with strict academic detachment. The United States seems to pursue uncritically a social policy of reductive utilitarianism, aimed at promoting the happiness of all its members severally. Each special interest accordingly clamors more loudly to be satisfied while the community as a whole becomes noticeably more and more infirm economically, environmentally, and politically.

The humane moralists, whether or not they are consciously and deliberately following Bentham on this particular, nevertheless, in point of fact, are committed to the welfare of certain kinds of animals distributively or reductively in applying their moral concern for nonhuman beings.[28] They lament the treatment of animals, most frequently farm and laboratory animals, and plead the special interests of these beings. We might ask, from the perspective of the land ethic, what the effect upon the natural environment taken as whole would be if domestic animals were actually liberated? There is, almost certainly, very little real danger that this might actually happen, but it would be instructive to speculate on the ecological consequences.

Ethical Holism

Before we take up this question, however, some points of interest remain to be considered on the matter of a holistic versus a reductive environmental ethic. To pit the one against the other as I have done without further qualification would be mistaken. A society is constituted by its members, an organic body by its cells, and the ecosystem by the plants, animals, minerals, fluids, and gases which compose it. One cannot affect a system as a whole without affecting at least some of its components. An environmental ethic which takes as its *summum bonum* the integrity, stability, and beauty of the biotic community is not conferring moral standing on something *else* besides plants, animals, soils, and waters. Rather, the former, the good of the community as a whole, serves as a standard for the assessment of the relative value and relative ordering of its constitutive parts and therefore provides a means of adjudicating the often mutually contradictory demands of the parts considered separately for *equal* consideration. If diversity does indeed contribute to stability (a classical "law" of ecology), then *specimens* of rare and endangered species, for example, have a *prima facie* claim to preferential consideration from the perspective of the land ethic. Animals of those species, which, like the honey bee, function in ways critically important to the economy of nature, moreover, would be granted a greater claim to moral attention than psychologically more complex and sensitive ones, say, rabbits and moles, which seem to be plentiful, globally distributed, reproductively efficient, and only routinely integrated into the natural economy. Animals and plants, mountains, rivers, seas, the atmosphere are the *immediate* practical beneficiaries of the land ethic. The well-being of the biotic community, the biosphere as a whole, cannot be logically separated from their survival and welfare.

Some suspicion may arise at this point that the land ethic is ultimately grounded in *human* interests, not in those of nonhuman natural entities. Just as we might prefer a sound and attractive house to one in the opposite condition, so the "goodness" of a whole, stable, and beautiful environment seems rather to be of the instrumental, not the autochthonous, variety. The question of ultimate value is a very sticky one for environmental as well as for all ethics and cannot be fully addressed here. It is my view that there can be no value apart from an evaluator, that all value is as it were in the eye of the beholder. The value that is attributed to the ecosystem, therefore, is humanly dependent or (allowing that other living things may take a certain delight in the well-being of the whole of things, or that the gods may) at least dependent upon some variety of morally and aesthetically sensitive consciousness. Granting this, however, there is a further, very crucial distinction to be drawn. It is possible that while things may only have value because we (or someone) values them, they may nonetheless be valued for themselves as well as for the contribution they might make to the realization of our (or someone's) interests. Children are valued for themselves by most parents. Money, on the other hand, has only an instrumental or indirect value. Which sort of value has the health of the biotic community and its members severally for Leopold and the land ethic? It is especially difficult to separate these two general sorts of value, the one of moral significance, the other merely selfish, when something that may be valued in *both ways at once* is the subject of consideration. Are pets, for example, well-treated, like children, for the sake of themselves, or, like mechanical appliances, because of the sort of services they provide their owners? Is a healthy biotic community something we value because we are so utterly and (to the biologically well-informed) so obviously dependent upon it not only for our happiness but for our very survival, or may we also perceive it disinterestedly as having an independent worth? Leopold insists upon a noninstrumental value for the biotic community and *mutatis mutandis* for its constituents. According to Leopold, collective enlightened self-interest on the part of human beings does not go far enough; the land ethic in his opinion (and no doubt this reflects his own moral intuitions) requires "love, respect, and admiration for land, and a high regard for its value." The land ethic, in Leopold's view, creates "obligations over and above self-interest." And, "obligations have no meaning without conscience, and the problem we face is the extension of the social conscience from people to land."[29] If, in other words, any genuine ethic is possible, if it is possible to value *people* for the sake of themselves, then it is equally possible to value *land* in the same way.

Some indication of the genuinely biocentric value orientation of ethical environmentalism is indicated in what otherwise might appear to be gratuitous misanthropy. The biospheric perspective does not exempt *Homo sapiens* from moral evaluation in relation to the well-being of the community of nature taken as a whole. The preciousness of individual deer, as of any other specimen, is inversely proportional to the population of the species. Environmentalists, however reluctantly and painfully, do not omit to apply the same logic to their own kind. As omnivores, the population of human beings should, perhaps, be roughly twice that of bears, allowing for differences of size. A global population of more than four billion persons and showing no signs of an orderly decline presents an alarming prospect to humanists, but it is at present a global disaster (the more *per capita* prosperity, indeed, the more disastrous it appears) for the biotic community. If the land ethic were only a means of managing nature for the sake of man, misleadingly phrased in moral terminology, then man would be considered as having an ultimate value essentially different from that of his "resources." The extent of misanthropy in modern environmentalism thus may be taken as a measure of the degree to which it is biocentric. Edward Abbey in his enormously popular *Desert Solitaire* bluntly states that he would sooner shoot a man than a snake.[30] Abbey may not be simply depraved; this is perhaps only his way of dramaticcally making the point that the human population has become so disproportionate from the biological point of view that if one had to choose between a specimen of *Homo sapiens* and a specimen of a race even if unattractive species, the choice would be moot. Among academicians, Garret Hardin, a human ecologist by discipline who has written extensively on ethics, environmental and otherwise, has shocked philosophers schooled in the preciousness of human life with his "lifeboat" and "survival" ethics and his "wilderness economics." In context of the latter, Hardin recommends limiting access to wilderness by criteria of hardiness and woodcraft and would permit no emergency roads or airborne rescue vehicles to violate the pristine purity of wilderness areas. If a wilderness adventurer should have a serious accident, Hardin recommends that he or she get out on his or her own or die in the attempt. Danger, from the strictly human-centered, psychological perspective, is part of the wilderness experience, Hardin argues, but in all probability his more important concern is to protect from mechanization the remnants of wild country that remain even if the price paid is the incidental loss of human life which, from the perspective once more of the biologist, is a commodity altogether too common in relation to wildlife and to wild landscapes.[31] Hardin's recommendation of harsh policies in relation to desperate, starving nations is based strictly upon a utilitarian calculus, but reading between the lines, one can also detect the biologist's chagrin concerning the ecological dislocations which a human population explosion have already created and which if permitted to continue unchecked could permanently impoverish (if not altogether extinguish) an already stressed and overburdened economy of nature.[32]

Finally, it may be wondered if anything ought properly be denominated an "ethic" which on the basis of an impersonal, not to say abstract, good, "the integrity, stability, and beauty of the biotic community," permits and even requires *preferential* consideration. A "decision procedure," to give it for the moment a neutral rubric, which lavishes loving and expensive care on whooping cranes and (from the Benthamite point of view, villainous) timber wolves while simultaneously calculating the correct quotas for "harvesting" mallards and ruffed grouse should hardly be dignified, it might be argued, by the term *ethic.* Modern systems of ethics have, it must be admitted, considered the principle of the quality of persons to be inviolable. This is true, for example, of both major schools of modern ethics, the utilitarian school going back to Bentham and Mill, and the deontological, originating with Kant. The land ethic manifestly does not accord equal moral worth to each and every member of the biotic community; the moral worth of individuals (including, n.b., human individuals) is relative, to be assessed in accordance with the particular relation of each to the collective entity which Leopold called "land."

There is, however, a classical Western ethic, with the best philosophical credentials, which assumes a similar holistic posture (with respect to the social moral sphere). I have in mind Plato's moral and social philosophy. Indeed, two of the same analogies figuring in the conceptual foundations of the Leopold land ethic appear in Plato's value theory.[33] From the ecological perspective, according to Leopold as I have pointed out, land is like an organic body or like a human society. According to Plato, body, soul, and society have similar structures and corresponding virtues.[34] The goodness of each is a function of its structure or organization and the relative value of the parts or constituents of each is calculated according to the contribution made to the integrity, stability, and beauty of each whole.[35] In the *Republic*, Plato, in the very name of virtue and justice, is notorious for, among other things, requiring infanticide for a child whose only offense was being born without the sanction of the state, making presents to the enemy of guardians who allow themselves to be captured alive in combat, and radically restricting the practice of medicine to the dressing of wounds and the curing of seasonal maladies on the principle that the infirm and chronically ill not only lead miserable lives but contribute nothing to the good of the polity.[36] Plato, indeed, seems to regard individual human life and certainly human pain and suffering with complete indifference. On the other hand, he shrinks from nothing so long as it seems to him to be in the interest of the community. Among the apparently inhuman recommendations that he makes to better the community are a program of eugenics involving a phony lottery (so that those whose natural desires are frustrated, while breeding proceeds from the best stock as a kennel or stable, will blame chance, not the design of the rulers), the destruction of the pair bond and nuclear family (in the interests of greater military and bureaucratic efficiency and group solidarity), and the utter abolition of private property.[37]

When challenged with the compliant that he is ignoring individual human happiness (and the happiness of those belonging to the most privileged class at that), he replies that it is the well-being of the community as a whole, not that of any person or special class at which his legislation aims.[38] This principle is readily accepted, first of all, in our attitude toward the body, he reminds us—the separate interests of the parts of which we acknowledge to be subordinate to the health and well-being of the whole—and secondly, assuming that we accept his faculty psychology, in our attitude toward the soul—whose multitude of desires must be disciplined, restrained, and, in the case of some, altogether repressed in the interest of personal virtue and a well-ordered and morally responsible life.

Given these formal similarities to Plato's moral philosophy, we may conclude that the land ethic—with its holistic good and its assignment of differential values to the several parts of the environment irrespective of their intelligence, sensibility, degree of complexity, or any other characteristic discernible in the parts considered separately—is somewhat foreign to modern systems of ethical philosophy, but perfectly familiar in the broader context of classical Western ethical philosophy. If, therefore, Plato's system of public and private justice is properly an "ethical" system, then so is the land ethic in relation to environmental virtue and excellence.[39]

Reappraising Domesticity

Among the last philosophical remarks penned by Aldo Leopold before his untimely death in 1948 is the following: "Perhaps such a shift of values [as implied by the attempt to weld together the concepts of ethics and ecology] can be achieved by reappraising things unnatural, tame, and confined in terms of things natural, wild, and free."[40] John Muir, in a similar spirit of reappraisal, had noted earlier the difference between the wild mountain sheep of the Sierra and the ubiquitous domestic variety. The latter, which Muir described as "hooved locusts," were only, in his estimation, "half alive" in comparison with their natural and autonomous counterparts.[41] One of the more distressing aspects of the animal liberation movement is the failure of almost all its exponents to draw a sharp distinction between the very different plights (and rights) of wild and domestic animals.[42] But this distinction lies at the very center of the land ethic. Domestic animals are creations of man. They are living artifacts, but artifacts nevertheless, and they constitute yet another mode of extension of the works of man into the ecosystem. From the perspective of the land ethic a herd of cattle, sheep, or pigs is as much or more a ruinous blight on the landscape as a fleet of four-wheel drive off-road vehicles. There is thus something profoundly incoherent (and insensitive as well) in the complaint of some animal liberationists that the "natural behavior" of chickens and bobby calves is cruelly frustrated on factory farms. It would make almost as much sense to speak of the natural behavior of tables and chairs.

Here a serious disanalogy (which no one to my knowledge has yet pointed out) becomes clearly evident between the liberation of blacks from slavery (and more recently, from civil inequality) and the liberation of animals from a similar sort of subordination and servitude. Black slaves remained, as it were, metaphysically autonomous: they were by nature if not by convention free beings quite capable of living on their own. They could not be enslaved for more than a historical interlude, for the strength of the force of their freedom was too great. They could, in other words, be retained only by a continuous counter-force, and only temporarily. This is equally true of caged wild animals. African cheetas in American and European zoos are captive, not in-dentured, beings. But this is not true of cows, pigs, sheep, and chickens. They have been bred to docility, tractability, stupidity, and dependency. It is literally meaningless to suggest that they be liberated. It is, to speak in hyperbole, a logical impossibility.

Certainly it is a practical impossibility. Imagine what would happen if the people of the world became morally persuaded that domestic animals were to be regarded as oppressed and enslaved persons and accordingly *set free*. In one scenario we might imagine that like former American black slaves they would receive the equalivent of forty acres and a mule and be turned out to survive on their own. Feral cattle and sheep would hang around farm outbuildings waiting forlornly to be sheltered and fed, or would graze aimlessly through their abandoned and deteriorating pastures. Most would starve or freeze as soon as winter settled in. Reproduction which had been assisted over many countless generations by their former owners might be altogether impossible in the feral state for some varieties, and the care of infants would be an art not so much lost as never acquired. And so in a very short time, after much suffering and agony, these species would become abruptly extinct. Or, in another scenario beginning with the same simple emancipation from human association, survivors of the first massive die-off of untended livestock might begin to recover some of their remote wild ancestral genetic traits and become smaller, leaner, heartier, and smarter versions of their former selves. An actual contemporary example is afforded by the feral mustangs ranging over parts of the American West. In time such animals as these would become (just as the mustangs are now) competitors both with their former human masters and (with perhaps more tragic consequences) indigenous wildlife for food and living space.

Foreseeing these and other untoward consequences of immediate and unplanned liberation of livestock, a human population grown morally more perfect than at present might decide that they had a duty, accumulated over thousands of years, to continue to house and feed as before their former animal slaves (whom they had rendered genetically unfit to care for themselves), but not to butcher them or make other ill use of them, including frustrating their "natural" behavior, their right to copulate freely, reproduce, and enjoy the delights of being parents. People, no longer having meat to eat, would require more vegetables, cereals, and other plant foods, but the institutionalized animal incompetents would still consume all the hay and grains (and more since they would no longer be slaughtered) than they did formerly. This would require clearing more land and bringing it into agricultural production with further loss of wildlife habitat and ecological destruction. Another possible scenario might be a decision on the part of people not literally to liberate domestic animals but simply to cease to breed and raise them. When the last livestock have been killed and eaten (or permitted to die "natural" deaths), people would become vegetarians and domestic livestock species would thus be rendered deliberately extinct (just as they had been deliberately created). But there is surely some irony in an outcome in which the beneficiaries of a humane extension of conscience are destroyed in the process of being saved.[43]

The land ethic, it should be emphasized, as Leopold has sketched it, provides for the *right* of nonhuman natural beings to share in the life processes of the biotic community. The conceptual foundation of such rights, however, is less conventional than natural, based upon, as one might say, evolutionary and ecological entitlement. Wild animals and native plants have a particular place in nature, according to the land ethic, which domestic animals (because they are products of human art and represent an extended presence of human beings in the natural world) do not have. The land ethic, in sum, is as much opposed, though on different grounds, to commercial traffic in wildlife, zoos, the slaughter of whales and other marine mammals, etc. as is the humane ethic. Concern for animal (and plant) rights and well-being is as fundamental to the land ethic as to the humane ethic, but the difference between naturally evolved and humanly bred species is an essential consideration for the one, though not for the other.

The "shift of values" which results from our "reappraising things unnatural, tame, and confined in terms of things natural, wild, and free" is especially dramatic when we reflect upon the definitions of *good* and *evil* espoused by Bentham and Mill and uncritically accepted by their contemporary followers. Pain and pleasure seem to have nothing at all to do with good and evil if our appraisal is taken from the vantage point of ecological biology. Pain in particular is primarily information. In animals, it informs the central nervous system of stress, irritation, or trauma in outlying regions of the organism. A certain level of pain under optimal organic circumstances is indeed desirable as an indicator of exertion—of the degree of exertion needed to maintain fitness, to stay "in shape," and of a level of exertion beyond which it would be dangerous to go. An arctic wolf in pursuit of a caribou may experience pain in her feet or chest because of the rigors of the chase. There is nothing bad or wrong in that. Or, consider a case of injury. Suppose that a person in the course of a wilderness excursion sprains an ankle. Pain informs him or her of the injury and by its intensity the amount of further stress the ankle may endure in the course of getting to safety. Would it be better if pain were not experienced upon injury or, taking advantage of recent technology, anaesthetized? Pleasure appears to be, for the most part (unfortunately is not always so) a reward accompanying those activities which contribute to organic maintenance, such as the pleasures associated with eating, drinking, grooming, and so on, or those which contribute to social solidarity like the pleasures of dancing, conversation, teasing, etc., or those which contribute to the continuation of the species, such as the pleasures of sexual activity and of being parents. The doctrine that life is the happier the freer it is from pain and that the happiest life conceivable is one in which there is continuous pleasure uninterrupted by pain is biologically preposterous. A living mammal which experienced no pain would be one which had a lethal dysfunction of the nervous system. The idea that pain is evil and ought to be minimized or eliminated is as primitive a notion as that of a tyrant who puts to death messengers bearing bad news on the supposition that thus his well-being and security is improved.[44]

More seriously still, the value commitments of the humane movement seem at bottom to betray a world-denying or rather a life-loathing philosophy. The natural world as actually constituted is one in which one being lives at the expense of others.[45] Each organism, in Darwin's metaphor, struggles to maintain its own organic integrity. The more complex animals seem to experience (judging from our own case, and reasoning from analogy) appropriate and adaptive psychological accompaniments to organic existence. There is a palpable passion for self-preservation. There are desire, pleasure in the satisfaction of desires, acute agony attending injury, frustration, and chronic dread of death. But these experiences are the psychological substance of living. To live *is* to be anxious about life, to feel pain and pleasure in a fitting mixture, and sooner or later to die. That is the way the system works. If nature as a whole is good, then pain and death are also good. Environmental ethics in general require people to play fair in the natural system. The neo-Benthamites have in a sense taken the uncourageous approach. People have attempted to exempt themselves from the life/death reciprocities of natural processes and from ecological limitations in the name of a prophylactic ethic of maximizing rewards (pleasure) and minimizing unwelcome information (pain). To be fair, the humane moralists seem to suggest that we should attempt to project the same values into the nonhuman animal world and to widen the charmed circle—no matter that it would be biologically unrealistic to do so or biologically ruinous if, per impossible, such an environmental ethic were implemented.

There is another approach. Rather than imposing our alienation from nature and natural processes and cycles of life on other animals, we human beings could reaffirm our participation in nature by accepting life as it is given without a sugar coating. Instead of imposing artificial legalities, rights, and so on on nature, we might take the opposite course and accept and affirm natural biological laws, principles, and limitations in the human personal and social spheres. Such appears to have been the posture toward life of tribal peoples in the past. The chase was relished with its dangers, rigors, and hardships as well as its rewards: animal flesh was respectfully consumed; a tolerance for pain was cultivated; virtue and magnanimity were prized; lithic, floral, and faunal spirits were worshipped; population was routinely optimized by sexual continency, abortion, infanticide, and stylized warfare; and other life forms, although certainly appropriated, were respected as fellow players in a magnificent and awesome, if not altogether idyllic, drama of life. It is impossible today to return to the symbiotic relationship of Stone Age man to the natural environment, but the ethos of this by far the longest era of human existence could be abstracted and integrated with a future human culture seeking a viable and mutually beneficial relationship with nature. Personal, social, and environmental *health* would, accordingly, receive a premium value rather than comfort, self-indulgent pleasure, and anaesthetic insulation from pain. Sickness would be regarded as a worse evil than death. The pursuit of health or wellness at the personal, social, and environmental levels would require self-discipline in the form of simple diet, vigorous exercise, conservation, and social responsibility.

Leopold's prescription for the realization and implementation of the land ethic—the reappraisal of things unnatural, tame, and confined in terms of things natural, wild, and free—does not stop, in other words, with a reappraisal of nonhuman domestic animals in terms of their wild (or willed) counterparts; the human ones should be similarly reappraised. This means, among other things, the reappraisal of the comparatively recent values and concerns of "civilized" *Homo sapiens* in terms of those of our "savage" ancestors.[46] Civilization has insulated and alienated us from the rigors and challenges of the natural environment. The hidden agenda of the humane ethic is the imposition of the anti-natural prophylactic ethos of comfort and soft pleasure on an even wider scale. The land ethic, on the other hand, requires a shrinkage, if at all possible, of the domestic sphere; it rejoices in a recrudescence of wilderness and a renaissance of tribal cultural experience.

The converse of those goods and evils, axiomatic to the humane ethic, may be illustrated and focused by the consideration of a single issue raised by the humane morality: a vegetarian diet. Savage people seem to have had, if the attitudes and values of surviving tribal cultures are representative, something like an intuitive grasp of ecological relationships and certainly a morally charged appreciation of eating. There is nothing more intimate than eating, more symbolic of the connectedness of life, and more mysterious. What we eat and how we eat is by no means an insignificant ethical concern.

From the ecological point of view, for human beings universally to become vegetarians is tantamount to a shift of trophic niche from omnivore with carnivorous preferences to herbivore. The shift is a downward one on the trophic pyramid, which in effect shortens those food chains terminating with man. It represents an increase in the efficiency of the conversion of solar energy from plant to human biomass, and thus, by bypassing animal intermediates, increases available food resources for human beings. The human population would probably, as past trends overwhelmingly suggest, expand in accordance with the potential thus afforded. The net result would be fewer nonhuman beings and more human beings, who, of course, have requirements of life far more elaborate than even those of domestic animals, requirements which would tax other "natural resources" (trees for shelter, minerals mined at the expense of topsoil and its vegetation etc.) more than under present circumstances. A vegetarian human population is therefore *probably* ecologically catastrophic.

Meat eating as implied by the foregoing remarks may be more *ecologically* responsible than a wholly vegetable diet. Meat, however, purchased at the supermarket, externally packaged and internally laced with petrochemicals, fattened in feed lots, slaughtered impersonally, and, in general, mechanically processed from artificial insemination to microwave roaster, is an affront not only to physical metabolism and bodily health but to conscience as well. From the perspective of the land ethic, the immoral aspect of the factory farm has to do far less with the suffering and killing of nonhuman animals than with the monstrous transformation of living things from an organic to a mechanical mode of being. Animals, beginning with the Neolithic Revolution, have been debased through selective breeding, but they have nevertheless remained animals. With the Industrial Revolution an even more profound and terrifying transformation has overwhelmed them. They have become, in Ruth Harrison's most apt description, "animal machines." The very presence of animals, so emblematic of delicate, complex organic tissue, surrounded by machines, connected to machines, penetrated by machines in research laboratories or crowded together in space-age "production facilities" is surely the more real and visceral source of our outrage at vivisection and factory farming than the contemplation of the quantity of pain that these unfortunate beings experience. I wish to denounce as loudly as the neo–Benthamites this ghastly abuse of animal life, but also to stress that the pain and suffering of research and agribusiness animals is not greater than that endured by free-living wildlife as a consequence of predation, disease, starvation, and cold—indicating that there is something immoral about vivisection and factory farming which is not an ingredient in the natural lives and deaths of wild beings. That immoral something is the transmogrification of organic to mechanical processes.

Ethical vegetarianism to all appearances insists upon the human consumption of plants (in a paradoxical moral gesture toward those animals whose very existence is dependent upon human carnivorousness), even when the tomatoes are grown hydroponically, the lettuce generously coated with chlorinated hydrocarbons, the potatoes pumped up with chemical fertilizers, and the cereals stored with the help of chemical preservatives. The land ethic takes as much exception to the transmogrification of plants by mechanicochemical means as to that of animals. The important thing, I would think, is not to eat vegetables as opposed to animal flesh, but to resist factory farming in all its manifestations, including especially its liberal application of pesticides, herbicides, and chemical fertilizers to maximize the production of *vegetable* crops.

The land ethic, with its ecological perspective, helps us to recognize and affirm the organic integrity of self and the untenability of a firm distinction between self and environment. On the ethical question of what to eat, it answers, not vegetables instead of animals, but organically as opposed to mechanicochemically produced food. Purists like Leopold prefer, in his expression, to get their "meat from God," i.e., to hunt and consume wildlife and to gather wild plant foods, and thus to live within the parameters of the aboriginal human ecological niche.[47] Second best is eating from one's own orchard, garden, henhouse, pigpen, and barnyard. Third best is buying or bartering organic foods from one's neighbors and friends.

Conclusion

Philosophical controversy concerning animal liberation/rights has been most frequently represented as a polar dispute between traditional moral humanists and seemingly *avant garde* humane moralists. Further, animal liberation has been assumed to be closely allied with environmental ethics, possibly because in Leopold's classical formulation moral standing and indeed rights (of some unspecified sort) is accorded nonhuman beings, among them animals. The purpose of this discussion has been to distinguish sharply environmental ethics from the animal liberation/rights movement both in theory and practical application and to suggest, thereupon, that there is an underrepresented, but very important, point of view respecting the problem of the moral status of nonhuman animals. The debate over animal liberation, in short, should be conceived as triangular, not polar, with land ethics or environmental ethics, the third and, in my judgment, the most creative, interesting, and practicable alternative. Indeed, from this third point of view moral humanism and humane moralism appear to have much more in common with one another than either have with environmental or land ethics. On reflection one might even be led to suspect that the noisy debate between these parties has served to drown out the much deeper challenge to "business-as-usual" ethical philosophy represented by Leopold and his exponents, and to keep ethical philosophy firmly anchored to familiar modern paradigms.

Moral humanism and humane moralism, to restate succinctly the most salient conclusions of this essay, are *atomistic* or distributive in their theory of moral value, while environmental ethics (again, at least, as set out in Leopold's outline) is *holistic* or collective. Modern ethical theory, in other words, has consistently located moral value in individuals and set out certain metaphysical reasons for including some individuals and excluding others. Humane moralism remains firmly within this modern convention and centers its attention on the competing criteria for moral standing and rights holding, while environmental ethics locates ultimate value in the "biotic community" and assigns differential moral value to the constitutive individuals relative to that standard. This is perhaps the most fundamental theoretical difference between environment ethics and the ethics of animal liberation.

Allied to this difference are many others. One of the more conspicuous is that in environmental ethics, plants are included within the parameters of the ethical theory as well as animals. Indeed, inanimate entities such as oceans and lakes, mountains, forests, and wetlands are assigned a greater value than individual animals and in a way quite different from systems which accord them moral considerability through a further multiplication of competing individual loci of value and holders of rights.

There are intractable practical differences between environmental ethics and the animal liberation movement. Very different moral obligations follow in respect, most importantly, to domestic animals, the principal beneficiaries of the humane ethic. Environmental ethics sets a very low priority on domestic animals as they very frequently contribute to the erosion of the integrity, stability, and beauty of the biotic communities into which they have been insinuated. On the other hand, animal liberation, if pursued at the practical as well as rhetorical level, would have ruinous consequences on plants, soils, and waters, consequences which could not be directly reckoned according to humane moral theory. As this last remark suggests, the animal liberation/animal rights movement is in the final analysis utterly unpracticable. An imagined society in which all animals capable of sensibility received equal consideration or held rights to equal consideration would be so ludicrous that it might be more appropriately and effectively treated in satire than in philosophical discussion. The land ethic, by contrast, even though its ethical purview is very much wider, is nevertheless eminently practicable, since, by reference to a single good, competing individual claims may be adjudicated and relative values and priorities assigned to the myraid components of the biotic community. This is not to suggest that the implementation of environmental ethics as social policy would be easy. Implementation of the land ethic would require discipline, sacrifice, retrenchment, and massive economic reform, tantamount to a virtual revolution in prevailing attitudes and life styles. Nevertheless, it provides a unified and coherent practical principle and thus a decision procedure at the practical level which a distributive or atomistic ethic may achieve only artificially and so imprecisely as to be practically indeterminate.

Notes

1. Aldo Leopold, *A Sand County Almanac* (New York: Oxford University Press, 1949), pp. 202-3. Some traditional Western systems of ethics, however, have accorded moral standing to nonhuman beings. The Pythagorean tradition did, followed by Empedocles of Acragas; Saint Francis of Assisi apparently believed in the animal soul; in modern ethics Jeremy Bentham's hedonic utilitarian system is also an exception to the usual rule. John Passmore ("The Treatment of Animals," *Journal of the History of Ideas* 36 [1975]: 196-218) provides a well-researched and eye-opening study of historical ideas about the moral status of animals in Western thought. Though exceptions to the prevailing attitudes have existed, they are exceptions indeed and represent but a small minority of Western religious and philosophical points of view.

2. The tag "animal liberation" for this moral movement originates with Peter Singer whose book *Animal Liberation* (New York: New York Review, 1975) has been widely influential. "Animal rights" have been most persistently and unequivocally championed by Tom Regan in various articles, among them: "The Moral Basis of Vegetarianism," *Canadian Journal of Philosophy* 5 (1975): 181-214; "Exploring the Idea of Animal Rights" in *Animal Rights: A Symposium*, eds. D. Patterson and R. Ryder (London: Centaur, 1979); "Animal Rights, Human Wrongs," *Environmental Ethics* 2 (1980): 99-120. A more complex and qualified position respecting animal rights has been propounded by Joel Feinberg, "The Rights of Animals and Unborn Generations" in *Philosophy and Environmental Crisis*, ed. William T. Blackstone (Athens: University of Georgia Press, 1974), pp. 43-68, and "Human Duties and Animal Rights," in *On the Fifth Day*, eds. R. K. Morris and M. W. Fox (Washington: Acropolis Books, 1978), pp. 45-69. Lawrence Haworth ("Rights, Wrongs and Animals," *Ethics* 88 [1978]: 95-105), in the context of the contemporary debate, claims limited rights on behalf of animals. S. R. L. Clark's *The Moral Status of Animals* (Oxford: Clarendon Press, 1975) has set out arguments which differ in some particulars from those of Singer, Regan, and Feinberg with regard to the moral considerability of some nonhuman animals. In this discussion, as a tribute to Singer, I use the term *animal liberation* generically to cover the several philosophical rationales for a humane ethic. Singer has laid particular emphasis on the inhumane usage of animals in agribusiness and scientific research. Two thorough professional studies from the humane perspective of these institutions are Ruth Harrison's *Animal Machines* (London: Stuart, 1964) and Richard Ryder's *Victims of Science* (London: Davis-Poynter, 1975), respectively.

3. Peter Singer and Tom Regan especially insist upon *equal* moral *consideration* for nonhuman animals. Equal moral consideration does not necessarily imply equal treatment, however, as Singer insists. Cf. Singer, *Animal Liberation*, pp. 3, 17–24, and Singer, "The Fable of the Fox and the Unliberated Animals," *Ethics* 88 (1978): 119–20. Regan provides an especially clear summary of both his position and Singer's in "Animal Rights, Human Wrongs," pp. 108–12.

4. We have Richard Ryder to thank for coining the term *speciesism*. See his *Speciesism: The Ethics of Vivisection* (Edinburgh: Scottish Society for the Prevention of Vivisection, 1974). Richard Routley introduced the term *human chauvinism* in "Is There a Need for a New, an Environmental Ethic?" *Proceedings of the Fifteenth World Congress of Philosophy* 1 (1973); 205–10. Peter Singer ("All Animals Are Equal," in *Animal Rights and Human Obligations*, eds. Tom Regan and Peter Singer [Englewood Cliffs, N.J.: Prentice-Hall, 1976], pp. 148–62) developed the egalitarian comparison of speciesism with racism and sexism in detail. To extend the political comparison further, animal liberation is also a reformist and activist movement. We are urged to act, to become vegetarians, to boycott animal products, etc. The concluding paragraph of Regan's "Animal Rights, Human Wrongs" (p. 120) is especially zealously hortatory.

5. Leopold, *Sand County Almanac*, p. 204.

6. Ibid., pp. 201–3. A more articulate historical representation of the parallel expansion of legal rights appears in C. D. Stone's *Should Trees Have Standing?* (Los Altos: William Kaufman, 1972), pp. 3–10, however without specific application to animal liberation.

7. Leopold, *Sand County Almanac*, p. 203.

8. Ibid., p. 204.

9. Ibid., p. 221 (trees); pp. 129–33 (mountains); p. 209 (streams).

10. John Benson ("Duty and the Beast," *Philosophy* 53 [1978]: 547–48) confesses that in the course of considering issues raised by Singer et al. he was "obliged to change my own diet as a result." An elaborate critical discussion is Philip E. Devine's "The Moral Basis of Vegetarianism" (*Philosophy* 53 [1978]: 481–505).

11. For a biography of Leopold including particular reference to Leopold's career as a "sportsman," see Susan L. Flader, *Thinking Like a Mountain* (Columbia: University of Missouri Press, 1974).

12. See especially, Leopold, *Sand County Almanac*, pp. 54–58; 62–66; 120–22; 149–54; 177–87.

13. A most thorough and fully argued dissent is provided by John Rodman in "The Liberation of Nature," *Inquiry* 20 (1977): 83–131. It is surprising

that Singer, whose book is the subject of Rodman's extensive critical review, or some of Singer's philosophical allies, has not replied to these very penetrating and provocative criticisms. Another less specifically targeted dissent is Paul Shepard's "Animal Rights and Human Rites" (*North American Review* [Winter, 1974]: 35-41). More recently Kenneth Goodpaster ("From Egoism to Environmentalism" in *Ethics and Problems of the 21st Century*, eds. K. Goodpaster and K. Sayre [Notre Dame: Notre Dame University Press, 1979], pp. 21-35) has expressed complaints about the animal liberation and animal rights movement in the name of environmental ethics. "The last thing we need," writes Goodpaster, "is simply another 'liberation movement'" (p. 29).

14. Singer, "All Animals are Equal" (p. 159), uses the term *humanist* to convey a speciesist connotation. Rationality and future-conceiving capacities as criteria for rights holding have been newly revived by Michael E. Levin with specific reference to Singer in "Animal Rights Evaluated," *The Humanist* (July/August, 1977): 12; 14-15. John Passmore, in *Man's Responsibility for Nature* (New York: Charles Scribner's Sons, 1974), cf., p. 116, has recently insisted upon having interests as a criterion for having rights and denied that nonhuman beings have interests. L. P. Francis and R. Norman ("Some Animals Are More Equal than Others," Philosophy 53 [1978]: 507-27) have argued, again with specific reference to animal liberationists, that linguistic abilities are requisite for moral status. H. J. McCloskey ("The Rights to Life," *Mind* 84 [1975]: 410-13, and "Moral Rights and Animals," *Inquiry* 22 [1979]: 23-54), adapting an idea of Kant's, defends *autonomy* as the main ingredient of human nature which entitles human beings to rights. Michael Fox ("Animal Liberation: A Critique," *Ethics* 88 [1978]: 106-18) defends, among other exclusively human qualifications for rights holding, *self*-awareness. Richard A. Watson ("Self-Consciousness and the Rights of Nonhuman Animals and Nature," *Environmental Ethics* 1 [1979]: 99-129) also defends self-consciousness as a criterion for rights holding, but allows that some nonhuman animals also possess it.

15. In addition to the historical figures, who are nicely summarized and anthologized in *Animal Rights and Human Obligations*, John Passmore has recently defended the reactionary notion that cruelty toward animals is morally reprehensible for reasons independent of any obligation or duties people have to animals as such (*Man's Responsibility*, cf., p. 117).

16. "Humane moralists" is perhaps a more historically accurate designation than animal liberationists." John Rodman, "The Liberation of Nature" (pp. 88-89), has recently explored in a programmatic way the connection between the contemporary animal liberation/rights movements and the historical humane societies movement.

17. Tom Regan styles more precise formulations of this argument, "the argument from marginal cases," in "An Examination and Defense of One Argument Concerning Animal Rights," *Inquiry* 22 (1979): 190. Regan directs our attention to Andrew Linzey, *Animal Rights* (London: SCM Press, 1976) as well

as to Singer, *Animal Liberation*, for paradigmatic employment of this argument on behalf of moral standing for animals (p. 144).

18. A particularly lucid advocacy of this notion may be found in Feinberg, "Human Duties and Animal Rights," especially pp. 53ff.

19. Again, Feinberg in "Human Duties and Animal Rights" (pp. 57–59) expresses this point especially forcefully.

20. John Rodman's comment in "The Liberation of Nature" (p. 91) is worth repeating here since it has to all appearances received so little attention elsewhere: "If it would seem arbitrary... to find one species claiming a monopoly on intrinsic value by virtue of its allegedly exclusive possession of reason, free will, soul, or some other occult quality, would it not seem almost as arbitrary to find that same species claiming a monoploy of intrinsic value for itself and those species most resembling it (e.g. in type of nervous system and behavior) by virtue of their common and allegedly exclusive possession of sentience [i.e., sensibility]?" Goodpaster ("From Egoism to Environmentalism," p. 29) remarks that in modern moral philosophy "a fixation on egoism and a consequent loyalty to a model of moral sentiment or reason which in essence generalizes or universalizes that egoism... makes it particularly inhospitable to our recent felt need for an environmental ethic.... For such an ethic does not readily admit of being reduced to 'humanism'—nor does it sit well with any class or generalization model of moral concern."

21. John Rodman, "The Liberation of Nature" (p. 95), comments: "Why do our 'new ethics' seem so old?... Because the attempt to produce a 'new ethics' by the process of 'extension' perpetuates the basic assumptions of the conventional modern paradigm, however much it fiddles with the boundaries." When the assumptions remain conventional, the boundaries are, in my view, scalar, but triangular when both positions are considered in opposition to the land ethic. The scalar relation is especially clear when two other positions, not specifically discussed in the text, the reverence-for-life ethic and pan-moralism, are considered. The reverence-for-life ethic (as I am calling it in deference to Albert Schweitzer) seems to be the next step on the scale after the humane ethic. William Frankena considers it so in "Ethics and the Environment," *Ethics and Problems of the 21st Century*, pp. 3–20. W. Murray Hunt ("Are *Mere Things* Morally Considerable," *Environmental Ethics* 2 [1980]: 59–65) had gone a step past Schweitzer, and made the bold suggestion that *everything* should be accorded moral standing, pan-moralism. Hunt's discussion shows clearly that there is a similar logic ("slippery slope" logic) involved in taking each downward step, and thus a certain commonality of underlying assumptions among all the ethical types to which the land ethic stands in opposition. Hunt is not unaware that his suggestion may be interpreted as a *reductio ad absurdum* of the whole matter, but insists that that is not his intent. The land ethic is not part of this linear series of steps and hence may be represented as a point off the scale. The principal difference, as I explain below, is that the land ethic is collective or "holistic" while the others are distrib-

utive or "atomistic." Another relevant difference is that moral humanism, humane moralism, reverence-for-life ethics, and the limiting case, pan-moralism, either openly or implicitly espouse a pecking-order model of nature. The land ethic, founded upon an ecological model of nature emphasizing the contributing roles played by various species in the economy of nature, aban- dons the "higher"/"lower" ontological and axiological schema, in favor of a functional system of value. The land ethic, in other words, is inclined to estab- lish value distinctions not on the basis of higher and lower orders of being, but on the basis of the importance of organisms, minerals, and so on to the biotic community. Some bacteria, for example, may be of greater value to the health or economy of nature than dogs, and thus command more respect.

22. Rodman, "The Liberation" of Nature (p. 86), says in reference to Singer's humane ethic that "the weakness . . . lies in the limitation of its horizon to the late eighteenth and early nineteenth century Utilitarian humane movement [and] its failure to live up to its own noble declaration that 'philosophy ought to question the basic assumptions of the age'. . . ."

23. Leopold, *Sand County Almanac*, pp. 224–25.

24. Anthropologist Clifford Geertz ("Ethos, World View, and the Analy- sis of Sacred Symbols," in *The Intepretation of Culture*, ed. Clifford Geertz [New York: Basic Books, 1973], p. 127) remarks that in cultures the world over "the powerfully coercive 'ought' is felt to grow out of a comprehensive factual 'is'. . . . The tendency to synthesize world view and ethos at some level, if not logically necessary, is at least empirically coercive; if it is not philosophically justified, it is at least pragmatically universal." Rodman, "The Liberation of Nature" (p. 96), laments the preoccupation of modern moral philosophy with the naturalistic fallacy, and comments that "thanks to this, the quest for an ethics is reduced to prattle about 'values' taken in abstraction from the 'facts' of experience; the notion of an ethics as an organic ethos, a way of life, remains lost to us."

25. By "first," "second," and "third" order wholes I intend paradigmat- ically single cell organisms, multicell organisms, and biocoenoses, respec- tively.

26. "Some Fundamentals of Conservation in the Southwest," composed in the 1920s but unpublished until it appeared last year (*Environmental Ethics* 1 [1979]: 131–41), shows that the organic analogy, conceptually repre- senting the nature of the whole resulting from ecological relationships, ante- dates the community analogy in Leopold's thinking, so far at least as its moral implications are concerned. "The Land Ethic" of *Sand County Almanac* em- ploys almost exclusively the community analogy but a rereading of "The Land Ethic" in the light of "Some Fundamentals" reveals that Leopold did not en- tirely abandon the organic analogy in favor of the community analogy. For example, toward the end of "The Land Ethic" Leopold talks about "land health" and "land the collective organism" (p. 258). William Morton Wheeler,

Essays in Philosophical Biology (New York: Russell and Russell, 1939), and Lewis Thomas, *Lives of a Cell* (New York: Viking Press, 1974), provide extended discussions of holistic approaches to social, ethical, and environmental problems. Kenneth Goodpaster, almost alone among academic philosophers, has explored the possibility of a holistic environmental ethical system in "From Egoism to Environmentalism."

27. *An Introduction to the Principles of Morals and Legislation* (Oxford: Oxford University Press, 1823), chap. 1, sec. 4.

28. This has been noticed and lamented by Alastair S. Gunn ("Why Should We Care About Rare Species?" *Environmental Ethics* 2 [1980]: 36) who comments, "Environmentalism seems incompatible with the 'Western' obsession with individualism, which leads us to resolve questions about our treatment of animals by appealing to the essentially atomistic, competitive notion of rights...." John Rodman, "The Liberation of Nature" (p. 89), says practically the same thing: "The moral atomism that focuses on individual animals and their subjective experiences does not seem well adapted to coping with ecological systems." Peter Singer has in fact actually stressed the individual focus of his humane ethic in "Not for Humans Only: The Place of Nonhumans in Environmental Issues" (*Ethics and Problems of the 21st Century*, pp. 191–206) as if it were a virtue! More revealingly, the only grounds that he can discover for moral concern over species, since species are *per se* not sensible entities (and that is the extent of his notion of an ethically relevant consideration), are anthropocentric grounds, human aesthetics, environmental integrity for humans, etc.

29. Leopold, *Sand County Almanac*, pp. 223 and 209.

30. Edward Abbey, *Desert Solitaire* (New York: Ballantine Books, 1968), p. 20.

31. Garrett Hardin, "The Economics of Wilderness," *Natural History* 78 [1969]: 173–77. Hardin is blunt: "Making great and spectacular efforts to save the life of an individual makes sense only when there is a shortage of people. I have not lately heard that there is a shortage of people" (p. 176).

32. See, for example, Garrett Hardin, "Living on Lifeboat," *Bioscience* 24 (1974): 561–68.

33. In *Republic* 5 Plato directly says that "the best governed state most nearly resembles an organism" (462D) and that there is no "greater evil for a state than the thing that distracts it and makes it many instead of one, or a greater good than that which binds it together and makes it one" (462A). Goodpaster in "From Egoism to Environmentalism" (p. 30) has in a general way anticipated this connection: "The oft-repeated plea by some ecologists and environmentalists that our thinking needs to be less atomistic and more 'holistic' translates in the present context into a plea for a more embracing object of moral consideration. In a sense it represents a plea to return to the

richer Greek conception of man by nature social and not intelligibly removable from his social and political context though it goes beyond the Greek conception in emphasizing that societies too need to be understood in a context, an ecological context, and that it is this larger whole that is the 'bearer of value.'"

34. See especially *Republic* 4.444A-E.

35. For a particularly clear statement by Plato of the idea that the goodness of anything is a matter of the fitting order of the parts in relation to respective wholes see *Gorgias* 503D-507A.

36. Cf., *Republic* 5.461C (infanticide); 468A (disposition of captives); *Republic* 3.405D-406E (medicine).

37. Cf., *Republic* 5.459A-460E (eugenics, nonfamily life and child rearing), *Republic* 3.416D-417B (private property).

38. Cf., *Republic* 4.419A-421C and *Republic* 7.419D-521B.

39. After so much strident complaint has been registered here about the lack of freshness in self-proclaimed "new" environmental ethics (which turn out to be "old" ethics retreaded) there is surely an irony in comparing the (apparently brand new) Leopoldian land ethic to Plato's ethical philosophy. There is, however, an important difference. The humane moralists have simply revived and elaborated Bentham's historical application of hedonism to questions regarding the treatment of animals with the capacity of sensibility. There is nothing new but the revival and elaboration. Plato, on the other hand, never develops anything faintly resembling an *environmental* ethic. Plato never reached an ecological view of living nature. The wholes of his universe are body, soul, society, and cosmos. Plato is largely, if not exclusively, concerned with moral problems involving individual human beings in a political context and he has the temerity to insist that the good of the whole transcends individual claims. (Even in the *Crito* Plato is sympathetic to the city's claim to put *Socrates* to death however unjust the verdict against him.) Plato thus espouses a holistic ethic which is valuable as a (very different) paradigm to which the Leopoldian *land* ethic, which is also holistic but in relation to a very different whole, may be compared. It is interesting further that some (but not all) of the analogies which Plato finds useful to convey his holistic social values are also useful to Leopold in his effort to set out a land ethic.

40. Leopold, *Sand County Almanac*, p. ix.

41. See John Muir, "The Wild Sheep of California," *Overland Monthly* 12 (1874): 359.

42. Roderick Nash (*Wilderness and the American Mind*, rev. ed. [New Haven and London: Yale University Press, 1973], p. 2) suggests that the English word *wild* is ultimately derived from *will*. A wild being is thus a willed

one—"self-willed, willful, or uncontrollable." The humane moralists' indifference to this distinction is rather dramatically represented in Regan's "Animal Rights, Human Wrongs" (pp. 99–104) which begins with a bid for the reader's sympathy through a vivid description of four concrete episodes of human cruelty toward animals. I suspect that Regan's intent is to give examples of four principal categories of animal abuse at the hands of man: whaling, traffic in zoo captives, questionable scientific experimentation involving unquestionable torture, and intensive meat production. But his illustration, divided according to precepts central to land ethics, concern two episodes of wanton slaughter of *wild animals, a blue whale and a gibbon, aggravated by the consideration that both are specimens of disappearing species, and two episodes of routine cruelty toward domestic* animals, a "bobby calf" (destined to become veal) and a laboratory rabbit. The misery of the calf and the agony of the rabbit are, to be sure, reprehensible, from the perspective of the land ethic, for reasons I explain shortly, but it is, I think, a trivialization of the deeper environmental and ecological issues involved in modern whaling and wildlife traffic to discuss the exploitation and destruction of blue whales and gibbon apes as if they are wrong for the same reasons that the treatment of laboratory rabbits and male dairy calves is wrong. The inhumane treatment of penned domestics should not be, I suggest, even discussed in the same context as whaling and wildlife traffic; it is a disservice to do so.

43. John Rodman, "The Liberation of Nature" (p. 101), castigates Singer for failing to consider what the consequences of wholesale animal liberation might be. With tongue in cheek he congratulates Singer for taking a step toward the elimination of a more subtle evil, the genetic debasement of other animal beings, i.e., domestication *per se.*

44. A particularly strong statement of the ultimate value commitment of the neo-Benthamites is found in Feinberg's "Human Duties and Animal Rights" (p. 57): "We regard pain and suffering as an intrinsic evil... simply because they are pain and suffering.... The question 'What's wrong with pain anyway?' is never allowed to arise." I shall raise it. I herewith declare in all soberness that I see nothing wrong with pain. It is a marvelous method, honed by the evolutionary process, of conveying important organic information. I think it was the late Alan Watts who somewhere remarks that upon being asked if he did not think there was too much pain in the world replied, "No, I think there's just enough."

45. Paul Shepard, "Animal Rights and Human Rites" (p. 37), comments that "the humanitarian's projection onto nature of illegal murder and the rights of civilized people to safety not only misses the point but is exactly contrary to fundamental ecological reality: the structure of nature is a sequence of killings."

46. This matter has been ably and fully explored by Paul Shepard, *The Tender Carnivore and the Sacred Game* (New York: Scribner's Sons, 1973). A

more empirical study has been carried out by Marshall Sahlins, *Stone Age Economics* (Chicago: Aldine/Atherton, 1972).

47. The expression "our meat from God" is found in Leopold, *Sand County Almanac*, p. viii. Leopold mentions "organic farming" as something intimately connected with the land ethic; in the same context he also speaks of "biotic farming" (p. 222).

3

Environmental Ethics and Nonhuman Rights

Bryan G. Norton

Introduction

The rapidly deteriorating natural environment provides convincing evidence that human decisions are often made without adequate attention to environmental concerns.[1] In controversies between developers and preservationists, the former usually win over the latter. One reason is the preservationists' lack of a coherent theoretical rationale around which to rally. Appeals are made to a number of fragmentary ideals, and this often leads to confusion within the movement, as well as to misinterpretations by others. Most environmentalists agree that present decisions are being made mainly on the basis of calculations of costs and benefits based upon relatively short-term benefits for human beings only. I agree with environmentalists who believe this approach provides an inadequate basis for environmental protection and wish to join their search for a complete and coherent rationale for environmental protection. I examine a much discussed proposal that nonhuman elements of the environment have or should be ascribed rights as a counterpoise to human interests and rights, questioning whether this proposal has promise as a basis for such a rationale.[2]

While I agree that there are important moral considerations presently being ignored in decisions with environmental impact, I doubt that appeals to rights provide the best means to conceptualize these moral concerns.

The Need for an Environmental Rationale

Two recent controversies illustrate my point that the environmentalists' fragmentary approach damages their goals. The Tellico dam project on the Tennessee River was halted temporarily, near completion, because it threatened the only known habitat of the snail darter, a three-inch fish of the perch family. Similarly, the Dickey-Lincoln hydroelectric project on the St. John River in Maine has been questioned because it would drown more than half of the population of furbish louseworts, a rare relative of the snapdragon. Both of these controversies have been complex, with appeals to save threatened species accounting for only a small part of the disputation. Proponents of both projects appealed to the need for hydroelectric power, recreational opportunities, increases in real estate values for residential and commercial uses, and so forth, values (relatively) easily factored into monetary benefits. The counter-case by environmentalists has been ineffective because it was fragmented, shifting, and not easily quantified.

Serious splits developed within the movements to halt the dams. Environmentalists disagreed as to whether the dams should be opposed for human economic reasons, independent of the endangered species in question, whether they should be opposed because an incalculable price must be placed upon eradicating a species, or whether the eradication of the species was to be considered as one cost among others. Conflicting accounts as to how to value a species were widely reported. An Associated Press story attributed to one botanist the view that the furbish louseworts had "little intrinsic worth." The discoverer of the colony of louseworts (thought for thirty years to be extinct) was quoted as saying "The furbish lousewort has no commercial value. It's not pretty or beautiful. It's scientific entirely. It's a rare plant that might become extinct."[3]

Other biologists offered far graver interpretations, finding the loss of a species "very frightening," saying that "such a loss has a direct bearing on and cannot be separated from a larger problem—the biotic impoverishment of the earth, which is reducing the capacity of the environment to produce services. It is one of the great issues of our time, right up there with nuclear proliferation,... The ultimate resource is the biota—there is no other. And we are destroying it."[4]

These splits from within caused confusion among outsiders with a resulting backlash. Even members of the public generally well disposed to environmental causes intrepret appeals to the Endangered Species Act as cynical attempts to use legal technicalities to obstruct human progress. In the process, the Endangered Species Act was significantly weakened in substance,[5] and a precedent for circumvention was set. The final upshot of the Tellico case (the controversy concerning the Dickey-Lincoln Dam continues), then, was severely damaging to the cause of environmentalists. They failed to stop a project which a nonpartisan committee concluded (unanimously) was too costly and destructive independently of danger to the snail darter. Further, the case left environmentalists on the defensive against a serious public backlash, causing them to be wary of appeals to the Endangered Species Act, for fear that if they forced a single confrontation over the act, it would be repealed.

Having been battered and beaten publicly in an attempt to defend the environment against developmental interests on noneconomic grounds, leaders were reluctant to continue with that strategy and resolved to fight on purely economic grounds. Accordingly, opponents of the Dickey-Lincoln project reportedly attempted to dissociate themselves from the endangered species issue:

> To those fighting the Dickey-Lincoln project, the plight of the furbish lousewort poses a particularly sticky problem. While they are against any deliberate attempt to extinguish a species, they recognize that the weed is being turned into a scapegoat by proponents of the dam. "The lousewort is actually damaging to our efforts to save the river because people think it is ridiculous that a weed should hold up a project costing millions of dollars," said Wayne Cobb, former assistant director of the Natural Resources Council of Maine, which is leading the battle to save the St. John from drowning.
>
> "There are a lot of good reasons for not building those dams," said Mr. Cobb. He explained that the dams would destroy one of the last wild rivers in the East and eliminate many miles of some of the best whitewater canoeing anywhere. It would submerge 88,000 acres of valuable timberland while supplying virtually no power to impoverished northern Maine because most of the electricity that would be generated is destined for the Boston area[6]

This attitude, it could be argued, plays directly into the hands of developmental interests who find it much easier to list concrete and more or less immediate economic gains to specifiable beneficiaries, whereas environmental advantages are often deferred, difficult to quantify, and diffused.

These illustrative cases support my contention that there is a serious need for a coherent rationale for environmental protection.[7] Appeals to stop developmental projects on immediate economic grounds are seldom convinccing. Even where they are, such arguments should be seen as only an incidental part of broader, long-term considerations. Such a coherent package is the environmental rationale which I am advocating.

Anthropocentric Utilitarianism

Environmental decision makers have normally applied cost-benefit analyses based on the theory of utilitarianism—actions are good if they maximize the aggregated happiness of the totality of humans, ignoring benefits or harms to nonhuman individuals.[8] Does this approach, which I call "anthropocentric utilitarianism," provide an adequate basis for environmental preservation? Many writers have answered this question negatively, and I fully agree with them.

John N. Martin claims, nevertheless, that utilitarianism can (usually) be used to account for our intuitions as to which features of the natural environment ought to be preserved:

> A reason frequently given for preserving species and ecosystems is their unique ecological properties. Sometimes these items are held to be valuable because their properties are of scientific interest, but many times their importance lies in the beneficial effects the object has on the human environment. In either case, objects with these properties are valuable because of their long-term effect on social utility. Such arguments are properly seen as being consistent with economic utilitarianism.[9]

But Eric Katz points out that Mark Sagoff had already effectively demolished Martin's line of reasoning. In reply to an essay by Martin Krieger entitled "What's Wrong With Plastic Trees?" Sagoff treats Krieger's willingness to modify human desires for preservation as a *reductio ad absurdum* of utilitarian arguments for preservation. If the only reason for preservation rests on human preferences, and if human preferences can be modified, no natural object is safe from destruction.[10] This result conflicts with the powerful intuition of environmentalists that some wonders of nature deserve preservation even if human beings find this in conflict with their preferences. Katz emphasizes the failure of anthropocentric utilitarianism by showing that "human needs are connected only contingently with the preservation of any given natural object, resource, or ecological system." It is possible that some technological advance will provide more efficient alternative means to satisfy the desire or, alternatively, the desire may be modified as a matter of changing fashions or policies.[11] Gunn presents a detailed discussion of several formulations of the utilitarian basis. Gunn's criticisms complement those stressed here.

Rather than elaborate arguments so convincingly stated elsewhere, I shall only supplement these criticisms with a concrete example. The North American timber wolf is an endangered species which all committed preservationists desire to protect from extinction. But wolves do not make good pets, they mix badly with human and domesticated animal populations, and they can require as much as ten square miles of wilderness in order to survive.[12] As human interests require the development of more and more land for agricultural or residential uses, the wolf will become, by human standards, a luxury at best.

The preservation of species such as the wolf must be understood as having a temporal dimension. Given present population levels, one might balance the costs to humans (setting aside of space, some loss of livestock, etc.) against the benefits to humans (the preservation of diversity, the inspiration some people find in the wolf, the enjoyment from hearing their howl, etc.) and conclude that an effort to save them from extinction is warranted. The costs involved, however, will increase through time. And two sorts of decisions affecting the viability of the wolf species are being made at present. Besides deciding whether the present costs outweigh present benefits of providing large preserves for wolves, humans are making decisions (in a much more haphazard way) affecting future human population levels. If choices are made which lead to further overcrowding, the costs of preserving wolves will increase—human demands to develop open spaces will increase and eventually the costs of preserving wolves will exceed the benefits. Even if wolves are presently beneficial by human standards, they will not be in a situation of acute overpopulation and food scarcity. The shifting character of human interests, then, provides no firm basis for the preservation of wolves. Some independent principles must be applied to constrain human reproductive choices so as to avoid the emergence of future conflicts between human interests and rare species. I proceed to inquire whether appeals to the rights of nonhumans provide a coherent rationale for preservation and, consequently, a counterpoise to ever growing human demands upon the environment.

Minimal Conditions Essential to Rights Holding

Before assessing the value to environmentalists of appeals to rights, one must undertake a theoretical examination of the concept of a right. Here, I follow Ruth Macklin's line of reasoning (put forward in the context of appeals to rights in medical situations):

> I should like to argue this: appeals to abstract notions of rights, in the absence of a moral theory in which appeals might be grounded, are bound to be arbitrary, *ad hoc*, or give rise to controversies that are impossible to settle in principle.... In other words, in the absence of a broader moral theory—in particular, a theory of justice—a well-grounded account of human rights will not be forthcoming. It is, then, within the framework of an overall theory of justice that we might expect to resolve at least some of the debates and uncertainties about questions of rights. Without such a generally accepted theory, claims about the existence and nature of specific rights cannot be adequately grounded or justified; yet they may still serve as expressions of moral outrage or as demands for social and legislative reform.[13]

Macklin is, I believe, correct. Failure to embed rights in a theoretical framework can only lead to question begging. Appeals to an unexplicated concept of rights are little more than expressions of moral sensitivity. Lacking a theoretical account of what a right is, there is no objective criterion for distinguishing justified from unjustified claims to rights. In such a subjective situation, it is possible to appeal to a "right" in order to defend any policy position one pleases, and such appeals amount to little more than (perhaps) morally persuasive ways of saying "I prefer policy X." In arguing for the preservation of the Mineral King mountain range from recreation development, Justice W. O. Douglas says, "With all respect, the problem is to make certain that the inanimate objects, which are the very core of America's beauty, have spokesmen before they are destroyed."[14] To this end, Douglas proposes, following Christopher Stone, that legal standing or rights be accorded to natural objects.[15] Here, rights are introduced in order to bolster an already firmly entrenched idea. But in cases where ideals are controversial among disputants, such appeals to rights are indecisive, for, lacking a theory which allows rational adjudication of conflicting rights claims, the developers of Mineral King could just as well argue that Mineral King has a right to be "perfected," to have its true potentials developed. Appeals to rights can only be supported objectively by an appeal to theoretically justifiable conceptions of rights with an attendant criterion of rights holding.

Many writers ask whether we need appeals to rights of nonhumans in order to protect the environment.[16] This question is usually posed in such a manner as to presuppose that *if* such rights exist, then they provide, *ipso facto*, an adequate environmental ethic. I adopt a more skeptical stance, asking whether a rights-based ethic will be adequate, given the goals of environmentalists.

It might appear that I have now set for myself a virtually impossible task, to present and defend an unexceptionable theory of rights. Fortunately, this awesome task can be avoided. If I show that there are certain ideas essential to and shared by all theories of rights, I can then derive from these ideas the minimal characteristics of all rights holders. As minimal conditions for rights holding they can then serve as the basis for a partial evaluation of imputations of rights to new, nonhuman rights holders and allow an estimate of whether this sort of ethic will prove adequate for the goals of environmentalists.[17]

To forestall unnecessary controversies about the proper theory of rights, I defend no particular theory. Rather I limit my claims about the nature of rights to four noncontroversial conditions which follow from the very concept of a right. My minimal claims are only that the attribution of a right to X implies that:

1. X is an identifiable individual, and

2. it is in some meaningful sense possible to say that X has interests;

3. attributions of interests to X are not sufficient to entail corresponding rights had by X;

4. if it is determined that an interest of X is also a right of X, this determination must depend, perhaps among other factors, upon characteristics of X rather than solely on characteristics of others.[18]

Claim (1) implies that rights are individualistic in nature, in the sense that they govern the treatment of one individual by another. Here, I use the term *individual* in a neutral manner, not assuming that individuals must be human beings, or even, for that matter, living beings. I require only that a rights holder be an identifiable individual, the denotatum of a singular referring expression.

Requirements (2) and (3) jointly reflect the view that interests are necessary, though not sufficient for rights. My claim is merely that one cannot properly attribute rights to an individual to whom one cannot attribute interests.[19] Not all interests entail rights, and differing theories suggest differing elements or processes which qualify some interests as rights. In general, however, there seems to be agreement that, perhaps among other things, legitimation by a set of rules is an important added requirement. That is, individual interests, when asserted, become claims. Not all claims are justified (rights). When claims cannot all be honored, a system of rules adjudicates conflicts. Rights then are claims which have been given validity by a system of rules for adjudicating conflicting claims.[20]

Condition (4) rules out attributions of rights for an individual, X, when the claim on which the right is based is purely a claim of a second party. For example, if it is illegal or immoral to harm a farmer's horse, this prohibition does not reflect a right of the horse when it is based merely on the fact that the horse is owned and used by the farmer. If the same prohibition governs horses and tractors and is supported purely on the basis of the usefulness to, and ownership of, the object by another party, any rights involved are property rights of the owner, not rights of the owned object.

The minimal conditions (1) through (4) merely give expression to these central conceptual features of discourse about rights. Rights govern the treatment of individuals and rest upon the interests or claims made by individuals. At the same time, no theory of rights takes interests to be sufficient—the purpose of a theory of rights is to provide rules for adjudicating disputes as to which *interest*, among competing ones, is a *right*. A theory cannot credit all claims, or it would provide no distinction between legitimate and illegitimate interests.

Besides forestalling controversies concerning the nature of rights, my minimalist approach has the advantage of being applicable to utilitarian as well as deontological attempts to attribute moral concepts to nonhumans. While I have rejected (anthropocentric) utilitarian theory as an adequate guide in environmental matters, some environmentalists may find the expansion of a utilitarian calculus to include the interests of nonhumans to be an attractive basis for an environmental ethic. The treatment of expanded versions of utilitarianism as one among other theories of rights may startle readers who are accustomed to treating utilitarian theory as an attempt to avoid references to rights altogether. If care is taken on this point, however, I can avoid confusion and gain considerable generality. Utilitarians must decide, prior to calculating which action leads to the greatest happiness, which beings count as moral individuals. A moral individual, for utilitarians, is one whose interests must be taken into account in the calculus. The utilitarian, then, faces considerations essentially similar to those faced by rights theorists. Both must decide who and/or what is to be considered a moral individual and, on a sufficiently abstract level, it is indifferent as to whether one formulates this question as one concerning rights holding or one of legitimate interest holding.

It may well be that there are reasons to think that rights holding is a more restricted characteristic than is that of legitimate interest holding. This distinction is, I believe, the motivation for Kenneth Goodpaster's introduction of the category of *moral considerability*.[21] Goodpaster intends to raise utilitarian considerations favoring moral concern for animals without becoming embroiled in the difficulties involved in attributing the more problematic concept of rights to them. Peter Singer, however, uses less cautious terminology, claiming to defend the animals' "rights" to equal consideration of their interests as a necessary consequence of utilitarianism. While Singer spoke freely of rights in his early publication, *Animal Liberation*, he later explained that his use of the concept of rights was inessential, arguing that he had only used the concept as a means of referring to the necessity of according equality of consideration for interests of animals.[22] Since my argument is negative, however, and since it applies equally to utilitarian and to deontological attempts to develop an environmental ethic based upon an expanded group of moral individuals, I choose to use the them *right* in the broader sense. That is, when I speak of the class of rights holders I refer to the entire class of moral individuals and, hence, I am using the term in a sense equivalent to Goodpaster's *moral considerability*. I believe that this broad interpretation is justified both by the added scope which is thereby afforded my argument as well as by the fact that this usage seems to square with that of environmentalists who appeal to rights. I have never encountered an attribution of rights in the context of a defense for preservationist values which would demand the narrower sense of rights usually associated with deontological ethics.

Rights of Nonhumans and Environmental Ethics

Armed with the four minimal conditions set out in the last section, I can now proceed to inquire whether rights attributed to nonhumans can provide an adequate basis for an environmental ethic. As a starting point in this inquiry, I cite the well-known work of animal liberationists who ascribe rights to animals in the process of arguing for vegetarianism and antivivisectionism. The central line of reasoning of the animal liberationists is that (a) (at least some) individual animals can suffer; (b) (at least some) animals have interests; therefore, (c) it is in the interests of (at least some) individual animals not to suffer. But (d) the interests of every being affected by an action are to be taken into account and given the same weight as the like interests of another being; (e) it is the right of humans not to be subjected to unnecessary suffering (that is, a human interest in avoiding pain becomes a right, provided that the suffering is unnecessary for some more important good or for the fulfillment of some higher obligation); and (f) some nonhumans experience suffering comparable to some human suffering. Therefore, (g) those cases of animal suffering which are similar to human suffering and which are unnecessary should give rise to a right, unless rights are limited to members of the human species merely because of this species membership. But (h) mere membership in a species cannot, in and of itself, justify a difference in moral treatment; therefore, (i) under some circumstances, some nonhuman animals have the right not to suffer.[23]

This line of reasoning is not, of course, noncontroversial. Premises (b), (d), (f), and (h) have all been questioned with some cogency. In the context of the present article, however, it is unnecessary to resolve these controversies, as I intend not to question the truth of attributions of rights to nonhumans, but to argue that even if these are true, they are inadequate as a basis for an environmental ethic. Rights attributed to nonhumans according to this argument successfully fulfill the minimal conditions (1) through (4). Since suffering is a characteristic of individuals, rights attributed by this argument apply to individuals in the sense of being individual organisms, not just in the broader sense of being the referent of an individual referring expresion. Likewise, condition (2) is fulfilled because the argument, in premise (b), states that the rights in question presuppose interests. But not all of the interests are assumed to entail corresponding rights (thereby fulfilling condition [3]), because interests must (by premise [e]) be judged not to be overriden by the most important goods or obligations. Finally, condition (4) is fulfilled because the attribution of a right to an interest-holding nonhuman depends at least upon the individual in question being capable of experiencing suffering comparable to the suffering of other rights holders.

Having granted that rights attributed to nonhumans by animal liberationists fulfill the minimal conditions (1) through (4), it remains to inquire whether such rights are sufficient to support an environmental ethic. Initially, this line of reasoning seems promising. One important source of individual suffering among wild, nonhuman animals is destruction of habitat. In cases where human destruction of a habitat caused the suffering of individual animals unnecessarily, the animal liberationists' line of reasoning would, perhaps, provide a rights-based prohibition. And such prohibitions against destruction might extend further than to the species in question, as other species (not included in the argument as rights holders) and even geophysical characteristics of an area are usually necessary for the members of a species to flourish.

It is difficult to assess the extent of the usefulness to environmentalists of this line of reasoning, however, because of the vagueness embodied in the phrase *some animals*. If only primates, for example, can suffer comparably to humans, then such an argument is worthless to environmentalists except in those areas where primates live indigenously. If all higher mammals have rights, then the application is wider, but still does not affect actions in areas not containing any higher mammals. That is, whenever one draws the line as to what has interests and rights, there will, undoubtedly, be some area of earth or sea which environmentalists feel deserving of preservation, but which serves as the habitat for none of the species above the line as drawn. If, of course, interests and rights are extended to all living things or even to all things existent, these problems are, in one sense, minimized.[24] But, in another sense, such problems might even be exacerbated. As one expands the class of rights holders to larger and larger portions of nature, one necessarily increases the number of conflicts. If not just animals, but plants also, have rights, then vegetarians must develop criteria for justified eating of plant life. It may turn out that in the hierarchy required by such extreme expansion some nonhuman elements of the universe may end up faring no better than in a system where only humans have rights.

Of course, these objections may have no theoretical importance. It could be argued that, in principle, there exists a complex theory of rights of nonhumans accompanied by a hierarchy of types of rights which yields a rational system *and* supports all legitimate interests in environmental preservation. But even if this were the case, the practical difficulties of such a proposal would be overwhelming. If such a theoretical system were to be the basis of an environmental ethic, arguments based upon it would have to await the development of such a system. Since even the central claim that *some* nonhuman animals have rights is extremely controversial and is presently accepted by only a small minority of both philosophers and the general population, it is unrealistic to hope that such an ethic will be available in the near future. Indeed, considering the current rate of environmental destruction and the seeming intractability of the theoretical problems in ranking rights on a hierarchy, it seems highly doubtful that such a theory will gain enough agreement to provide a real force for environmental preservation before it is too late.

One aspect of these practical difficulties has already made itself felt. The animal liberationists' concern for individuals is obvious and well-known. Environmentalists, on the other hand, show concern for groups, species, habitats, etc., and very little concern for the suffering of individual creatures.[25] Leopold, for example, advocates hunting (under certain wilderness situations) as an ideal form of human recreation in the same book in which he introduces his famous land ethic. Likewise, environmentalists advocate the culling of deer and buffalo herds in the absence of natural predators. Or, somewhat less shortsightedly, they attempt to reintroduce predators to perform this task for them. Such an ethic has little in common with that of ethical vegetarians and antivivisectionists who see as their duty the elimination of suffering.[26] Indeed, there is a growing rift between the humane organizations and traditional wildlife organizations as these very different goals and approaches become evident.[27]

I do not, however, intend to rest my case on purely practical difficulties, as theoretical ones abound as well. In order to illustrate these theoretical difficulties, I assume that animal liberationists can settle upon a class of rights holders based upon the argument sketched above. First, note that such a class is, in the context of a search for an environmental ethic, constrained on both sides. Such a class must be more general than some plausible cutoff points, since an adequate environmental ethic must apply to a broad range of endangered species and to many types of environmentally sensitive areas. As mentioned above, if the class of rights holders is restricted to primates, the resulting ethic will not be sufficient to protect many environmentally crucial species or areas, because many environmentally damaging actions affect no nonhuman primates.

But, on the other side, if rights holding is construed too broadly, the crucial analogy to human interests breaks down. Any expansion of the class of rights holders based upon the above argument must maintain a plausible analogy with human interests. Failing this, premise (h), whereby failures to accord rights without appeal to relevant characteristics other than mere species membership are branded as unjustified *speciesism*, becomes implausible, and the argument from analogy to human interests collapses. Singer and other animal liberationists have cited the characteristic of sentience, shared by humans and at least other higher mammals, to secure premise (b) that some nonhumans have interests—interests in avoiding their own suffering. The question of whether rights based upon individual interests in avoiding suffering can support a comprehensive and general environmental ethic, then, reduces to the question of whether every case of unacceptable environmental destruction causes the suffering of some sentient individual. At first glance, this latter question sounds as if it can be resolved positively if it can be verified that all destruction of environmentally sensitive areas does not in fact cause sentient beings to suffer. Thus, the issue seems to require only the affirmation of a plausible empirical hypothesis. But a more careful analysis shows that the relationship between environmental destruction and suffering must be stronger than an empirical correlation if a general environmental ethic is to be built upon avoidance of suffering. It is possible, that is, for humans to accept the obligation to avoid unnecessary suffering resulting from their actions without accepting the obligation to save environmentally important areas. They could, for example, humanely capture and relocate all creatures in an area slated to become a parking lot or a condominium complex, thereby sparing them suffering. Indeed, if such animals were moved to zoos or other preserves, protected from predators, given food and shelter, it could be argued that the destruction of the area has minimized suffering.[28] Or, alternately, developers could, several years prior to disrupting an area, put a sterilizing drug in the food source of all indigenous species deemed to be "sentient."

The relationship between habitat destruction and individual suffering is, then, a contingent one. I am arguing that such a contingent relationship cannot form the basis of an adequate environmental ethic because it will always be possible for humans, if the anticipated benefits to themselves are considered valuable enough, to devise means to protect the individuals in question from the suffering attendant upon the destruction of their habitat. Wide acceptance of the humane attitude of the animal liberationists might, then, be accompanied not by environmental preservation, but with a growth in technological means whereby individual members of species indigenous to areas slated for development can be spared individual suffering. The humane ethic might, then, provide a decisive element in the justification of the destruction of wilderness areas.

Perhaps because they have recognized this problem, some writers have eschewed the argument based upon the analogy between human and nonhuman suffering, opting instead for claims that rights or moral considerability apply to nonsentient living beings or even to all existent things.[29] Rights construed this broadly, of course, avoid the problem of narrowness just raised. It is difficult to imagine a case of environmental destruction that harms no living thing, animal or plant, and impossible to imagine a case which harms no existing thing. Such an approach, however, should not be viewed as yet one more liberation movement based upon analogy to human rights and interests. To apply rights and/or moral considerability this broadly is to abandon the analogical argument attributed above to animal liberationists. Some proponents of this position have recognized the necessity of parting ways with the animal liberationists. As Goodpaster says, "What I want to suggest is that the *last* thing we need is simply another 'liberation movement'."[30] And he summarizes his line of argument as follows:

> I have been arguing so far that the two major foundational accounts of morality share, both in their classic formulations and in their contemporary interpretations, a fixation on egoism and a consequent loyalty to a model of moral sentiment or reason which in essence generalizes or universalizes that very egoism. And I have suggested that it is this fact about modern moral philosophy that makes it particularly inhospitable to our recent felt need for an environmental ethic—an ethic which, in the words of Leopold, takes the integrity, stability and beauty of the biotic community as its central touch-stone. For such an ethic does not readily admit of being reduced to "humanism"—nor does it sit well with any class or generalization model of moral concern.[31]

Goodpaster is correct because the ethic he advocates abandons the attempt to generate obligations to, and rights of, individuals of any sort. Such an approach involves no rights, as is implied by condition (1).

Anyone who ignores Goodpaster's arguments and attempts to support an environmental ethic with individual rights attributed to all living or all existing things must abandon the argument from human analogy. The animal liberationists' argument exploits the fact that human interests and the capacity to suffer are given unquestioned moral weight and emphasizes the similarity of certain other creatures to humans in these respects. It is thus possible to argue for moral standards for these individuals on a basis of fairness or impartiality. But the characteristics of being alive and being in existence are not given unquestioned (or any) moral weight at present. Thus, the argument for very widespread moral standing cannot be based upon an argument of *fairness*—it appeals to characteristics not given moral significance for any beings, human or otherwise.

But lacking a human analogy and the sorts of priority rules which apply in human-centered ethics, rights attributions are quite arbitrary. Since the reasons given for attributing rights to all living things or all nonhuman things grow out of the environmental crisis, *not* out of concern to eliminate individual suffering, problems arise with this view. Rights are assigned for environmental reasons, not individual reasons. Such assignments must employ some conception of what may be done, environmentally speaking. That is, if there is a conflict in "interest" between two plants, for example, the one which is environmentally more crucial will be saved. This presupposes that rights attributions are also quite arbitrary from the point of view of considerations concerning individuals. But then such rights violate condition (4). They depend not on characteristics of the individual itself, but on its centrality in the environmental concerns felt by others.

Even if such rights attributions did not violate condition (4), they would be worthless anyway. Since they are assigned to individuals on the basis of environmental priority, such assignments presuppose knowledge as to what ought to be preserved. If that is known, there must already be an accepted environmental ethic and appeals to rights are otiose. The assignments of such rights presuppose the very system of rules they are designed to yield.

Ascribing rights to nonhuman individuals does not, then, provide a promising basis for an environmental ethic. The problem with this suggestion can be put most simply as follows: the relationship between the individual interests of organisms, individual plants, and nonliving objects, on the one hand, and the healthy functioning and integrity of the ecosystem, on the other hand, is a contingent one. Actions which damage an environmentally sensitive area usually or always damage some individuals or some species. This fact accounts, no doubt, for the persistence of suggestions that the recognition of interests and rights of nonhuman objects is a useful basis for a new environmental consciousness or ethic. But environmental destruction need not result in harm to any individual. It is possible to accept a humane ethic extended as broadly as one wishes and take this ethic to require steps to protect all individuals affected, rather than to protect the habitat, the community, or the ecosystem in question. Once the contingency of this relationship is recognized, the temptation is to continue the expansion of rights to apply to greater and greater portions of the environment—hence, the implausible suggestions that all existent things have rights. This seems to insure that, whenever the environment is damaged, some rights holder will be affected and the rights-based ethic will become relevant. This ploy works only at the expense of trivializing the environmental ethic in question. Every action with environmental consequences must, on this view, affect some rights holder. If this result is not to be totally paralyzing, there must be some means of deciding which actions are to be prohibited from those which need not be. And since the original use of the terms *rights* and *interests* applies to human rights and interests, no guidance for behavior is forthcoming from those concepts alone, as the analogy with human rights and interests has been abandoned. Worse, the reason it has been abandoned is precisely the same reason the expansion was necessary. In order to insure that all environmentally damaging actions affect some individual, the class of individuals is made identical to the class of objects affected. If this trivializing move is not to paralyze human action, some independent principle is necessary to isolate actions which are to be prohibited. But if such an independent principle were available, the appeal to individual rights would be redundant. I conclude that rights and interests of individuals are not a helpful basis for an environmental ethic.

I began this examination of the possibility of resting an environmental ethic on rights with the recognition that the concept of rights is, necessarily, an individualistic concept. I have now shown that it is exactly this individualistic character of rights which makes the attempt to generate an environmental ethic from rights unpromising—I would even say impossible.

At this point, it is tempting to close the discussion and conclude that interests and rights are inadequate as a support for an environmental ethic. One further possibility must be considered, however, as condition (1), requiring that rights holders must be individuals, was stated in neutral terms, leaving open the possibility that the individuals in question might not be organisms, but collectivities of some sort. I chose a neutral definition because some environmentalists have suggested a rights-based environmental ethic on which various sorts of collectivities are rights holder. For example, Stone ascribes rights to forests and to the Mineral King mountain range and Leopold speaks of a "land ethic" which might be (and has been) construed as an ascription of rights to the land or the biotic community as a whole.[32] At first glance, this suggestion seems to stretch condition (1) beyond recognition and even to trivialize it. Condition (1) seems to be designed to anchor rights ascriptions to the human analogy—the concept of a right applies most straightforwardly to human individuals—and a stringent enforcement of condition (1) rules out this suggestion as nonsensical. I have chosen to discuss it substantively, however, because there is an analogy other than the human one which might be thought to give it plausibility. Corporations are, according to law, treated as fictional persons and are ascribed rights. Stone has appealed to this precedent and, admittedly, it is difficult to rule out ascriptions of rights to species and habitats on the basis of condition (1) without ruling out the widely accepted precedent of rights for corporations.[33] For this reason I grant such ascriptions can pass condition (1) and base my argument against them on the remaining conditions.

It makes sense to say that corporations have interests because they are formed for a human purpose, such as profit making. Given this, one can say that a particular piece of legislation or a government regulation is against the interest of such a corporation, meaning that the law or regulation makes it more difficult for the corporation to fulfill the purpose for which it has been formed. But there is no sense in which a species, an ecosystem, or a mountain range is constructed for a purpose. It may be that humans assign or ascribe purposes to them. Two possibilities arise here. Humans could ascribe purposes to these collectivities by insisting that they behave teleologically in themselves and, consequently, that they have, in themselves, interests in achieving certain goals, such as preservation, or humans could ascribe interests to these collectivities because they are useful to the fulfillment of human purposes.

The latter possibility, which is implied by the analogy with corporations, is easily dismissed as useless for an environmental ethic. First, since the interests are not interests of the collectives but of humans, it seems doubtful if this suggestion can succeed in fulfilling condition (4) whereby rights assigned to an object must be assigned, at least to some extent, on the basis of characteristics of that object rather than solely on the characteristics of other beings. Since all of the interests of the collectives, on this interpretation, are derived from human interests, conflicts between interests will be adjudicated, ultimately, on the basis of human needs. Therefore, the rights so assigned are not, strictly speaking, rights of the collectives at all. Rather, the collectives are just convenient repositories for human rights. Even more importantly, however, this interpretation holds no hope for an environmental ethic. An environmental ethic based upon nonhuman rights seeks to identify rights which will serve as a counterpoise to human claims on the environment. The rights presently suggested merely embody human rights in a new form. While one might suggest that the environment would be preserved if all human rights to a clean and unspoiled environment were honored, such claims to human rights have to be weighed against other human claims such as property rights, the right to sustenance of human life, etc. Hence, the ascriptions of rights based upon this line of reasoning suffers all of the disadvantages which environmentalists presently experience in convincing others that saving the environment is actually in the interest of humankind.

The other interpretation—that environmental collectives have interests in their own rights—is, perhaps, more promising. But it must be recognized that this approach embodies a curious amalgamation of analogies. Condition (1) is satisfied by virtue of the legal convention that personhood may be assigned to a humanly created entity as a legal fiction. Once this step has been taken, it also seems reasonable to assign interests to this legal fiction on the basis of the purpose its human creators had in bringing the entity into existence. But I have already shown that assigning human purposes to elements of the environment and deriving interests from this source yields no acceptable environmental ethic. So, to satisfy condition (2) in a manner which shows promise in the search for an environmental ethic, the entities which are assigned individual moral status by convention must then be seen as having interests independent of their conventionally assigned individuality. Hence, a switch is necessitated from the conventional assignment of moral individuality for collectives drawn from the corporate analogy to the human analogy in the attribution of interests—otherwise, the entities assigned moral individuality do not have the independence of interests necessary to provide a counterpoise to human interests in environmental conflicts. But collectives such as mountain ranges, species, and ecosystems have no significant analogues to human sentience on which to base assignments of interests, and the whole enterprise of assigning interests becomes virtually arbitrary. This is seen to be especially so as one notes that the original choices as to which entities to assign conventional individuality seem arbitrary in themselves. Ecologists have often noted the arbitrary nature of concepts such as that of an ecosystem, a species, etc. How could Stone, for example, justify his offhand suggestion that the Mineral King mountain range has legal standing rather than parallel suggestions that individual rocks or individual mountains should have it?[34] And these parallel suggestions could give rise to substantive conflicts. If one assigns rights to individual mountains, there seems to be no basis for deciding which mountain is to be sacrificed for a four-lane highway through the range, whereas if the range as a whole has rights, one might be led to sacrifice a smaller and less integral mountain on the edges of the range for a highway, as long as this seems the best means to preserve the "integrity" of the range itself. Lest I be accused of having based my argument on the worst case, note that ambiguities arise on what may seem to be the best case for this suggestion as well. It may seem easier to assign interests to a species—it is in the interest of a species to persist. But since the suggestion is that this is a species interest, not an individual interest, it is unclear whether it is in the species' interest to survive in its present form or to be allowed to evolve in response to changing environmental situations (perhaps including human development of its present habitat), which might create a new species, the members of which might not count as members of the original species, but which are more likely to survive.

There is yet one more puzzle involved in the present proposal. Note that the ascription of individual rights to collectives is an inherently odd idea because every environmental collective is a part of a larger such collective. A habitat is a part of an ecosystem and ecosystems can be embedded in larger and larger ecosystems until all individuals and all collectives can be seen as parts of the entire ecosystem which makes up the universe. Once this is noted, it becomes obvious that the original motivation for the suggestion that rights be assigned to collectives—that individual rights do not capture the central holistic idea of environmentalists—is self-defeating. Assigning rights to collectives which in turn can conflict with those of individuals and other collectives is not to achieve a holistic ethic; it is only to treat collectives as if they are individuals and to add more individuals with more claims and to exacerbate conflicts.

Perhaps none of these considerations add up to a straightforward proof that the suggestion that rights be ascribed to environmental collectives is hopeless. But the unnatural ring of the entire idea of rights of collectives treated as individuals, the extraordinary arbitrariness which would be introduced in making detailed ascriptions of rights to collectives, and the recognition that such an approach does not, ultimately, achieve the goal of a holistic ethic convinces me that little help to environmentalists will be forthcoming from this suggestion.

Conclusion

It is worthwhile to examine, in conclusion, the deeper explanation for the failure of individualistic appeals to rights and interests as a basis for an environmental ethic. Human demands on the environment are individual demands. As the population increases, these demands are increased and a principle of adjudication is required. The animal liberation movement is based upon an analogy between human and animal suffering and its main thrust is *not* to provide a means to adjudicate between conflicting demands that human individuals make on the environment, but rather it introduces a whole new category of demands—the demands of animals. Recognition of such demands has the overall effect of exacerbating the problem. It also has the contingent effect of calling attention to destruction of habitat as one source of animal suffering, and many have seen this as a plausible route to an environmental ethic. But as the class of rights holders is expanded further and further in order to insure that environmentally damaging results affect some rights holder, more and more demands are made. Expanding the number and types of rights holders does not address the problem of deciding which individual claims have priority over others—it only increases these demands and makes it more and more difficult to satisfy them. The basic problem, then, lies precisely in the emphasis on individual claims and interests. An environmental ethic must support the holistic functioning of an ongoing system. One cannot generate a holistic ethic from an individualistic basis, regardless of how widely that basis is expanded

Notes

1. Throughout this paper, I refer to "environmentalists," "environmental preservationists," and "preservationists" interchangeably and in an intuitive, nontechnical sense. These terms have an intuitive basis—they refer to those individuals who, other things being equal, are more likely to oppose large, artificial projects, who support the maintenance (even at considerable cost) of natural, unspoiled areas, and who find the extinction of a species through intentional or careless actions to be abhorrent. My intuitive use of these terms can, I think, be justified in that the meaning of environmental preservation is significantly clarified as the argument of the paper unfolds.

2. This is the first in a series of three essays which search for a more adequate environmental ethic. In the second paper, I examine the suggestion that rights of future generations could provide such an ethic. In the third and

final paper, I propose an alternative based upon value of life as an ongoing enterprise plus principles from ecological theory.

3. Associated Press, "Rare Wild Flowers May Halt Project," *Sarasota Herald-Tribune*, 11 November 1976.

4. George Woodwell, quoted in an article by Philip Shabecoff, "New Battles Over Endangered Species: Birds and Fish vs. Highways and Dams," *New York Times Magazine*, 4 June 1978, p. 43.

5. Congress passed legislation allowing a cabinet-level committee to exempt projects from the act when it concluded that the benefits of the project "clearly outweigh the alternatives." The committee subsequently refused to exempt Tellico and, consequently, Congress overturned its own committee's finding by voting the direct exemption. President Carter signed this legislation on 25 September 1979.

6. Shabecoff, "New Battles," p. 39.

7. I here discount such claims as that of R. J. Nelson who argues for "directing our moral energies away from self-defeating moral suasion, which is so prevalent today in the most concerned circles, to deliberation on our social choice practices. The imperatives posed by the environment are simply not going to be met by harping on traditional moral desiderata—even and especially when extended to sentient beings other than humans." See "Ethics and Environmental Decision Making," *Environmental Ethics* 1 (1979): 269. Nelson may be correct in claiming that moral suasion of a purely abstract sort has limited efficacy in changing people's minds. But he is wrong in believing that one can avoid ethical theory. His supposed alternative, that of presuming that deciding parties "in environmental affairs are utilitarians" does just that —it presumes a theory of morality which may or may not be correct. Interestingly, he interprets utilitarianism as the view that one judges "a good environment to be part of a state of well-being and maximum happiness for everything in the natural order capable of it" (p. 269). If this very liberal form of utilitarianism were universally accepted as he presumes, there would already have been a radical shift in human treatment of the environment. Note, also, that later in the essay, Nelson's argument becomes confused in just the ways one would expect, given that he eschews any attempt at a coherent rationale. On p. 273 he uses the vague phrase "everyone's preferences." Does this phrase refer to every human being, every decision maker, or every affected individual, including nonhumans, as his brand of "utilitarianism" would suggest? Most disturbingly, he uses this vague phrase to "secure" his procedure "as ethically correct." But what this really amounts to is a covert sliding from procedural considerations on aggregating utilities to the conclusion that the resulting composite decision "must fairly represent the collective." The deliberative procedure does not, even, involve all humans, much less everything in the natural order capable of happiness. Nothing other than a question-begging equivo-

cation allows him to move from choices by some humans to the conclusion that the happiness and well-being of the entire natural order will be served. What is necessary in order to make such moves in argument is some general moral rationale enforcing upon human decision makers the obligation to take the well-being of the entire natural order into account in their choices.

8. It is true that Bentham claimed that the ability to suffer is the only criterion that utilitarians should use in deciding who or what is to be considered in the utilitarian calculus; Jeremy Bentham, *An Introduction to the Principles of Morals and Legislation* (New York: Hafner Publishing Company, 1948), p. 311. But Bentham's claim has been, in practice, universally ignored.

9. John N. Martin, "The Concept of the Irreplaceable," *Environmental Ethics* 1 (1979): 40.

10. Eric Katz, "Utilitarianism and Preservation," *Environmental Ethics* 1 (1979): 362; Mark Sagoff, "On Preserving the Natural Environment," *Yale Law Journal* 84 (1974): 205; Martin H. Krieger, "What's Wrong with Plastic Trees?" *Science* 179 (1973): 446-55.

11. Katz, "Utilitarianism and Preservation," p. 362. Also see David W. Ehrenfeld, "The Conservation of Non-Resources," *American Scientist* 64 (1976): 648-56, and Alastair Gunn, "Why Should We Care About Rare Species?" *Environmental Ethics* 2 (1980): 17-37, esp. 22-29.

12. L. David Mech, *The Wolf: The Ecology and Behavior of an Endangered Species* (Garden City: Natural History Press, 1970), p. 324.

13. Ruth Macklin, "Moral Concerns and Appeals to Rights and Duties," *Hastings Center Report* 6 (1976): 31.

14. William O. Douglas, "Sierra Club vs. Morton: Minority Opinion," reprinted in Christopher Stone, *Should Trees Have Standing?* (Los Altos, Calif.: William Kaufmann, 1974), p. 76.

15. Stone, pp. 53-54.

16. See, for example, Richard Routley, "Is There a Need for a New, an Environmental, Ethic?" *Proceedings of the XVth World Congress of Philosophy* 1 (1973): 203-9.

17. My approach is somewhat similar to that of Richard Watson in "Self-Consciousness and the Rights of Nonhuman Animals and Nature," *Environmental Ethics* 1 (1979): 99-129. However, I believe that Watson's emphasis on self-consciousness, rationality, and the ability to reciprocate in acceptance of moral duty as necessary conditions on rights-holding are too restrictive. These substantive conditions appear far too strong to advocates of nonhuman rights and Watson's otherwise admirable analysis has proved unpersuasive because it appears to beg the question against advocates of nonhuman rights. Chapter 1, this volume.

18. I hope that my assertion of (1) through (4) as minimal conditions on rights holding does not appear overly dogmatic. To show for every actual and possible theory of rights that (1) through (4) hold would be both tedious and outside the scope of this paper. My goal has been to concentrate on cental ideas which seem to be conceptual consequences of any rights attribution. I leave it to the reader to judge my success on this point.

19. See Joel Feinberg, "The Rights of Animals and Unborn Generations," in William Blackstone, ed., *Philosophy and Environmental Crisis* (Athens, Ga.: University of Georgia Press, 1974), p. 49.

20. Feinberg, "The Nature and Value of Rights," *Journal of Value Inquiry* 4 (1970): 243-57. While Feinberg's theory is not noncontroversial in all of its aspects, all competitors either accept his reference to claims or substitute some other concept such as entitlements, which equally presuppose interests. See H. J. McCloskey, "Rights," *Philosophy Quarterly* 15 (1965): 115-27.

21. Kenneth Goodpaster, "On Moral Considerability," *Journal of Philosophy* 75 (1978): 308-25.

22. See Peter Singer, *Animal Liberation* (New York: New York Review, 1975); and "The Fable of the Fox and the Unliberated Animals," *Ethics* 88 (1978): 122.

23. I offer this argument as an encapsulation of Singer's argument as it appears in chapter 1 of *Animal Liberation*, qualified by clarifications offered in "The Fable of the Fox and the Unliberated Animals."

24. See Goodpaster, "On Moral Considerability," and W. Murray Hunt, "Are *Mere Things* Morally Considerable?" *Environmental Ethics* 2 (1980): 59-65.

25. Alastair Gunn, "Why Should We Care about Rare Species?" *Environmental Ethics* 2 (1980): 20-21. Also, see Peter Singer, "Not for Humans Only: The Place of Nonhumans," in Goodpaster and Sayre, eds., *Ethics and Problems of the 21st Century* (Notre Dame: University of Notre Dame Press, 1979): 191-206; J. Baird Callicott's comprehensive consideration of these issues in "Animal Liberation: A Triangular Affair," *Environmental Ethics* 2 (1980): 311-38.

26. Note that the disanalogy with individual rights is not avoided by emphasizing the right to be spared *unnecessary* suffering and by arguing that herd culling, etc., is *necessary* for the survival of the herd. In order for this analogy to hold, it would, contrary to fact, have to be considered permissible for the problem of human famine to be solved by the "culling" of human populations.

27. For an excellent discussion of this rift, see Peter Steinhart, "Essay: Advance of the Ethic," *Audubon* 82 (January 1980): 126-27.

28. This point is convincingly made several times by John Rodman in "The Liberation of Nature?" *Inquiry* 20 (1977): 83-131.

29. See Goodpaster, "On Moral Considerability," and Hunt, "Are *Mere Things* Morally Considerable?"

30. Goodpaster, "From Egoism to Environmentalism," in Goodpaster and Sayre, *Problems in the 21st Century*, p. 29.

31. Ibid., p. 28.

32. Aldo Leopold, *Sand County Almanac* (New York: Oxford University Press, 1949), pp. 202-3.

33. See Stone, *Should Trees Have Standing?* p. 18. This precedent is, it would seem, more plausible in the context of legal rights than when speaking of moral rights.

34. Ibid., p. xiii. Note that Stone, in this first statement on Mineral King, attributes the rights in question "to Mineral King—the park itself." At other points he suggests attributions of rights to rivers and forests, etc., p. 24.

4

The Ethics of Respect for Nature

Paul W. Taylor

1. Human-Centered and Life-Centered Systems of Environmental Ethics

In this paper I show how the taking of a certain ultimate moral attitude toward nature, which I call "respect for nature," has a central place in the foundations of a life-centered system of environmental ethics. I hold that a set of moral norms (both standards of character and rules of conduct) governing human treatment of the natural world is a rationally grounded set if and only if, first, commitment to those norms is a practical entailment of adopting the attitude of respect for nature as an ultimate moral attitude, and second, the adopting of that attitude on the part of all rational agents can itself be justified. When the basic characteristics of the attitude of respect for nature are made clear, it will be seen that a life-centered system of environmental ethics need not be holistic or organicist in its conception of the kinds of entities that are deemed the appropriate objects of moral concern and consideration. Nor does such a system require that the concepts of ecological homeostasis, equilibrium, and integrity provide us with normative principles from which could be derived (with the addition of factual knowledge) our obligations with regard to natural ecosystems. The "balance of nature" is not itself a moral norm, however important may be the role it plays in our general outlook on the natural world that underlies the attitude of respect for nature. I argue that finally it is the good (well-being, welfare) of individual organisms, considered as entities having inherent worth, that determines our moral relations with the Earth's wild commun-

95

ities of life.

In designating the theory to be set forth as life-centered, I intend to contrast it with all anthropocentric views. According to the latter, human actions affecting the natural environment and its nonhuman inhabitants are right (or wrong) by either of two criteria: they have consequences which are favorable (or unfavorable) to human well-being, or they are consistent (or inconsistent) with the system of norms that protect and implement human rights. From this human-centered standpoint it is to humans and only to humans that all duties are ultimately owed. We may have responsibilities *with regard to* the natural ecosystems and biotic communities of our planet, but these responsibilities are in every case based on the contingent fact that our treatment of those ecosystems and communities of life can further the realization of human values and/or human rights. We have no obligation to promote or protect the good of nonhuman living things, independently of this contingent fact.

A life-centered system of environmental ethics is opposed to human-centered ones precisely on this point. From the perspective of a life-centered theory, we have prima facie moral obligations that are owed to wild plants and animals themselves as members of the Earth's biotic community. We are morally bound (other things being equal) to protect or promote their good for *their* sake. Our duties to respect the integrity of natural ecosystems, to preserve endangered species, and to avoid environmental pollution stem from the fact that these are ways in which we can help make it possible for wild species populations to achieve and maintain a healthy existence in a natural state. Such obligations are due those living things out of recognition of their inherent worth. They are entirely additional to and independent of the obligations we owe to our fellow humans. Although many of the actions that fulfill one set of obligations will also fulfill the other, two different grounds of obligation are involved. Their well-being, as well as human well-being, is something to be realized *as an end in itself.*

If we were to accept a life-centered theory of environmental ethics, a profound reordering of our moral universe would take place. We would begin to look at the whole of the Earth's biosphere in a new light. Our duties with respect to the "world" of nature would be seen as making prima facie claims upon us to be balanced against our duties with respect to the "world" of human civilization. We could no longer simply take the human point of view and consider the effects of our actions exclusively from the perspective of our own good.

2. The Good of a Being and the Concept of Inherent Worth

What would justify acceptance of a life-centered system of ethical principles? In order to answer this it is first necessary to make clear the fundamental moral attitude that underlies and makes intelligible the commitment to live by such a system. It is then necessary to examine the considerations that would justify any rational agent's adopting that moral attitude.

Two concepts are essential to the taking of a moral attitude of the sort in question. A being which does not "have" these concepts, that is, which is unable to grasp their meaning and conditions of applicability, cannot be said to have the attitude as part of its moral outlook. These concepts are, first, that of the good (well-being, welfare) of a living thing, and second, the idea of an entity possessing inherent worth. I examine each concept in turn.

(1) Every organism, species population, and community of life has a good of its own which moral agents can intentionally further or damage by their actions. To say that an entity has a good of its own is simply to say that, without reference to any *other* entity, it can be benefited or harmed. One can act in its overall interest or contrary to its overall interest, and environmental conditions can be good for it (advantageous to it) or bad for it (disadvantageous to it). What is good for an entity is what "does it good" in the sense of enhancing or preserving its life and well-being. What is bad for an entity is something that is detrimental to its life and well-being.[1]

We can think of the good of an individual nonhuman organism as consisting in the full development of its biological powers. Its good is realized to the extent that it is strong and healthy. It possesses whatever capacities it needs for successfully coping with its environment and so preserving its existence throughout the various stages of the normal life cycle of its species. The good of a population or community of such individuals consists in the population or community maintaining itself from generation to generation as a coherent system of genetically and ecologically related organisms whose average good is at an optimum level for the given environment. (Here *average good* means that the degree of realization of the good of *individual organisms* in the population or community is, on average, greater than would be the case under any other ecologically functioning order of interrelations among those species populations in the given ecosystem.)

The idea of a being having a good of its own, as I understand it, does not entail that the being must have interests or take an interest in what affects its life for better or for worse. We can act in a being's interest or contrary to its interest without its being interested in what we are doing to it in the sense of wanting or not wanting us to do it. It may, indeed, be wholly unaware that favorable and unfavorable events are taking place in its life. I take it that trees, for example, have no knowledge or desires or feelings. Yet is it undoubtedly the case that trees can be harmed or benefited by our actions. We can crush their roots by running a bulldozer too close to them. We can see to it that they get adequate nourishment and moisture by fertilizing and water-ing the soil around them. Thus we can help or hinder them in the realization of their good. It is the good of trees themselves that is thereby affected. We can similarly act so as to further the good of an entire tree population of a certain species (say, all the redwood trees in a California valley) or the good of a whole community of plant life in a given wilderness area, just as we can do harm to such a population or community.

When construed in this way, the concept of a being's good is not coextensive with sentience or the capacity for feeling pain. William Frankena has argued for a general theory of environmental ethics in which the ground of a creature's being worthy of moral consideration is its sentience. I have offered some criticisms of this view elsewhere, but the full refutation of such a position, it seems to me, finally de-pends on the positive reasons for accepting a life-centered theory of the kind I am defending in this essay.[2]

It should be noted further that I am leaving open the question of whether machines—in particular, those which are not only goal-directed, but also self-regulating—can properly be said to have a good of their own.[3] Since I am concerned only with human treatment of wild organisms, species populations, and communities of life as they occur in our planet's natural ecosystems, it is to those entities alone that the concept "having a good of its own" will here be applied. I am not denying that other living things, whose genetic origin and environ-mental conditions have been produced, controlled, and manipulated by humans for human ends, do have a good of their own in the same sense as do wild plants and animals. It is not my purpose in this essay, however, to set out or defend the principles that should guide our conduct with regard to their good. It is only insofar as their produc-tion and use by humans have good or ill effects upon natural ecosys-tems and their wild inhabitants that the ethics of respect for nature comes into play.

(2) The second concept essential to the moral attitude of respect

for nature is the idea of inherent worth. We take that attitude toward wild living things (individuals, species populations, or whole biotic communities) when and only when we regard them as entities possessing inherent worth. Indeed, it is only because they are conceived in this way that moral agents can think of themselves as having validly binding duties, obligations, and responsibilities that are *owed* to them as their *due*. I am not at this juncture arguing why they *should* be so regarded; I consider it at length below. But so regarding them is a presupposition of our taking the attitude of respect toward them and accordingly understanding ourselves as bearing certain moral relations to them. This can be shown as follows:

What does it mean to regard an entity that has a good of its own as possessing inherent worth? Two general principles are involved: the principle of moral consideration and the principle of intrinsic value.

According to the principle of moral consideration, wild living things are deserving of the concern and consideration of all moral agents simply in virtue of their being members of the Earth's community of life. From the moral point of view their good must be taken into account whenever it is affected for better or worse by the conduct of rational agents. This holds no matter what species the creature belongs to. The good of each is to be accorded some value and so acknowledged as having some weight in the deliberations of all rational agents. Of course, it may be necessary for such agents to act in ways contrary to the good of this or that particular organism or group of organisms in order to further the good of others, including the good of humans. But the principle of moral consideration prescribes that, with respect to each being an entity having its own good, every individual is deserving of consideration.

The principle of intrinsic value states that, regardless of what kind of entity it is in other respects, if it is a member of the Earth's community of life, the realization of its good is something *intrinsically* valuable. This means that its good is prima facie worthy of being preserved or promoted as an end in itself and for the sake of the entity whose good it is. Insofar as we regard any organism, species population, or life community as an entity having inherent worth, we believe that it must never be treated as if it were a mere object or thing whose entire value lies in being instrumental to the good of some other entity. The well-being of each is judged to have value in and of itself.

Combining these two principles, we can now define what it means for a living thing or group of living things to possess inherent worth. To say that it possesses inherent worth is to say that its good is deserving of the concern and consideration of all moral agents, and that the realization of its good has intrinsic value, to be pursued as an end in itself and for the sake of the entity whose good it is.

The duties owed to wild organisms, species populations, and communities of life in the Earth's natural ecosystems are grounded on their inherent worth. When rational, autonomous agents regard such entities as possessing inherent worth, they place intrinsic value on the realization of their good and so hold themselves responsible for performing actions that will have this effect and for refraining from actions having the contrary effect.

3. The Attitude of Respect for Nature

Why should moral agents regard wild living things in the natural world as possessing inherent worth? To answer this question we must first take into account the fact that, when rational, autonomous agents subscribe to the principles of moral consideration and intrinsic value and so conceive of wild living things as having that kind of worth, such agents are *adopting a certain ultimate moral attitude toward the natural world*. This is the attitude I call "respect for nature." It parallels the attitude of respect for persons in human ethics. When we adopt the attitude of respect for persons as the proper (fitting, appropriate) attitude to take toward all persons as persons, we consider the fulfillment of the basic interests of each individual to have intrinsic value. We thereby make a moral commitment to live a certain kind of life in relation to other persons. We place ourselves under the direction of a system of standards and rules that we consider validly binding on all moral agents as such.[4]

Similarly, when we adopt the attitude of respect for nature as an ultimate moral attitude we make a commitment to live by certain normative principles. These principles constitute the rules of conduct and standards of character that are to govern our treatment of the natural world. This is, first, an *ultimate* commitment because it is not derived from any higher norm. The attitude of respect for nature is not grounded on some other, more general, or more fundamental attitude. It sets the total framework for our responsibilities toward the natural world. It can be justified, as I show below, but its justification cannot consist in referring to a more general attitude or a more basic normative principle.

Second, the commitment is a *moral* one because it is understood to be a disinterested matter of principle. It is this feature that distinguishes the attitude of respect for nature from the set of feelings and dispositions that comprise the love of nature. The latter stems from one's personal interest in and response to the natural world. Like the affectionate feelings we have toward certain individual human beings, one's love of nature is nothing more than the particular way one feels about the natural environment and its wild inhabitants. And just as our love for an individual person differs from our respect for all persons as such (whether we happen to love them or not), so love of nature differs from respect for nature. Respect for nature is an attitude we believe all moral agents ought to have simply as moral agents, regardless of whether or not they also love nature. Indeed, we have not truly taken the attitude of respect for nature ourselves unless we believe this. To put it in a Kantian way, to adopt the attitude of respect for nature is to take a stance that one wills to be a universal law for all rational beings. It is to hold that stance categorically, as being validly applicable to every moral agent without exception, irrespective of whatever personal feelings toward nature such an agent might have or might lack.

Although the attitude of respect for nature is in this sense a disinterested and universalizable attitude, anyone who does adopt it has certain steady, more or less permanent dispositions. These dispositions, which are themselves to be considered disinterested and universalizable, comprise three interlocking sets: dispositions to seek certain ends, dispositions to carry on one's practical reasoning and deliberation in a certain way, and dispositions to have certain feelings. We may accordingly analyze the attitude of respect for nature into the following components. (a) The disposition to aim at, and to take steps to bring about, as final and disinterested ends, the promoting and protecting of the good of organisms, species populations, and life communities in natural ecosystems. (These ends are "final" in not being pursued as means to further ends. They are "disinterested" in being independent of the self-interest of the agent.) (b) The disposition to consider actions that tend to realize those ends to be prima facie obligatory *because* they have that tendency. (c) The disposition to experience positive and negative feelings toward states of affairs in the world *because* they are favorable or unfavorable to the good of organisms, species populations, and life communities in natural ecosystems.

The logical connection between the attitude of respect for nature and the duties of a life-centered system of environmental ethics can now be made clear. Insofar as one sincerely takes that attitude and so has the three sets of dispositions, one will at the same time be disposed to comply with certain rules of duty (such as nonmaleficence and non-interference) and with standards of character (such as fairness and benevolence) that determine the obligations and virtues of moral agents with regard to the Earth's wild living things. We can say that the actions one performs and the character traits one develops in fulfilling these moral requirements are the way one *expresses* or *embodies* the attitude in one's conduct and character. In his famous essay, "Justice as Fairness," John Rawls describes the rules of the duties of human morality (such as fidelity, gratitude, honesty, and justice) as "forms of conduct in which recognition of others as persons is manifested."[5] I hold that the rules of duty governing our treatment of the natural world and its inhabitants are forms of conduct in which the attitude of respect for nature is manifested.

4. The Justifiability of the Attitude of Respect for Nature

I return to the question posed earlier, which has not yet been answered: why *should* moral agents regard wild living things as possessing inherent worth? I now argue that the only way we can answer this question is by showing how adopting the attitude of respect for nature is justified for all moral agents. Let us suppose that we were able to establish that there are good reasons for adopting the attitude, reasons which are intersubjectively valid for every rational agent. If there are such reasons, they would justify anyone's having the three sets of dispositions mentioned above as constituting what it means to have the attitude. Since these include the disposition to promote or protect the good of wild living things as a disinterested and ultimate end, as well as the disposition to perform actions for the reason that they tend to realize that end, we see that such dispositions commit a person to the principles of moral consideration and intrinsic value. To be disposed to further, as an end in itself, the good of any entity in nature just because it is that kind of entity, is to be disposed to give consideration to *every* such entity and to place intrinsic value on the realization of its good. Insofar as we subscribe to these two principles we regard living things as possessing inherent worth. Subscribing to the principles is what it *means* to so regard them. To justify the attitude of respect for nature, then, is to justify commitment to these principles and thereby to justify regarding wild creatures as possessing inherent worth.

We must keep in mind that inherent worth is not some mysterious sort of objective property belonging to living things that can be discovered by empirical observation or scientific investigation. To ascribe inherent worth to an entity is not to describe it by citing some feature discernible by sense perception or inferable by inductive reasoning. Nor is there a logically necessary connection between the concept of a being having a good of its own and the concept of inherent worth. We do not contradict ourselves by asserting that an entity that has a good of its own lacks inherent worth. In order to show that such an entity "has" inherent worth we must give good reasons for ascribing that kind of value to it (placing that kind of value upon it, conceiving of it to be valuable in that way). Although it is humans (persons, valuers) who must do the valuing, for the ethics of respect for nature, the value so ascribed is not a human value. That is to say, it is not a value derived from considerations regarding human well-being or human rights. It is a value that is ascribed to nonhuman animals and plants themselves, independently of their relationship to what humans judge to be conducive to their own good.

Whatever reasons, then, justify our taking the attitude of respect for nature as defined above are also reasons that show why we *should* regard the living things of the natural world as possessing inherent worth. We saw earlier that, since the attitude is an ultimate one, it cannot be derived from a more fundamental attitude nor shown to be a special case of a more general one. On what sort of grounds, then, can it be established?

The attitude we take toward living things in the natural world depends on the way we look at them, on what kind of beings we conceive them to be, and on how we understand the relations we bear to them. Underlying and supporting our attitude is a certain *belief system* that constitutes a particular world view or outlook on nature and the place of human life in it. To give good reasons for adopting the attitude of respect for nature, then, we must first articulate the belief system which underlies and supports that attitude. If it appears that the belief system is internally coherent and well-ordered, and if, as far as we can now tell, it is consistent with all known scientific truths relevant to our knowledge of the object of the attitude (which in this case includes the whole set of the Earth's natural ecosystems and their communities of life), then there remains the task of indicating why scientifically informed and rational thinkers with a developed capacity of reality awareness can find it acceptable as a way of conceiving of the natural world and our place in it. To the extent we can do this we provide at least a reasonable argument for accepting the belief system and the ultimate moral attitude it supports.

I do not hold that such a belief system can be *proven* to be true, either inductively or deductively. As we shall see, not all of its components can be stated in the form of empirically verifiable propositions. Nor is its internal order governed by purely logical relationships. But the system as a whole, I contend, constitutes a coherent, unified, and rationally acceptable "picture" or "map" of a total world. By examining each of its main components and seeing how they fit together, we obtain a scientifically informed and well-ordered conception of nature and the place of humans in it.

This belief system underlying the attitude of respect for nature I call (for want of a better name) "the biocentric outlook on nature." Since it is not wholly analyzable into empirically confirmable assertions, it should not be thought of as simply a compendium of the biological sciences concerning our planet's ecosystems. It might best be described as a philosophical world view, to distinguish it from a scientific theory or explanatory system. However, one of its major tenets is the great lesson we have learned from the science of ecology: the interdependence of all living things in an organically unified order whose balance and stability are necessary conditions for the realization of the good of its constituent biotic communities.

Before turning to an account of the main components of the biocentric outlook, it is convenient here to set forth the overall structure of my theory of environmental ethics as it has now emerged. The ethics of respect for nature is made up of three basic elements: a belief system, an ultimate moral attitude, and a set of rules of duty and standards of character. These elements are connected with each other in the following manner. The belief system provides a certain outlook on nature which supports and makes intelligible an autonomous agent's adopting, as an ultimate moral attitude, the attitude of respect for nature. It supports and makes intelligible the attitude in the sense that, when an autonomous agent understands its moral relations to the natural world in terms of this outlook, it recognizes the attitude of respect to be the only *suitable* or *fitting* attitude to take toward all wild forms of life in the Earth's biosphere. Living things are now viewed as the appropriate objects of the attitude of respect and are accordingly regarded as entities possessing inherent worth. One then places intrinsic value on the promotion and protection of their good. As a consequence of this, one makes a moral commitment to abide by a set of rules of duty and to fulfill (as far as one can by one's own efforts) certain standards of good character. Given one's adoption of the attitude of respect, one makes that moral commitment because one considers those rules and standards to be validly binding on all moral agents. They are seen as embodying forms of conduct and character structures in which the attitude of respect for nature is manifested.

This three-part complex which internally orders the ethics of respect for nature is symmetrical with a theory of human ethics grounded on respect for persons. Such a theory includes, first, a conception of oneself and others as persons, that is, as centers of autonomous choice. Second, there is the attitude of respect for persons as persons. When this is adopted as an ultimate moral attitude it involves the disposition to treat every person as having inherent worth or "human dignity." Every human being, just in virtue of her or his humanity, is understood to be worthy of moral consideration, and intrinsic value is placed on the autonomy and well-being of each. This is what Kant meant by conceiving of persons as ends in themselves. Third, there is an ethical system of duties which are acknowledged to be owed by everyone. These duties are forms of conduct in which public recognition is given to each individual's inherent worth as a person.

This structural framework for a theory of human ethics is meant to leave open the issue of consequentialism (utilitarianism) versus nonconsequentialism (deontology). That issue concerns the particular kind of system of rules defining the duties of moral agents toward persons. Similarly, I am leaving open in this paper the question of what particular kind of system of rules defines our duties with respect to the natural world.

5. The Biocentric Outlook on Nature

The biocentric outlook on nature has four main components. (1) Humans are thought of as members of the Earth's community of life, holding that membership on the same terms as apply to all the nonhuman members. (2) The Earth's natural ecosystems as a totality are seen as a complex web of interconnected elements, with the sound biological functioning of each being dependent on the sound biological functioning of the others. (This is the component referred to above as the great lesson that the science of ecology has taught us.) (3) Each individual organism is conceived of as a teleological center of life, pursuing its own good in its own way. (4) Whether we are concerned with standards of merit or with the concept of inherent worth, the claim that humans by their very nature are superior to other species is a groundless claim and, in the light of elements (1), (2), and (3) above, must be rejected as nothing more than an irrational bias in our own favor.

The conjunction of these four ideas constitutes the biocentric outlook on nature. In the remainder of this paper I give a brief account of the first three components, followed by a more detailed analysis of the fourth. I then conclude by indicating how this outlook provides a way of justifying the attitude of respect for nature.

6. Humans as Members of the Earth's Community of Life

We share with other species a common relationship to the Earth. In accepting the biocentric outlook we take the fact of our being an animal species to be a fundamental feature of our existence. We consider it an essential aspect of "the human condition." We do not deny the differences between ourselves and other species, but we keep in the forefront of our consciousness the fact that in relation to our planet's natural ecosystems we are but one species population among many. Thus we acknowledge our origin in the very same evolutionary process that gave rise to all other species and we recognize ourselves to be confronted with similar environmental challenges to those that confront them. The laws of genetics, of natural selection, and of adaptation apply equally to all of us as biological creatures. In this light we consider ourselves as one with them, not set apart from them. We, as well as they, must face certain basic conditions of existence that impose requirements on us for our survival and well-being. Each animal and plant is like us in having a good of its own. Although our human good (what is of true value in human life, including the exercise of individual autonomy in choosing our own particular value systems) is not like the good of a nonhuman animal or plant, it can no more be realized than their good can without the biological necessities for survival and physical health.

When we look at ourselves from the evolutionary point of view, we see that not only are we very recent arrivals on Earth, but that our emergence as a new species on the planet was originally an event of no particular importance to the entire scheme of things. The Earth was teeming with life long before we appeared. Putting the point metaphorically, we are relative newcomers, entering a home that has been the residence of others for hundreds of million of years, a home that must now be shared by all of us together.

The comparative brevity of human life on Earth may be vividly depicted by imagining the geological time scale in spatial terms. Suppose we start with algae, which have been around for at least 600 million years. (The earliest protozoa actually predated this by several *billion* years.) If the time that algae have been here were represented by the length of a football field (300 feet), then the period during which sharks have been swimming in the world's oceans and spiders have been spinning their webs would occupy three quarters of the length of the field; reptiles would show up at about the center of the field; mammals would cover the last third of the field; hominids (mammals of the family *Hominidae*) the last two feet; and the species *Homo sapiens* the last six inches.

Whether this newcomer is able to survive as long as other species remains to be seen. But there is surely something presumptuous about the way humans look down on the "lower" animals, especially those that have become extinct. We consider the dinosaurs, for example, to be biological failures, though they existed on our planet for 65 million years. One writer has made the point with beautiful simplicity:

> We sometimes speak of the dinosaurs as failures; there will be time enough for that judgment when we have lasted even one tenth as long....[6]

The possibility of the extinction of the human species, a possibility which starkly confronts us in the contemporary world, makes us aware of another respect in which we should not consider ourselves privileged beings in relation to other species. This is the fact that the well-being of humans is dependent upon the ecological soundness and health of many plant and animal communities, while their soundness and health does not in the least depend upon human well-being. Indeed, from their standpoint the very existence of humans is quite unnecessary. Every last man, woman, and child could disappear from the face of the Earth without any significant detrimental consequence for the good of wild animals and plants. On the contrary, many of them would be greatly benefited. The destruction of their habitats by human "developments" would cease. The poisoning and polluting of their environment would come to an end. The Earth's land, air, and water would no longer be subject to the degradation they are now undergoing as the result of large-scale technology and uncontrolled population growth. Life communities in natural ecosystems would gradually return to their former healthy state. Tropical forests, for example, would again be able to make their full contribution to a life-sustaining atmosphere for the whole planet. The rivers, lakes, and oceans of the world would (perhaps) eventually become clean again. Spilled oil, plastic trash, and even radioactive waste might finally, after many centuries, cease doing their terrible work. Ecosystems would return to their proper balance, suffering only the disruptions of natural events such as volcanic eruptions and glaciation. From these the community of life could recover, as it has so often done in the past. But the ecological disasters now perpetrated on it by humans—disasters from which it might never recover—these it would no longer have to endure.

If, then, the total, final, absolute extermination of our species (by our own hands?) should take place and if we should not carry all the others with us into oblivion, not only would the Earth's community of life continue to exist, but in all probability its well-being would be enhanced. Our presence, in short, is not needed. If we were to take the standpoint of the community and give voice to its true interest, the ending of our six-inch epoch would most likely be greeted with a hearty "Good riddance!"

7. The Natural World as an Organic System

To accept the biocentric outlook and regard ourselves and our place in the world from its perspective is to see the whole natural order of the Earth's biosphere as a complex but unified web of interconnected organisms, objects, and events. The ecological relationships between any community of living things and their environment form an organic whole of functionally interdependent parts. Each ecosystem is a small universe itself in which the interactions of its various species populations comprise an intricately woven network of cause-effect relations. Such dynamic but at the same time relatively stable structures as food chains, predator-prey relations, and plant succession in a forest are self-regulating, energy-recycling mechanisms that preserve the equilibrium of the whole.

As far as the well-being of wild animals and plants is concerned, this ecological equilibrium must not be destroyed. The same holds true of the well-being of humans. When one views the realm of nature from the perspective of the biocentric outlook, one never forgets that in the long run the integrity of the entire biosphere of our planet is essential to the realization of the good of its constituent communities of life, both human and nonhuman.

Although the importance of this idea cannot be overemphasized, it is by now so familiar and so widely acknowledged that I shall not further elaborate on it here. However, I do wish to point out that this "holistic" view of the Earth's ecological systems does not itself constitute a moral norm. It is a factual aspect of biological reality, to be understood as a set of causal connections in ordinary empirical terms. Its significance for humans is the same as its significance for nonhumans, namely, in setting basic conditions for the realization of the good of living things. Its ethical implications for our treatment of the natural environment lie entirely in the fact that our *knowledge* of these causal connections is an essential *means* to fulfilling the aims we set for ourselves in adopting the attitude of respect for nature. In addition, its theoretical implications for the ethics for nature lie in the fact that it (along with the other elements of biocentric outlook) makes the adopting of that attitude a rational and intelligible thing to do.

8. Individual Organisms as Teleological Centers of Life

As our knowledge of living things increases, as we come to a deeper understanding of their life cycles, their interactions with other organisms, and the manifold ways in which they adjust to the environment, we become more fully aware of how each of them is carrying out its biological functions according to the laws of its species-specific nature. But besides this, our increasing knowledge and understanding also develop in us a sharpened awareness of the uniqueness of each individual organism. Scientists who have made careful studies of particular plants and animals, whether in the field or in laboratories, have often acquired a knowledge of their subjects as identifiable individuals. Close observation over extended periods of time has led them to an appreciation of the unique "personalities" of their subjects. Sometimes a scientist may come to take a special interest in a particular animal or plant, all the while remaining strictly objective in the gathering and recording of data. Nonscientists may likewise experience this development of interest when, as amateur naturalists, they make accurate observations over sustained periods of close acquaintance with an individual organism. As one becomes more and more familiar with the organism and its behavior, one becomes fully sensitive to the particular way it is living out its life cycle. One may become fascinated by it and even experience some involvement with its good and bad fortunes (that is, with the occurrence of environmental conditions favorable or unfavorable to the realization of its good). The organism comes to mean something to one as a unique, irreplaceable individual. The final culmination of this process is the achievement of a genuine understanding of its point of view and, with that understanding, an ability to "take" that point of view. *Conceiving of it as a center of life, one is able to look at the world from its perspective.*

This development from objective knowledge to the recognition of individuality, and from the recognition of individuality to full awareness of an organism's standpoint, is a process of heightening our consciousness of what it means to be an individual living thing. We grasp the particularity of the organism as a teleological center of life, striving to preserve itself and to realize its own good in its own unique way.

It is to be noted that we need not be falsely anthropomorphizing when we conceive of individual plants and animals in this manner. Understanding them as teleological centers of life does not necessitate "reading into" them human characteristics. We need not, for example, consider them to have consciousness. Some of them may be aware of the world around them and others may not. Nor need we deny that different kinds and levels of awareness are exemplified when consciousness in some form is present. But conscious or not, all are equally teleological centers of life in the sense that each is a unified system of goal-oriented activities directed toward their preservation and well-being.

When considered from an ethical point of view, a teleological center of life is an entity whose "world" can be viewed from the perspective of *its* life. In looking at the world from that perspective we recognize objects and events occurring in its life as being beneficent, maleficent, or indifferent. The first are occurrences which increase its powers to preserve its existence and realize its good. The second decrease or destroy those powers. The third have neither of these effects on the entity. With regard to our human role as moral agents, we can conceive of a teleological center of life as a being whose standpoint we can take in making judgments about what events in the world are good or evil, desirable or undesirable. In making those judgments it is what promotes or protects the being's own good, not what benefits moral agents themselves, that sets the standard of evaluation. Such judgments can be made about anything that happens to the entity which is favorable or unfavorable in relation to its good. As was pointed out earlier, the entity itself need not have any (conscious) *interest* in what is happening to it for such judgments to be meaningful and true.

It is precisely judgments of this sort that we are disposed to make when we take the attitude of respect for nature. In adopting that attitude those judgments are given weight as reasons for action in our practical deliberation. They become morally relevant facts in the guidance of our conduct.

9. The Denial of Human Superiority

This fourth component of the biocentric outlook on nature is the single most important idea in establishing the justifiability of the attitude of respect for nature. Its central role is due to the special relationship it bears to the first three components of the outlook. This relationship will be brought out after the concept of human superiority is examined and analyzed.[7]

In what sense are humans alleged to be superior to other animals? We are different from them in having certain capacities that they lack. But why should these capacities be a mark of superiority? From what point of view are they judged to be signs of superiority and what sense of superiority is meant? After all, various nonhuman species have capacities that humans lack. There is the speed of a cheetah, the vision of an eagle, the agility of a monkey. Why should not these be taken as signs of *their* superiority over humans?

One answer that comes immediately to mind is that these capacities are not as *valuable* as the human capacities that are claimed to make us superior. Such uniquely human characteristics as rational thought, aesthetic creativity, autonomy and self-determination, and moral freedom, it might be held, have a higher value than the capacities found in other species. Yet we must ask: valuable to whom, and on what grounds?

The human characteristics mentioned are all valuable to humans. They are essential to the preservation and enrichment of our civilization and culture. Clearly it is from the human standpoint that they are being judged to be desirable and good. It is not difficult here to recognize a begging of the question. Humans are claiming human superiority from a strictly human point of view, that is, from a point of view in which the good of humans is taken as the standard of judgment. All we need to do is to look at the capacities of nonhuman animals (or plants, for that matter) from the standpoint of *their* good to find a contrary judgment of superiority. The speed of the cheetah, for example, is a sign of its superiority to humans when considered from the standpoint of the good of its species. If it were as slow a runner as a human, it would not be able to survive. And so for all the other abilities of nonhumans which further their good but which are lacking in humans. In each case the claim to human superiority would be rejected from a nonhuman standpoint.

When superiority assertions are interpreted in this way, they are based on judgments of *merit*. To judge the merits of a person or an organism one must apply grading or ranking standards to it. (As I show below, this distinguishes judgments of merit from judgments of inherent worth.) Empirical investigation then determines whether it has the "good-making properties" (merits) in virtue of which it fulfills the standards being applied. In the case of humans, merits may be either moral or nonmoral. We can judge one person to be better than (superior to) another from the moral point of view by applying certain standards to their character and conduct. Similarly, we can appeal to nonmoral criteria in judging someone to be an excellent piano player, a fair cook, a poor tennis player, and so on. Different social purposes and roles are implicit in the making of such judgments, providing the frame of reference for the choice of standards by which the nonmoral merits of people are determined. Ultimately such purposes and roles stem from a society's way of life as a whole. Now a society's way of life may be thought of as the cultural form given to the realization of human values. Whether moral or nonmoral standards are being applied, then, all judgments of people's merits finally depend on human values. All are made from an exclusively human standpoint.

The question that naturally arises at this juncture is: why should standards that are based on human values be assumed to be the only valid criteria of merit and hence the only true signs of superiority? This question is especially pressing when humans are being judged superior in merit to nonhumans. It is true that a human being may be a better mathematician than a monkey, but the monkey may be a better tree climber than a human being. If we humans value mathematics more than tree climbing, that is because our conception of civilized life makes the development of mathematical ability more desirable than the ability to climb trees. But is it not unreasonable to judge nonhumans by the values of human civilization, rather than by values connected with what it is for a member of *that* species to live a good life? If all living things have a good of their own, it at least makes sense to judge the merits of nonhumans by standards derived from *their* good. To use only standards based on human values is already to commit oneself to holding that humans are superior to nonhumans, which is the point in question.

A further logical flaw arises in connection with the widely held conviction that humans are *morally* superior beings because they possess, while others lack, the capacities of a moral agent (free will, accountability, deliberation, judgment, practical reason). This view rests on a conceptual confusion. As far as moral standards are concerned, only beings that have the capacities of a moral agent can properly be judged to be *either* moral (morally good) *or* immoral (morally deficient). Moral standards are simply not applicable to beings that lack such capacities. Animals and plants cannot therefore be said to be morally inferior in merit to humans. Since the only beings that can have moral merits *or be deficient in such merits* are moral agents, it is conceptually incoherent to judge humans as superior to nonhumans on the ground that humans have moral capacities while nonhumans don't.

Up to this point I have been interpreting the claim that humans are superior to other living things as a grading or ranking judgment regarding their comparative merits. There is, however, another way of understanding the idea of human superiority. According to this interpretation, humans are superior to nonhumans not as regards their merits but as regards their inherent worth. Thus the claim of human superiority is to be understood as asserting that all humans, simply in virtue of their humanity, have *a greater inherent worth* than other living things.

The inherent worth of an entity does not depend on its merits.[8] To consider something as possessing inherent worth, we have seen, is to place intrinsic value on the realization of its good. This is done regardless of whatever particular merits it might have or might lack, as judged by a set of grading or ranking standards. In human affairs, we are all familiar with the principle that one's worth as a person does not vary with one's merits or lack of merits. The same can hold true of animals and plants. To regard such entities as possessing inherent worth entails disregarding their merits and deficiencies, whether they are being judged from a human standpoint or from the standpoint of their own species.

The idea of one entity having more merit than another, and so being superior to it in merit, makes perfectly good sense. Merit is a grading or ranking concept, and judgments of comparative merit are based on the different degrees to which things satisfy a given standard. But what can it mean to talk about one thing being superior to another in inherent worth? In order to get at what is being asserted in such a claim it is helpful first to look at the social origin of the concept of degrees of inherent worth.

The idea that humans can possess different degrees of inherent worth originated in societies having rigid class structures. Before the rise of modern democracies with their egalitarian outlook, one's membership in a hereditary class determined one's social status. People in the upper classes were looked up to, while those in the lower classes were looked down upon. In such a society one's social superiors and social inferiors were clearly defined and easily recognized.

Two aspects of these class-structured societies are especially relevant to the idea of degrees of inherent worth. First, those born into the upper classes were deemed more worthy of respect than those born into the lower orders. Second, the superior worth of upper class people had nothing to do with their merits nor did the inferior worth of those in the lower classes rest on their lack of merits. One's superiority or inferiority entirely derived from a social position one was born into. The modern concept of a meritocracy simply did not apply. One could not advance into a higher class by any sort of moral or nonmoral achievement. Similarly, an aristocrat held his title and all the privileges that went with it just because he was the eldest son of a titled nobleman. Unlike the bestowing of knighthood in contemporary Great Britain, one did not earn membership in the nobility by meritorious conduct.

We who live in modern democracies no longer believe in such hereditary social distinctions. Indeed, we would wholeheartedly condemn them on moral grounds as being fundamentally unjust. We have come to think of class systems as a paradigm of social injustice, it being a central principle of the democratic way of life that among humans there are no superiors and no inferiors. Thus we have rejected the whole conceptual framework in which people are judged to have different degrees of inherent worth. That idea is incompatible with our notion of human equality based on the doctrine that all humans, simply in virtue of their humanity, have the same inherent worth. (The belief in universal human rights is one form that this egalitarianism takes.)

The vast majority of people in modern democracies, however, do not maintain an egalitarian outlook when it comes to comparing human beings with other living things. Most people consider our own species to be superior to all other species and this superiority is understood to be a matter of inherent worth, not merit. There may exist thoroughly vicious and depraved humans who lack all merit. Yet because they are human they are thought to belong to a higher class of entities than any plant or animal. That one is born into the species *Homo sapiens* entitles one to have lordship over those who are one's inferiors, namely, those born into other species. The parallel with hereditary social classes is very close. Implicit in this view is a hierarchical conception of nature according to which an organism has a position of superiority or inferiority in the Earth's community of life simply on the basis of its genetic background. The "lower" orders of life are looked down upon and it is considered perfectly proper that they serve the interests of those belonging to the highest order, namely humans. The intrinsic value we place on the well-being of our fellow humans reflects our recognition of their rightful position as our equals. No such intrinsic value is to be placed on the good of other animals, unless we choose to do so out of fondness or affection for them. But their well-being imposes no moral requirement on us. In this respect there is an absolute difference in moral status between ourselves and them.

This is the structure of concepts and beliefs that people are committed to insofar as they regard humans to be superior in inherent worth to all other species. I now wish to argue that this structure of concepts and beliefs is completely groundless. If we accept the first three components of the biocentric outlook and from that perspective look at the major philosophical traditions which have supported that structure, we find it to be at bottom nothing more than the expression of an irrational bias in our own favor. The philosophical traditions themselves rest on very questionable assumptions or else simply beg the question. I briefly consider three of the main traditions to substantiate the point. These are classical Greek humanism, Cartesian dualism, and the Judeo-Christian concept of the Great Chain of Being.

The inherent superiority of humans over other species was implicit in the Greek definition of man as a rational animal. Our animal nature was identified with "brute" desires that need the order and restraint of reason to rule them (just as reason is the special virtue of those who rule in the ideal state). Rationality was then seen to be the key to our superiority over animals. It enables us to live on a higher plane and endows us with a nobility and worth that other creatures lack. This familiar way of comparing humans with other species is deeply ingrained in our Western philosophical outlook. The point to consider here is that this view does not actually provide an argument *for* human superiority but rather makes explicit the framework of thought that is implicitly used by those who think of humans as inherently superior to nonhumans. The Greeks who held that humans, in virtue of their rational capacities, have a kind of worth greater than that of any nonrational being, never looked at rationality as but one capacity of living things among many others. But when we consider rationality from the standpoint of the first three elements of the ecological outlook, we see that its value lies in its importance for *human* life. Other creatures achieve their species-specific good without the need of rationality, although they often make use of capacities that humans lack. So the humanistic outlook of classical Greek thought does not give us a neutral (nonquestion-begging) ground on which to construct a scale of degrees of inherent worth possessed by different species of living things.

The second tradition, centering on the Cartesian dualism of soul and body, also fails to justify the claim to human superiority. That superiority is supposed to derive from the fact that we have souls while animals do not. Animals are mere automata and lack the divine element that makes us spiritual beings. I won't go into the now familiar criticisms of this two-substance view. I only add the point that, even if humans are composed of an immaterial, unextended soul and a material, extended body, this in itself is not a reason to deem them of greater worth than entities that are only bodies. Why is a soul substance a thing that adds value to its possessor? Unless some theological reasoning is offered here (which many, including myself, would find unacceptable on epistemological grounds), no logical connection is evident. An immaterial something which thinks is better than a material something which does not think only if thinking itself has value, either intrinsically or instrumentally. Now it is intrinsically valuable to humans alone, who value it as an end in itself, and it is instrumentally valuable to those who benefit from it, namely humans.

For animals that neither enjoy thinking for its own sake nor need it for living the kind of life for which they are best adapted, it has no value. Even if "thinking" is broadened to include all forms of consciousness, there are still many living things that can do without it and yet live what is for their species a good life. The anthropocentricity underlying the claim to human superiority runs throughout Cartesian dualism.

A third major source of the idea of human superiority is the Judeo-Christian concept of the Great Chain of Being. Humans are superior to animals and plants because their Creator has given them a higher place on the chain. It begins with God at the top, and then moves to the angels, who are lower than God but higher than humans, then to humans, positioned between the angels and the beasts (partaking of the nature of both), and then on down to the lower levels occupied by nonhuman animals, plants, and finally inanimate objects. Humans, being "made in God's image," are inherently superior to animals and plants by virtue of their being closer (in their essential nature) to God.

The metaphysical and epistemological difficulties with this conception of a hierarchy of entities are, in my mind, insuperable. Without entering into this matter here, I only point out that if we are unwilling to accept the metaphysics of traditional Judaism and Christianity, we are again left without good reasons for holding to the claim of inherent human superiority.

The foregoing considerations (and others like them) leave us with but one ground for the assertion that a human being, regardless of merit, is a higher kind of entity than any other living thing. This is the mere fact of the genetic makeup of the species *Homo sapiens*. But this is surely irrational and arbitrary. Why should the arrangement of genes of a certain type be a mark of superior value, especially when this fact about an organism is taken by itself, unrelated to any other aspect of its life? We might just as well refer to any other genetic make-up as a ground of superior value. Clearly we are confronted here with a wholly arbitrary claim that can only be explained as an irrational bias in our own favor.

That the claim is nothing more than a deep-seated prejudice is brought home to us when we look at our relation to other species in the light of the first three elements of the biocentric outlook. Those elements taken conjointly give us a certain overall view of the natural world and of the place of humans in it. When we take this view we come to understand other living things, their environmental conditions, and their ecological relationships in such a way as to awake in us a deep sense of our kinship with them as fellow members of the Earth's community of life. Humans and nonhumans alike are viewed together as integral parts of one unified whole in which all living things are functionally interrelated. Finally, when our awareness focuses on the individual lives of plants and animals, each is seen to share with us the characteristic of being a teleological center of life striving to realize its own good in its own unique way.

As this entire belief system becomes part of the conceptual framework through which we understand and perceive the world, we come to see ourselves as bearing a certain moral relation to nonhuman forms of life. Our ethical role in nature takes on a new significance. We begin to look at other species as we look at ourselves, seeing them as beings which have a good they are striving to realize just as we have a good we are striving to realize. We accordingly develop the disposition to view the world from the standpoint of their good as well as from the standpoint of our own good. Now if the groundlessness of the claim that humans are inherently superior to other species were brought clearly before our minds, we would not remain intellectually neutral toward that claim but would reject it as being fundamentally at variance with our total world outlook. In the absence of any good reasons for holding it, the assertion of human superiority would then appear simply as the expression of an irrational and self-serving prejudice that favors one particular species over several million others.

Rejecting the notion of human superiority entails its positive counterpart: the doctrine of species impartiality. One who accepts

that doctrine regards all living things as possessing inherent worth—
the *same* inherent worth, since no one species has been shown to be
either "higher" or "lower" than any other. Now we saw earlier that,
insofar as one thinks of a living thing as possessing inherent worth,
one considers it to be the appropriate object of the attitude of respect
and believes that attitude to be the only fitting or suitable one for all
moral agents to take toward it.

Here, then, is the key to understanding how the attitude of respect is rooted in the biocentric outlook on nature. The basic connection is made through the denial of human superiority. Once we reject
the claim that humans are superior either in merit or worth to other
living things, we are ready to adopt the attitude of respect. The denial
of human superiority is itself the result of taking the perspective on
nature built into the first three elements of the biocentric outlook.

Now the first three elements of the biocentric outlook, it seems
clear, would be found acceptable to any rational and scientifically informed thinker who is fully "open" to the reality of the lives of nonhuman organisms. Without denying our distinctively human characteristics, such a thinker can acknowledge the fundamental respects in
which we are members of the Earth's community of life and in which
the biological conditions necessary for the realization of our human
values are inextricably linked with the whole system of nature. In
addition, the conception of individual living things as teleological
centers of life simply articulates how a scientifically informed thinker
comes to understand them as the result of increasingly careful and
detailed observations. Thus, the biocentric outlook recommends itself
as an acceptable system of concepts and beliefs to anyone who is
clear-minded, unbiased, and factually enlightened, and who has a
developed capacity of reality awareness with regard to the lives of
individual organisms. This, I submit, is as good a reason for making the
moral commitment involved in adopting the attitude of respect for
nature as any theory of environmental ethics could possibly have.

10. Moral Rights and the Matter of Competing Claims

I have not asserted anywhere in the foregoing account that animals or
plants have moral rights. This omission was deliberate. I do not think
that the reference class of the concept, bearer of moral rights, should
be extended to include nonhuman living things. My reasons for taking
this position, however, go beyond the scope of this paper. I believe I
have been able to accomplish many of the same ends which those who

ascribe rights to animals or plants wish to accomplish. There is no reason, moreover, why plants and animals, including whole species populations and life communities, cannot be accorded *legal* rights under my theory. To grant them legal protection could be interpreted as giving them legal entitlement to be protected, and this, in fact, would be a means by which a society that subscribed to the ethics of respect for nature could give public recognition to their inherent worth.

There remains the problem of competing claims, even when wild plants and animals are not thought of as bearers of moral rights. If we accept the biocentric outlook and accordingly adopt the attitude of respect for nature as our ultimate moral attitude, how do we resolve conflicts that arise from our respect for persons in the domain of human ethics and our respect for nature in the domain of environmental ethics? This is a question that cannot adequately be dealt with here. My main purpose in this paper has been to try to establish a base point from which we can start working toward a solution to the problem. I have shown why we cannot just begin with an initial presumption in favor of the interests of our own species. It is after all within our power as moral beings to place limits on human population and technology with the deliberate intention of sharing the Earth's bounty with other species. That such sharing is an ideal difficult to realize even in an approximate way does not take away its claim to our deepest moral commitment.

Notes

1. The conceptual links between an entity *having* a good, something being good *for* it, and events doing good *to* it are examined by G. H. Von Wright in the *The Varieties of Goodness* (New York: Humanities Press, 1963), chaps. 3 and 5.

2. See W. K. Frankena, "Ethics and the Environment," in K. E. Goodpaster and K. M. Sayre, eds., *Ethics and Problems of the 21st Century* (Notre Dame: University of Notre Dame Press, 1979), pp. 3-20. I critically examine Frankena's views in "Frankena on Environmental Ethics," *Monist* 64 (1981): 313-24.

3. In the light of considerations set forth in Daniel Dennett's *Brainstorms: Philosophical Essays on Mind and Psychology* (Montogomery, Vermont: Bradford Books, 1978), it is advisable to leave this question unsettled at this time. When machines are developed that function in the way our brains do, we may well come to deem them proper subjects of moral consideration.

4. I have analyzed the nature of this commitment of human ethics in "On Taking the Moral Point of View," *Midwest Studies in Philosophy*, vol. 3, *Studies in Ethical Theory* (1978), pp. 35-61.

5. John Rawls, "Justice as Fairness," *Philosophical Review* 67 (1958): 183.

6. Stephen R. L. Clark, *The Moral Status of Animals* (Oxford: Clarendon Press, 1977), p. 112.

7. My criticisms of the dogma of human superiority gain independent support from a carefully reasoned essay by R. and V. Routley showing the many logical weaknesses in arguments for human-centered theories of environmental ethics. R. and V. Routley, "Against the Inevitability of Human Chauvinism," in K.E. Goodpaster and K.M. Sayre, eds., *Ethics and Problems of the 21st Century* (Notre Dame: University of Notre Dame Press, 1979), pp. 36-59.

8. For this way of distinguishing between merit and inherent worth, I am indebted to Gregory Vlastos, "Justice and Equality," in R. Brandt. ed., *Social Justice* (Englewood Cliffs, N.J.: Prentice-Hall, 1962), pp. 31-72.

5

The Significance of Species

Mary Midgley

1. Real and Unreal Groups

The term *speciesism* was invented... for a particular purpose, as a device to winkle out exclusively humanistic radicals from an inconsistent position. It quite properly followed, as the night the day, the similar invention of the term sexism. *Ad hominem*, for their original purposes, both these explosive charges were well placed and fully justified. Self-righteous revolutionaries who expected their women to type the manifestoes and bring the coffee, but remain otherwise dutifully silent, could scarcely complain if their theory was publicly contrasted with their practice. Their position was not improved if they cheerfully consumed battery pork and chicken. We have already touched on the distressing subject of endemic revolutionary humbug. We have also noticed that the rest of us are probably in no position to get very bloody-minded about it. Humbug, like flu, is extremely common. But it is still dangerous and must be attended to. The more exalted are the principles which people put forward, the more urgently do their inconsistencies need to be pointed out. Moreover, the closer their critics stick to the original wording, the plainer does their point become. That is why the original term *racism* has proved so fertile, spawning in turn sexism, ageism, speciesism, and uglyism to date, no doubt with more to come.

For destructive purposes, I repeat, these terms are useful. But once the dust clears and the possible inconsistency is admitted, we need something more. To earn their keep, concepts must do more than suggest a surface likeness. What deeper parallels do these ideas

121

show? In the case of speciesism, there appears at once a most awkward and damaging difference. Race in humans is not a significant grouping at all, but species in animals certainly is. It is never true that, in order to know how to treat a human being, you must first find out what race he belongs to. (Cases where this might seem to matter always really turn on culture.) But with an animal, to know the species is absolutely essential. A zoo-keeper who is told to expect an animal, and get a place ready for it, cannot even begin to do this without far more detailed information. It might be a hyaena or a hippopotamus, a shark, an eagle, an armadillo, a python or a queen bee. Even members of quite similar and closely related species can have entirely different needs about temperature and water-supply, bedding, exercise-space, solitude, company and many other things. Their vision and experience of the world must therefore be profoundly different.

To liken a trivial human grouping such as race to this enormous, inconceivably varied range of possibilities is to indulge in what revolutionaries call 'patronizing' thinking—a failure to recognize the scale of difference between others and oneself. Overlooking somebody's race is entirely sensible. Overlooking their species is a supercilious insult. It is no privilege, but a misfortune, for a gorilla or a chimpanzee to be removed from its forest and its relatives and brought up alone among humans to be given what those humans regard as an education. If we ourselves were on another planet, among beings who considered themselves, and perhaps were, superior to us in intellect and other ways, we would have no doubt rejecting such an offer for ourselves or our children. We must shortly consider why this is so and how far the objection goes, but the general point is that we are not just disembodied intellects, but beings of particular kinds, and to ignore our particular qualities and capacities is insolent. This applies, not only to species, but also to age, sex and culture, though the point is not so extreme and glaring in these cases.

2. The Ambiguities of 'Racism'

To deal with this difficuty about speciesism, we have to understand what the parallel between species and race is really meant to do. As soon as we attempt this, we find to our alarm that *racism* itself is an ill-formed, spineless, impenetrably obscure concept, scarcely capable of doing its own work, and quite unfit to generate a family of descendants which can be useful elsewhere. To say this is not, of course, to make any criticism at all of the cause for which it has been used. As we have seen before, very vague and confused concepts can sometimes be used effectively in reform, just so long as everyone concerned understands what they are after and makes it explicit by other means. It is when we turn from this initial, familiar context to use the words elsewhere that the trouble arises. Then it becomes essential to understand their weakness.

What is *racism*? It differs from *racialism*—which means the holding of special theories asserting the importance of race—in being concerned with practice rather than theory. It names the offence of treating somebody—for whatever reasons—in a way determined by race, not by individual qualities and needs. But this offence is too wide. It is committed in all cases of 'reverse discrimination'—that is, of redressing injustice by deliberately giving privileges to members of previously oppressed groups. On this simple definition, therefore, the state of Israel, various black power groups and other reverse discriminators are racist. One way to deal with this unwelcome conclusion is to treat the term as a neutral one, like *killing* rather than *murder* and *bargain* rather than *cheat*, and rule that there can sometimes be justified racism. But then the word ceases to be the name of an offence, which is what it was wanted for in the first place.

The alternative is to give it a more complicated definition. But it will not be easy to find one which will do what is needed. It does not help to say that racism consists in determining the treatment *only* by race, and that reverse discriminators are moved by historical considerations as well. This is no good because race prejudice also invokes beliefs about history. A concept like race never is used alone, but always because of beliefs about the other factors associated with it. And the individuals involved are still being treated in a way determined by their race, not by their own personal qualities and needs. Nor can we say that the essence of racism is discrimination which favours *one's own* race. This would allow judges or landlords of races A and B to oppress members of their own and each other's races, identifying their own interests, as successful persons, with those of the dominant group C. And it still blocks reverse discrimination arranged by the oppressed groups themselves, when they acquire a state—or even a neighborhood—in which to practise it. The same disadvantage follows on a definition referring instead to 'the dominant or privileged race', since those who were formerly oppressed can always come to occupy this position.

This obscurity about reverse discrimination has done so much obvious damage to the cause of reform about race that the need for better concepts is probably clear by now. The term *racism* combines unthinkingly three quite distinct ideas—the triviality of the distinction drawn, group selfishness, and the perpetuation of an existing power hierarchy. The word *discrimination* re-emphasizes the first element. When we try to use these terms for other cases or even for race itself outside the narrow context which was originally taken for granted, the separateness of the three elements at once becomes clear.

In the case of species the first element does not apply at all. The distinction drawn is not trivial; it is real and crucial. This is also true, though less drastically, for age and sex. Certainly these distinctions have been misunderstood and misused, but they are real. One can be different without being inferior. Serious injustice can be done to women or the old by insisting on giving them exactly the same treatment as men or the young. The term *discrimination* probably cannot now be got out of this use, but it is not really suitable for the work at all. It still needs to be used sometimes in its familiar, favourable sense. To be undiscriminating is not a virtue. As for the second and third elements, they are of the first importance, and they need to be described plainly, not as part of a confused package. They are aspects of justice, and plenty of terms already exist for discussing them directly. Concepts like oppression, partiality, conceit, bias, exploitation, prejudice, entrenched self-interest, narrow-mindedness, privilege, self-importance and the like, with all the enrichments, both political and psychological, which they have received and are still receiving, will do the various jobs concerned all right. What cannot be done is to pile all these jobs into a single package and label it with a single word, such as racism or one of its derivatives.

3. What 'Speciesism' Means

Turning then from the objectionable concept to the real work it is used for, what points does the word *speciesism* exist to make? Its most obvious use is to deny the contention which we have repeatedly discussed under the heading of absolute dismissal—the supposition that the species boundary not only makes a difference, but makes the gigantic difference of setting the limits of morality, of deciding whether a given creature can matter to us at all. Here speciesism corresponds to the most extreme form of racism, which takes the same line. ('Pigs or Indians, it's all the same to me'—'We don't stop for Lascars'. A similar view seems to be held in many small cultures which use their own tribal name as the word for 'human being', and regard all outsiders impartially as fair game.) This extreme position, however, is obviously only the tip of the iceberg of prejudice, which can take far more subtle forms. Those concerned with melting it have in fact often been appalled at its capacity for persisting under endless transformations. The demolition of extreme positions by no means gets rid of all unfair habits of thought. If we want a clear view of the enterprise involved in removing prejudice, we need to consider what defines it. This, it seems clear, is unfairness itself, unreasonable bias. A belief is not a prejudice simply because it indicates a difference.

4. The Reality of Natural Bonds

Differences, as we have noticed, can be real and can need to be respected for the dignity and interests of those most closely involved in them. Thus, the insistence of many minority groups on retaining and emphasizing their distinct cultures, rather than becoming assimilated to somebody else's, is no prejudice. Neither is a belief necessarily a prejudice simply because it points out some individuals, regardless of their merits or capacities, as objects of concern before others. The special interest which parents feel in their own children is not a prejudice, nor is the tendency which most of us would show to rescue, in a fire or other emergency, those closest to us sooner than strangers.[1] These habits of thought and action are not unfair, though they can probably be called discriminatory. There is good reason for such a preference. We are bond-forming creatures, not abstract intellects. The question which people who want to use the notion of speciesism have to decide is, does the species barrier also give some ground for such a preference or not? Is cannibalism just the same thing as meat-eating, or is there a significant difference? Leaving aside the moral crudities of absolute dismissal, how is the priority question to be handled? Ought the distinction which Singer recognizes in degree of capacity to be compounded by another which evenly down-grades all non-human species? If so, how far? Should a gibbon, if taken to have one-tenth of the emotional capacity of a human being, go down by one-tenth again on account of being non-human, and settle at one-hundredth of human value? Or is it a twentieth? To look at it another way, do the Quongs from Alpha Centauri, who are ten times as intelligent as ourselves, finish up at par for us, while for them we go down to one-hundredth or a twentieth of Quong value? The question about gibbons is specially poignant since there are tribes in Borneo who used to regard them as kin, and therefore to treat them with the same sort of respect that was given to humans—until they discovered that Europeans thought this mistaken, on which they began to hunt them like any other creature. At which point, if any, were they wrong? Ought an understanding of the theory of evolution to affect their decision? How does extra-specific kinship compare arithmetically with the intra-specific kind? Does the Quongs' alien origin make an important difference to their claim?

Attempts of this kind at detailed arithmetical estimation of claims seem to be quite useless. The results they produce cannot possibly be made consistent; they are usually also morally shocking. This, however, would be just as true if we were talking about purely human affairs. We cannot compare arithmetically the claims of those near to us with the claims of outsiders, nor indeed any other competing sets of claims. There are no definite quantities here, no units. But it still makes very good sense to say that some claims are stronger than others, and even roughly how much stronger. Less formal ideas of *more* and *less* can very well be applied, because these relations are constantly being worked out in the course of conflicts, which continually arise between various sorts of claims. We all learn to compare them, and to show our working.

5. Why Is the Species-Bond So Serious?

Questions about the morality of species preference must certainly be put in the context of the other preferences which people give to those closest to them. These preferences do indeed cause problems. By limiting human charity, they can produce terrible misery. On the other hand they are also an absolutely central element in human happiness, and it seems unlikely that we could live at all without them. They are the root from which charity grows. Morality shows a constant tension between measures to protect the sacredness of these special claims and counter-measures to secure justice and widen sympathy for outsiders. To handle this tension by working out particular priorities is our normal moral business. In handling species conflicts, the notion of simply rejecting all discrimination as *speciesist* looks like a seductively simple guide, an all-purpose formula. I am suggesting that it is not simple, and that we must resist the seduction.

We have seen the difficulties which arise about its first element—the notion that all species other than our own should be treated alike. Singer himself, as it turns out, does not endorse this notion, since he takes account of their differing nervous capacities. What, then, about the more central component of speciesism, the preference normally given to our own species above others? Calling this preference a *prejudice* is treating it as unfair and unreasonable.

Now there are, broadly speaking, two things which can make a preference reasonable, namely value and bonding. There are difficulties about treating this preference as based simply on value. First, it is hard to find an impartial standpoint from which the judgment can be made. Second, there seems to be no attempt to weigh the value of the most evil, or even the least capable, of our species against the best and ablest of others. In so far as the preference does depend on value, it can be seen as a direct preference for the value itself, without reference to species. But it is not handled like this. It is automatic. Criminals, however odious, are in general granted a fair trial; it is only in extraordinary cases that people think it in order to 'shoot them down like dogs'. By contrast, the World Federation for the Protection of Animals estimates that, throughout Europe, some five million dogs are destroyed each year merely because they are unwanted, many by animal welfare groups.[2] Similarly, it is strongly argued that the lives of even the most miserably and incurably defective humans, even indeed of unconscious humans, or those anxious to die, may never be ended, that there can never be any question of 'putting them down' or even allowing them to release themselves. But primates may both be killed and experimented on freely. Degrees of capacity on either side of the human species-barrier are not allowed to affect this sharp divide. J. B. S. Haldane, one of the great biologists of this century, pointed out that this raises real problems. As he remarked, such a proposition as

> 'John Smith is a complete fool because he cannot oxidize phenylalanine' discloses a relation between mind and matter as surprising as transubstantiation, and a good deal better established. On the ethical side, it raises the problem of human rights in a rather sharp form. Has a hopeless idiot the right to life and care, though he or she is not a rational being nor likely to become one? If so, has a chimpanzee with considerably greater intelligence similar rights, and if not, why not?[3]

Haldane is certainly suggesting the answer 'yes' to both questions. The solution of current practice, however, is very different for the two cases. As we have seen it is hard to defend this difference on rationalist lines, by first insisting on the high value of human virtue, reason and language, and then building out awkward extensions to cover cases like John Smith's where some or all of these things are simply absent.

6. The Status of Natural Species-Bonding

Seeing this difficulty, people turn to a quite different line of defence and invoke bonding. An emotional, rather than a rational, preference for our own species is, they suggest, a necessary part of our social nature, in the same way that a preference for our children is, and needs no more justification. We must look seriously at this position, in which there is, I think, a great deal of truth. The species-bond *is* strong, even outside the institutions which have been devised to protect it. The kind of reaction which makes Crusoe risk his life to save Friday from the cannibals really works. Crusoe was not at all a scrupulous fellow; he had killed and cheated and made his pile as a slave-trader. All the same, he feels instant horror at Friday's predicament, and accepts at once the claim silently made on him by the mere helpless humanity of a stranger. The instinctive bond is a real one. But, as Crusoe's earlier behaviour as a slave-trader, and indeed that of the cannibals, shows, its workings are by no means simple or reliable. Before trying to weigh its moral significance, we had better look at the facts about it.

The natural preference for one's own species does exist. It is not, like race-prejudice, a product of culture. It is found in all human cultures, and in cases of real competition it tends to operate very strongly. We can still ask, however, how far it takes us. Is it an irresistible motive, forcing us to dismiss outsiders from consideration? To prove that it was, we would have to show that the differential response to our own species was a far stronger emotional tendency than our differential response to our own tribe or our own children, because nobody doubts that our duty can sometimes call on us to subordinate tribal or family interest to that of outsiders. It would have to be so strong that all attempts to extend consideration to animals were doomed to failure as unnatural.

This is quite a different kind of point from the rationalist one. It is empirical rather than *a priori*. It rests its case, not on the articulateness or rationality of man as an abstract feature, but on sheer physical kinship and its emotional effect. I would presumably produce different conduct in many imaginable cases. For instance, rational alien beings whold be honorary members of our moral community on the rationalist position, but not on this one, while non-rational human beings are a problem for rationalism, but not here. The suggestion is that our nature itself dictates where the border of morality shall fall, and aligns it once and for all with the species-barrier. What about this?

7. Zoological Probabilities

First, it is plausible enough that our tendency to respond differentially to our own species is a natural one. All social creatures attend mostly to members of their own species, and usually ignore others. This can be clearly seen in such places as the Serengeti Plain, where large mixed herds of grazing animals live together in harmony, but do not acquire each other's habits, nor those of the predators who often roam among them. For any serious social purpose such as mating or fighting or gathering to deal with a danger, each normally seeks out its own group. This direction of attention (which seems necessary to the production of a viable species, standardized enough to use its own ecological niche) is partly secured by imprinting in infancy. So it is often possible for an infant placed in an alien group to grow up imprinted on it, and to imitate many of its habits. This infant, however, is just as bigoted about having only one species as a normal specimen. Even if many models are available for it, it sticks to imitating and loving its partne-substitute and those like it. If brought face to face later with members of its own species, it may transfer its allegiance to them, or more often reach an uneasy compromise between the two. But that is not the same thing as general neutrailty.

The option of picking a mixed repertoire of behaviour from many species, of thinking all creatures literally and equally one's brothers, does not seem to be available. The tendency to species-choice as such does seem innate. Moreover, besides imprinting, there are always many detailed positive tendencies which are innate too. The adopted foal or duckling will never be fully integrated into its foster-species because many of the appropriate signals are impossible to it, and it has innate tastes of its own that will set it apart. It may live a reasonably contented life, and be unconscious of missing anything. But it will actually miss a great deal, because a whole range of its social capacities will never be tapped. A solitary duck reared among chickens will never get the clues it needs to perform many of its central behaviour-patterns. It shares some chicken activities, but by no means all. In some ways, too, it keeps getting itself misunderstood. It is therefore a deprived duck, just as it would be if it was kept away from water. Difficulties about mating illustrate this problem. Some species, even quite closely related ones, cannot mate together at all because of behavioural differences. Others can, but the hybrid offspring are not only themselves usually infertile, but unfitted for the full life of either species. Thus lion-tiger hybrids can exist in zoos, but would not have the neural co-ordinations needed for the very exacting, and totally different, hunting patterns of either species. They could therefore not rear young, even if they could produce them, so that if they survived in the wild, their lives would be very incomplete ones.

I think it is important to stress in this way that species-bonds are real, because unless we take account of them, the frequent exclusive attitude of our own species is hard to understand. There does indeed seem to be a deep emotional tendency, in us as in other creatures, to attend first to those around us who are like those who brought us up, and to take much less notice of others. And this, rather than some abstract judgment of value, does seem to be the main root of that relative disregard of other creatures which has been called 'species-ism'. I shall suggest in a moment that this natural tendency, though real, is nothing like so strong, simple and exclusive as is sometimes supposed, and has neither the force nor the authority to justify absolute dismissal of other species. A glance round the variety of human cultures will show that the extremely remote and contemptuous attitude sometimes taken in our own is neither typical nor necessary for *Homo sapiens*. But before coming to this issue, it may be necessary to justify the suggestion that the reasons for species-exclusiveness in humans are in general of the same kind as those that move other creatures.

8. The Difficulties of Species-Neutrality

To see this, we had better go back to our interplanetary situation. The virtuous and super-intelligent Quongs are offering to adopt human babies. Shall we let them? What do we need to know first? The first thing, I should guess, concerns emotional communication. Do the Quongs smile and laugh? Do they understand smiles and laughter? Do they cry or understand crying? Do they ever lose their temper? Does speech—or its equivalent—among them play the same sort of emotional part that it does in human life—for instance, do they greet, thank, scold, swear, converse, tell stories?[4] How much time do they give to their own children? Then—what about play? Do they play with their young at all? If so, how? Then, what are their gender arrangements—meaning, of course, not just sexual activity, but the division into roles of the two (or more) participating genders, throughout life? What singing, dancing or other such activities have they? What meaning do they attach to such words as love? Without going any further, it seems clear that, unless they are the usual cheap substitute for alien beings which appears in films—that is, more or less people in make-up —we shall find that the answers to these questions give us some reasons to refuse their offer completely, even if reluctantly. And these reasons will be of the same kind that applied to the duckling. A human being needs a human life.

Is this sort of objection mere prejudice? Zoology would not say so. It would back our impression that, for a full life, a developing social creature needs to be surrounded by beings very similar to it in all sorts of apparently trivial ways, ways which abstractly might not seem important, but which will furnish essential clues for the unfolding of its faculties. Are there any counter-examples which could show us humans as an exception to this principle because of our flexibility? Stories of wolf-children etc. are hard to evaluate, partly because the actual evidence is slight, partly because all have died soon after capture. It seem impossible that a child should be brought up *from the start* by wolves or any other terrestrial species, because the sheer physical work needed is beyond them. (Mowgli seems to have reached his wolves at about the age of two, which is still remarkably early.) If in this way the thing could be done, the wolf-person would, presumably, have mixed imprinting and have gained some foothold in both worlds, but would be lonely in both—would be excluded from many central joys, and would keep getting himself misunderstood on both sides. Certainly he might gain some kinds of understanding which would be some compensation for this. But the price paid would be terribly heavy—a far deeper variety of 'being at home nowhere' than that which afflicts people brought up to oscillate between two cultures.

A much better way of handling serious inter-species relations is described in C. S. Lewis's delightful novel *Out of the Silent Planet.* This shows a world where three quite different species co-exist. They live in peace, do business together and respect each other, giving the name *hnau*, rational creatures, to their whole class, and including under that heading, in spite of occasional doubts, the visiting human beings. But most of the time each keeps to its own way of life and its own preferred kind of country. When they do meet, they get on reasonably well, but tend to find each other very funny. They differ considerably in their habits and interests, admire each other's specialities, and do not raise the question whose life is best. This arrangement shows species-loyalty as a quite unpretentious emotional matter, a bond, not an evaluation. And it rightly suggests that it need not determine the borders of social intercourse.

9. Loyalty Is Not Exclusiveness

For we have to notice next that species-loyalty in social animals, strong though it is, is not necessarily exclusive. At an ordinary social level, creatures of different species are certainly often aware of each other, and are probably interacting quietly far more than we realize. (Would an observer of an alien species pick up all our social interactions?) This background awareness becomes visible at once when members of one's own species are removed. Thus, Jane Goodall describes how, even in the wild, a somewhat isolated juvenile chimp finds a playmate in a young baboon.[5] And the thing is well established in captivity. For instance, if a grazing animal—horse, cow, donkey, goat or the like—is left quite alone in a field, it grows very uneasy and depressed. But if a companion of some other species is brought in, it cheers up at once. They often do not seem to pay each other any particular attention, but the bond is there, apparently much as it would be with a conspecific. More remarkable still, an outsider may be cherished even when one's own species is present. A clear instance is the well-established tendency of race-horses to become attached to some apparently unimpressive stable-companion, such as a goat or even a cat, and to pine if they are separated from it.[6]

10. Species-Bonds Are Not Infallible

On the other side of the coin, we must notice that species-recognition does not necessarily lead to amity. The first attachment of social creatures is usually to their own group. Strangers, and even more strange bands, of one's own species are usually viewed at first with some alarm. They may eventually be accepted, but at least a period of familiarization is normally needed, and often some fighting, or at least sparring to determine dominance, must be gone through first. Chimps, who used to be cited as exceptions to this general rule, have turned out not to be so; their groups are indeed quite large, but they have limits, and outsiders do get sharply repelled.[7] Of course this tendency to exclude strangers is now rightly treated with some caution, because it was crassly over-emphasized by those who used to dramatize animal life as perpetually red in tooth and claw. But we have to take it seriously, because it illustrates a difficulty which is essential to social life. The more richly a social bond develops, the greater, inevitably, is the difference between those inside it and those without. Beings which treat acquaintances and strangers alike—as do those simpler creatures which merely go about in herds, without individual recognition —have no reason to be exclusive. They will accept, in their weak kind of acceptance, any conspecific who arrives and for them, therefore, their species is the only real community.[8] But the more lively and complex creatures cannot possibly do this. Their attachment to their own small community stands in the way of wider bonding. There are always some tendencies which counter this exclusiveness, some roads to the acceptance of strangers, but their capacity is limited.

11. Human Non-Humans

In animal cases, then, the species-bond does not exactly coincide with the area of concern; there are (as Singer rightly suggests) overlaps both ways. What, however, about *Homo sapiens?* A glance round the wide human scene suggests, on the face of things, that the discrepancy there is not narrower, but wider. On the one hand, even in explicit terms of language, not all humans admit all others as belonging to their species at all. The arrangement whereby the name of one's own tribe is also the word for 'human being' seems to be quite widespread. This can—though perhaps it need not—mean that outsiders are treated as 'only animals', notably in the two important respects of hunting them down without hesitation and rejecting with horror the idea of intermarrying with them. This attitude is part of the larger phenomenon called 'pseudo-speciation'—the tendency for human beings to regard their cultures as if they actually were separate species. Pseudo-speciation is what makes it possible for 'cultural evolution' to proceed so fast. Customs of all kinds are accepted by imprinting early in life, taken for granted as a part of one's constitution, in a way which makes it easy to go forward and make whatever new inventions are needed to supplement them. The price paid for this, however, is that people with different customs tend, at a glance, to seem like members of a different species, and so to be rejected. Of course it is possible to resist this process, but a glance around the world makes it clear that this needs a positive effort. Baboons, presumably, do not ask themselves whether the baboons of a strange invading band are really proper baboons at all, but people can ask this question, and can answer it with a no.

12. Non-Human Humans

Thus the social community which humans recognize does not necessarily contain their whole species. But neither, on the other hand, does it necessarily exclude all members of other species. Here we encounter the wide and confusing, but genuine, range of customs which has been roughly lumped together by theorists under the heading of *totemism*. Particular kinds of animals can be held sacred, protected, cherished and, most significantly, even viewed as ancestors. They can be worshipped as gods. They can be buried (as in ancient Egypt) with full human or super-human honours. Wives can be dedicated to them and mystical marriage-ceremonies performed. And offences against them can be resented exactly as though they were offences against tribal members. (Thus it is said that the origin of the Mau-Mau movement in Kenya was an incident when a white farmer shot a wild cat which he suspected of damaging his hens, and threw it to an African whose totem he knew it to be, saying 'OK, how about eating that?' The name Mau-Mau is a reference to this cat.)[9]

Thus I suggest that theorists who have hoped to find a clear, unmistakable definition of 'the human community' simply given as part of the natural history of our species are likely to be disappointed. They will no doubt find it irritating to be asked to pay attention, at the outset of this topic, to a set of customs which they probably regard as confused, primitive, superstitious and objectionable. But if the argument used here is really to be an empirical one, then the range of existing and reported customs is the proper evidence for it. It might have been true that people always and everywhere showed an unfailing regard for their species-barrier, that they naturally always accepted any member of their own species into fellowship without difficulty, and were never even tempted to form bonds with members of other species. We might have found too that they were always quite clear about their ancestral tree, and included in it no being who was not manifestly *sapiens*. We do not find this. Besides totemism, we find many links with particular species, such as that of the Masai with their cattle, and of nomads with their horses, which, while rather more utilitarian, play so important a part in social life that the community cannot be properly thought of without them. Tractors cannot be substituted. (Wherever there are horses, there are some people who actually prefer them to humans. This attitude is generally frowned upon, but it persists all the same.) Man does not naturally exist in species-isolation.

13. Nature Supplies No Plain Line

What should we conclude from all this? Obviously, we have no reason to conclude that existing views on this subject ought always to be accepted. On the issue of undue exclusion, no doubt we shall all agree that they ought not. Advancing morality has everywhere steadily worked to flatten out that side of the discrepancy, to insist that even foreigners are humans, and ought in principle to be treated as brothers. I think that there is in the West, though not in Buddhism, quite a widespread impression that flattening out the other side as well—excluding all non-humans to whom some sympathy and status have been extended—is merely a necessary part of this same enterprise, and ought obviously to be combined with it. This idea sometimes takes the form of assuming that the mere curtailing of sympathy and attention given to animals will, automatically, and as it were hydraulically, make more energy available for helping humans, rather as pushing in one bulge on a damaged can may straighten out another. This is not obvious. It would be so only if ... our duties could be represented by a series of concentric circles, each containing claims closer and more urgent than the one outside it, and if the species-barrier were clearly a circle right outside all those involving humans. But ... this set of concentric circles cannot be consistently drawn up at all. Claims are of different kinds. Those on behalf of one's own community certainly are strong, but they are not the only strong kind. And the species-barrier, as we now find, is not even accepted in the same form by all human communites. But also, more important than this, all these communities are themselves multi-species ones. It is one of the special powers and graces of our species not to ignore others, but to draw in, domesticate and live with a great variety of other creatures. No other animal does so on anything like so large a scale. Perhaps we should take this peculiar human talent more seriously and try to understand its workings....

Notes

1. A point well dealt with by Bernard Williams in 'Persons, Character and Morality'. See his book *Moral Luck* (Cambridge University Press, 1981).

2. Cited by Marian Dawkins, *Animal Suffering*, p. 6, from T. Carding (1974), 'Work at the International Level for Animal Protection; *Animalia*, I, 3.

3. Introduction to *The Biology of Mental Defect* by Lionel Penrose (1949).

4. See Wittgenstein on the use of language for such things as 'asking, thanking, cursing, greeting, praying' (*Philosophical Investigations*, Part 1, § 23).

5. Jan van Lawick-Goodall, *In the Shadow of Man* (Collins, 1971), pp. 151–54 and 193–95. See also Adrian Desmond, *The Ape's Reflexion*, p. 217.

6. For cats see Muriel Beadle, *The Cat, its History, Biology and Behaviour* (Collins and Harvill Press, 1977), p. 85.

7. See Adrian Desmond *The Ape's Reflexion*, pp. 223–23, summarizing Jane Goodall's Leakey Memorial Lecture of 1978.

8. This situation is well described by Lorenz in Chapter VIII of *On Aggression* (Methuen, 1966) and distinguished sharply from true social behaviour. He calls it 'the anonymity of the flock'.

9. See Credo Mutwa, *My People, the Writings of a Zulu Witch-Doctor* (Penguin Books, 1977), p. 175.

6

Moral Considerability and Extraterrestrial Life

J. Baird Callicott

1.

Ethics is more a *normative* than descriptive study of human behavior. That is, in ethics we want to know less how people might than how they *should* or *ought to* act, do, treat, or live. The sense of norm in normative is not the sense of norm in the vulgar meeting of normal— that is, average, mean, lowest common denominator. Rather, norm in normative (and in the medical meaning of normal) connotes a benchmark, a standard, an ideal.

The *ethical* question of this paper is how to treat extraterrestrial life—if there is any and if we ever find any. As an ethicist, I am not competent to predict how we will *in fact* treat extraterrestrial life if and when we encounter it. However, as it seems to me, an untrained observer, the human track record—average, or in that sense, normal human behavior—does not bode well for any extraterrestrial life unfortunate enough to be discovered by us. I am not at all sure that, as an ethicist, I can even address with confidence the question how we *ought to* treat extraterrestrial life. The question is made remote and speculative by two general uncertainties, one metaethical, the other epistemic.

Firstly, while today almost everyone of sound mind and good will agrees that *human* life without qualification is the subject of unambiguous and incontrovertible moral concern, there is by no means general agreement that other-than-human *terrestrial* life should be the subject of a similar concern. The suggestion that other-than-human terrestrial life possesses moral value—value, that is, apart from its utility to serve human ends—is greeted at best with skeptical indulgence and at worst with impatient ridicule, not only by popular moralists and their constituents, but more especially by mainstream Western moral philosophers.[1] In the prevailing contemporary ethical climate, the hypothesis that we might even entertain just the possibility of human moral obligations to *extra*terrestrial life, assuming that it is not anthropomorphic, therefore will likely be regarded as so absurd as to be beneath contempt.[2] Animal liberation/rights moral philosophers, who attempt to extend moral considerability to a narrow range of our closest terrestrial nonhuman relatives, are by their own estimation at the leading edge of ethical theory and, by the estimation of their mainstream philosophical critics, muddled sentimentalists.[3]

The chilly reception greeting even such comparatively modest proposals as animal welfare ethics for a more generous and expansive provision of moral considerability for nonhuman life forms cannot be attributed simply to the churlishness and/or niggardliness of reactionary guardians of the Western moral tradition. Rather, Western moral thought from Plato and St. Paul to Tillich and Hare provides few conceptual resources theoretically to underwrite such generosity of spirit and rigorously to effect such an expansion. But a more embracing ethic to be a proper ethic must have a sound conceptual basis and logical rigor, and it must somehow connect with historical moral theory. A life-centered—a literally biocentric—ethic discontinuous with traditional moral philosophy would not be recognizable as a species of ethics, and so could not be seriously entertained or critically appraised.

Secondly, not only is the very concept of extraterrestrial life problematic, but a critical exploration of the hypothesis that extraterrestrial life exists leads to a confounding paradox. Venus and Mars, the most likely planetary hosts for extraterrestrial life in our solar system, have been visited by unpeopled probes with disappointing results.[4] If life, however broadly defined, does not exist in the solar system—and it now seems more probable that it does not than that it does—may we suppose that it exists in the galaxy of which our solar system is a member?[5]

We know that our galaxy alone contains literally billions of stars. Thus, if our star, the Sun, is not unique or especially extraordinary in possessing a family of planets, and if we assume that life (defined so as not to be conceptually too terramorphic) is a natural, perhaps inevitable, stage in the progressive ordering of mature, suitably endowed and situated planetary surfaces, then the probability that extraterrestrial life exists in our galaxy beyond our solar system approaches unity and, thus, certainty.

But what of our chances to positively or empirically confirm this convincing *a priori* argument? Our spiral galaxy, the Milky Way, is on the average approximately 100,000 light years wide and 5,000 light years thick.[6] Exobiologist Valdermar Firsoff estimates there to be about two life-supporting planets per million cubic light years.[7] Let us now imagine ourselves actually setting out to find the other life-supporting planet in our million-cubic-light-year district. It ought to be only forty to sixty light years away.

The speed of light, however, is a limiting velocity—nothing can exceed it. And only particles of zero rest mass can actually attain the speed of light. Massy objects like spaceships are limited in principle to several fractional factors less than the speed of light. For purposes of calculating a time and energy budget for interstellar space exploration, Hewlett-Packard engineer Bernard Oliver suggests we generously posit a ship speed "far beyond our present technology," of $1/5$ the speed of light.[8] At that rate an expedition sent to our nearest stellar neighbor, Alpha Centauri, four light years away, would arrive in twenty years. In the forty-year working lifetime of a highly trained crew the next closest star beyond Alpha Centauri, regardless of its qualifications, could be visited and examined—and this assumes that our astronauts would be willing never to return home, would be willing to undertake, in effect, a suicide mission.[9] A search of a few more stars might be undertaken in a century by unpeopled probes, depending upon how many we sent and how far away their targets were. What would be the probability of finding in this way the other life supporting planet in our million-cubic-light-year district in a thousand years or a hundred thousand or a million, and at what expense of energy and other terrestrial resources?[10] My guess is that it would be very small, and prohibitively expensive.

Hence, and here is the epistemological paradox, we may take it as very nearly certain—given our knowledge of the size and stellar population of the galaxy, our understanding of biochemistry and organic evolution, and the reasonable assumption that our solar system is neither unique nor extraordinary—that life abounds in the galaxy. But this knowledge has no, or very nearly no, positive significance or operational translatability. To the extent that scientific epistemology remains positivistic, the seemingly very innocent and reasonable hypothesis that life abounds in the Milky Way turns out to be as scientifically nonsensical as the hypothesis that an electron has both a definite location and a definite velocity. The hypothesis is unverifiable *in principle* primarily because of the limitations on our autopsy imposed by Einstein's constant c, the speed of light, which functions in the large arena of interstellar space somewhat like Planck's constant, h, the quantum, in the small arena of subatomic space. An uncertainty principle, in other words, is operative in very large dimensions of space-time as it is in very small, at least in respect to the search for extraterrestrial life.

The metaethical and epistemological uncertainties surrounding the ethical question posed here lead to a third, more practical uncertainty: Can there be, really, any serious justification for this exercise? If animal-welfare ethics are controversial, if terrestrial biocentric and ecocentric environmental ethics are contemptuously ignored or ridiculed, isn't the construction of an ethic for the treatment of something we know not what or whether it may be more than just a little fatuous?

Right now, right here on Earth, anthropogenic species extinction grinds on at a catastrophic pace.[11] While we are wondering how to treat hypothetical life that may, for better or worse, lie forever beyond our ken, let alone our actions, the life we do partially understand and certainly know to exist is being stamped out—often without notice or comment and with very little remorse or protest—under our noses. Shouldn't we get our intellectual priorities straight and worry first about the treatment of terrestrial life, which is presently under such extreme and actual duress? Once we've got a persuasive ethic worked out to help address the more pressing real-world problem of wholesale terrestrial biocide, then maybe we can think about how we ought to treat extraterrestrial life—if there is any, if we should recognize it when we see it, and if we should ever encounter it!

I am not convinced by this criticism of the present enterprise, even though I have stated it as strongly as I can. It sounds a lot like the stock liberal diatribe against the Apollo project in the sixties: As a nation, so that argument went, we are allocating huge sums of money to put a man on the Moon, while here on Earth socioeconomic conditions for the urban minority underclasses in affluent America grow daily more desperate, and in the oppressed and impoverished Third and Fourth Worlds the "wretched of the Earth" die daily of preventable disease and outright starvation. Shouldn't we put our moral and financial resources to work addressing these earthly social problems before we consider a hollow technological vanity like putting a man on the Moon?

I thought then, and still think now, that even so the Apollo project was morally defensible and economically worthwhile, not so much because of the official rationale—the technical and scientific harvest forthcoming from lunar exploration—but primarily because of the impact of Apollo on human consciousness here on Earth.[12] We have known since the centuries of Copernicus and Galileo that the Earth is a planet and the Moon its satellite. But for one of us to stand on the Moon, look upon a distant Earth, and return to the rest of us photographs of our own small and very precious planet translated heretofore mere propositional knowledge into palpable human experience. We all participated vicariously in that experience. It was, indeed, a most signal event in the collective mind of mankind. Neil Armstrong was the Archimedes of human consciousness. Given the Moon to stand on, he moved the Earth. His lever was a camera. More than any other single phenomenon, those photographs of a soft, lake-blue planet, coyly swirled about with flouncy clouds, floating in empty space—with the utter desolation of the moonscape in the foreground—precipitated the ecological and environmental decade that immediately followed.[13] The photographs of the Earth taken from the Moon also helped bring to the forefront of social consciousness the concept of universal human community. We could all *see* our world as one. The concept of universal human rights immediately became public-policy rhetoric. We were all fellow citizens of a single small world, fellow passengers with all the other water-planet creatures on what then became spaceship Earth. Our indivisible collective dependency on Earth and its luxuriant life forms was made poignantly visceral by the empathy we all felt for the ill-fated Apollo XIII astronauts—their tenuous and precarious existence in space modules and spacesuits—on their desperate journey home to Earth.

The discussion of environmental ethics in the solar system, if not in the cosmos beyond, in a less far-reaching and certainly less dramatic way, might have a similar reflexive impact. To seriously entertain the ethical question, How ought we to treat exterrestrial life? may put into proper perspective the more immediate and pressing question, How ought we to treat life on Earth? To entertain a noble moral stance toward extraterrestrial life might help to shame us into taking more seriously a noble moral stance toward terrestrial life. And, as I have elsewhere argued, the Copernican revolution (made palpable by the Apollo project) is as much a conceptual foundation of environmental ethics as the subsequent Darwinian and ecological revolutions in thought.[14] Hence, reminding ourselves from time to time of these larger spatial and temporal parameters may be conceptually important for terrestrial environmental ethics.

And who knows, somewhere in the solar system we just might find some extraterrestrial life. In case we do, it would be better for us, wouldn't it, to be morally prepared for our first close encounter with extraterrestrial life than to shoot first and ask questions later?

Let me conclude these penultimate observations with the following ethical thought experiment. Imagine our astronauts finding something that seems to be more than just a mineral configuration of matter somewhere off the Earth. After performing some tests and consulting some criteria, they determine that they have indeed found extraterrestrial life or "living things." They then systematically eradicate all of it (or them) within reach. There seems to be something wrong, something morally wrong, with such an act of destruction—something more wrong than if the astronauts had found, say, some interesting patterns etched by solar winds on a planet's lifeless surface and erased them. Let us begin with this hopefully shared moral intuition as a touchstone and ask ourselves why we feel that the former act of otherworldly vandalism would be morally worse than the latter.[15]

2.

The most popularly known but philosophically least cultivated environmental ethic, the Leopold land ethic, provides little help for conceptually articulating our hopefully shared moral intuition respecting extraterrestrial life. The land ethic conceptually bases moral considerability for Earth's complement of animals, plants, waters, and soils upon evolutionary kinship and ecological community.[16] In other words, the land ethic confers moral standing on terrestrial plants and animals in part because they share with us a common evolutionary heritage. They are "fellow-voyagers...in the Odyssey of evolution"—indeed, perhaps we and they ultimately evolved from a single parent cell.[17] And Earth's plants and other animals along with the elemental components of Earth's biosphere are all, in Leopold's representation, also presently working members in good standing of Earth's biotic community. That is, terrestrial plants, animals, soils, and waters are ecologically integrated and mutually interdependent. This wholesale symbiosis of Earth's biota, by a moral logic that I have elsewhere elaborated, generates for us, according to Leopold, ethical duties and obligations to the ecosystem as a whole and to its members severally.[18] Extraterrestrial life forms, assuming that they were not of Earthly origin and inoculated somehow on some foreign body, or *vice versa*, would not be our kin—that is, descendants of a common paleontological parent stock—nor would they be participants in Earth's economy of nature or biotic community. Hence, they would lie outside the scope of Leopold's land ethic.

Pursuant to the general reflexive motif of this discussion, the consideration of the moral standing of extraterrestrial life sheds an interesting and very valuable light on Leopold's land ethic. It reveals the limitations of its conceptual foundations and thus highlights and more sharply defines its outlines. With our imaginations limited, as they often are in ethics and more especially in environmental ethics, by terrestrial horizons, Leopold's land ethic, which "enlarges the boundaries of the [biotic/moral] community to include soils, waters, plants, and animals, or collectively: the land," may seem to include everything "under the Sun" and thus to effectively include nothing, to be, in other words, impossibly dilute.[19] However, from the point of view of the Copernican spatiotemporal dimensions of our present discussion—the solar system, the galaxy, and the universe at large—the land ethic seems almost parochial in extent and even tribal in nature because it restricts itself to local—that is, terrestrial—beings and rests their moral value on kinship and mutual dependency. The very failure of the land ethic to provide moral considerability for extraterrestrial life reveals at once its strength for Earth-oriented environmental ethics—which is of course the only variety of environmental ethics with any genuine practical interest or application.

The land ethic, thus, could fairly be called a case of Earth chauvinism or terrestrialism. But unlike male chauvinism and racism, the land ethic is not anti-anything—extraterrestrial life in this case. It would not, in other words, encourage or necessarily sanction the suppression, enslavement, or destruction of extraterrestrial life. The land ethic simply has nothing to say about extraterrestrial life. If pressed to respond to the possibility that extraterrestrial life may exist in the solar system, that it may be found by human beings, and that it may be affected by human actions, an exponent of the land ethic might suggest that something analogous to diplomatic relations between autonomous and independent gens would be implied by it. But such an extension of the land ethic to moral problems with which it was not designed to deal is too speculative a matter to be pursued with confidence.

The advent and academic notoriety of the animal liberation/ rights ethics set in motion an intellectual dialectic that led to the development of an apparently novel life-principle ethic by Kenneth Goodpaster, building on suggestions of Joel Feinberg, and a revival of interest in Albert Schweitzer's popularly known reverence-for-life ethic.[20]

Animal liberationist Peter Singer argued that animals ought to be extended the same moral consideration as people because animals have the same capacity as people for suffering.[21] For Singer, sentiency, the capacity to experience pleasure and pain, should be the criterion for the moral considerability of beings.[22]

As this was obviously an inadequate basis for an environmental ethic, since most environmental entities are not sentient—all forms of plant life, for example, and many kinds of animals are not—Goodpaster attempted to extend Singer's moral logic a step further.[23] Sentiency, he argued, ought not to be the criterion for moral considerability, since sentiency exists in some beings only as a means to another end—life.[24] Life, therefore, being the end in reference to which sentiency evolved as a means, ought to be the characteristic in reference to which moral considerability should be conferred.

As I have elsewhere pointed out, Goodpaster's life-principle ethic and Schweitzer's reverence-for-life ethic, though they differ primarily in vocabulary, rhetoric, and historical resonance, have in the abstract a common metaethical foundation.[25] In the last analysis, both defend the moral considerability of living beings because they are conative (a capacity logically parallel to sentiency).

The Goodpaster life-principle and Schweitzer reverence-for-life ethics urge that we extend moral considerability to (and/or reverence for, in Schweitzer's case) only terrestrial life. I do not mean to suggest that either Goodpaster or Schweitzer expressly exclude extraterrestrial life; it is just clear that, quite naturally, the only life they are thinking about is terrestrial life, since that's all the life anyone knows to exist or imagines that s/he might actually affect.

But extraterrestrial life would be conative. I mean I guess it would be minimally conative—that is, in Feinberg's by now classical definition of conative, in possession of at least one of the following characteristics: "conscious wishes, desires, and hopes; *or* urges and impulses; *or* unconscious drives, aims, and goals; *or* latent tendencies, directions of growth and natural fulfillments."[26] Anything having the minimal characteristics of life—a growing, reproducing, dying thing— would have, it would seem necessarily, at least latent tendencies, directions of growth, and natural fulfillments if not unconscious drives, aims, and goals or conscious wishes, desires, and hopes. Such a thing would have therefore a "'good' of its own, the achievement of which can be its due," in Feinberg's words, and thus moral rights, as Feinberg grounds rights, or at least moral considerability, in Goodpaster's terms—if there is any significant difference between the possession of moral rights and moral considerability.[27]

Similarly, upon Schweitzer's more voluntarist and mystical rendering of conativity, I would suppose that extraterrestrial life, no less than terrestrial life, would be possessed by the will to live and therefore, according to Schweitzer, "[j]ust as in my own will-to-live there is a yearning for more life,... so the same obtains in all the will-to-live around me, equally whether it can express itself to my comprehension or whether it remains unvoiced." Schweitzer then goes on to say, "Ethics thus consists in this, that I experience the necessity of practising the same reverence for life toward all will-to-live, as toward my own."[28]

The life-principle/reverence-for-life ethics are, as it were, tailor-made for conceptually articulating and grounding our hopefully shared moral intuition that extraterrestrial life should be treated with respect, or reverence, if and when we may encounter it. The life-principle/reverence-for-life ethics, however, have a foible symmetrical to but opposite that of the Leopold land ethic. The land ethic is, because of its holistic or ecosystemic value orientation, practicable as a terrestrial environmental ethic, but, because of its conceptual foundations and logical structure, incapable of transference to life off the Earth. The life-principle/reverence-for-life ethics are, because of their conceptual foundations and logical structures, capable of transference off the Earth, but, because of their individualistic or atomistic biases, impracticable as terrestrial environmental ethics.[29] In other words, the life-principle/reverence-for-life ethics are serviceable as extraterrestrial environmental ethics, but, ironically, fail miserably as terrestrial environmental ethics.

Let me elaborate. Only individual living things are conative, at least as Feinberg and Schweitzer variously understand this shared basic idea. Populations, species, biocoenoses, ecotones, biomes, and the biosphere as a whole are not. Hence, only individual living things are properly rights bearers (Feinberg), morally considerable (Goodpaster), or objects of reverence and respect (Schweitzer). To consistently practice the life-principle/reverence-for-life ethics at home on Earth would require a life style so quiescent as to be suicidal, as Schopenhauer clearly recognized and affirmed.[30] To live is necessarily to exploit other living beings. Since we are integrated members of the terrestrial bioeconomy in which the life of one thing is purchased by the death of another, the exponents of life-principle/reverence-for-life ethics at home on Earth are caught in an unavoidable practical conundrum at every turn. However, since our astronauts would not be integrated members of some extraterrestrial ecosystem and would be bringing with them their own terrestrial foodstuff and other necessities of life, the life-principle/reverence-for-life ethics would be practicable, without continuous compromise between principle and necessity, in respect to life on other bodies in the solar system—should there be any and should our astronauts ever encounter it. Without the need to eat or otherwise exploit extraterrestrial life our astronauts could categorically respect and/or revere it.

But there is both a rational philosophical demand and a human psychological need for a self-consistent and all-embracing moral theory. We are neither good philosophers nor whole persons if for one purpose we adopt utilitarianism, another deontology, a third animal liberation, a fourth the land ethic, and a fifth a life-principle or reverence-for-life ethic, and so on. Such ethical eclecticism is not only rationally intolerable, it is morally suspect as it invites the suspicion of *ad hoc* rationalizations for merely expedient or self-serving actions.

Let me therefore recommend an environmental ethic that is sufficiently inclusive and consistent to provide at once for the moral considerability of extraterrestrial as well as for terrestrial life without neglecting the practical primacy of human life, human needs, and human rights.

Bryan Norton has distinguished between strong and weak anthropocentrism.[31] Anthropocentrism is the view that there exists no value independent from human experience. Whether such a view is ultimately justifiable or not, it seems to be the prevailing view in Western axiology.[32] In Norton's terms, strong anthropocentrism takes any valued human experience as in principle equal to any other—push-pin is as good as poetry, bird-shooting as botanizing, and dune-buggying as desert pup-fish habitat restoration. Nonhuman beings are merely resources for valued human experiences, and no constraints—except essentially economic constraints—are warranted when those resources are consumed or destroyed in the process of using them to satisfy human preferences. From the point of view of strong anthropocentrism, if when human astronauts encounter life on another planet they are more amused to eradicate it than leave it alone, and a majority of the rest of us feel better off or at least no worse off for their having done so, then that is what they should do.

Weak anthropocentrism on the other hand, the *locus classicus* of which Norton finds in Thoreau, regards certain uses of things as transforming and ennobling human nature.[33] Some human experiences therefore, are better than others because they expand and enlarge human consciousness, in short because they make better human beings of us.[34] Thus it is better to botanize than bird-shoot, save desert pup-fish than dune-buggy, and write poetry than play push-pin, bird-shooting, and dune-buggying stultify the human spirit and stupefy the human mind while literature, science, and species conservation elevate the human spirit and enlighten the human mind.

Now, as it seems to me, weak anthropocentrism would apply to our use of extraterrestrial as well as terrestrial life all to the greater good of mankind. I can think of nothing so positively transforming of human consciousness as the discovery, study, and conservation of life somewhere off the Earth. It would confirm experientially, palpably, viscerally what we presently believe in the abstract: that life is the expression of an inherent potentiality in physical nature. Such an event would immeasurably advance the ongoing process of the naturalization of human consciousness, which is presently progressing all too slowly. And to find life off the Earth, to discover a wholly exotic biology, to cherish it, and try to understand something about it would, I believe, transform our present view of life on Earth. In relation to extraterrestrial life, terrestrial organisms, ourselves included, comprise one great family, one gens. The current myopic prejudices regarding terrestrial species as somehow alien or exotic forms would perforce melt away in comparison with truly alien or exotic life forms. In short, the Archimedean adventure of the Apollo project would thereby be completed.

Notes

1. For an extended discussion ranging from skeptical indulgence to impatient ridicule see John Passmore, *Man's Responsibility for Nature: Ecological Problems and Western Traditions* (New York: Scribner's, 1974).

2. I was interested to learn that Michael Tooley, "Would ETIs Be Persons?" in James L. Christian, ed., *Extraterrestrial Intelligence: The First Encounter* (Buffalo, N.Y.: Prometheus Books, 1976), provides, by applying the usual ethical categories of mainstream Western moral thought, moral considerability for extraterrestrial intelligent beings of sci-fi fantasy, provided that they are also conative, self-conscious, and can envisage the future. Tooley does not address and his discussion suggests he could not philosophically support moral considerability for mere life—extraterrestrial or otherwise.

3. Peter Singer, *Animal Liberation: A New Ethics for Our Treatment of Animals* (New York: The New York Review, 1975), writes, "Philosophy ought to question the basic assumptions of the age" (p. 10), as if his extension of moral considerability to animals were really radical. See H. J. McCloskey, "Moral Rights and Animals," *Inquiry* 22 (1979): 23–59, for a humanistic rejection of animal liberation/rights.

4. Paul M. Henig, "Exobiologists Continue to Search for Life on Other Planets," *BioScience* 30 (1980), quotes physicist William G. Pollard as saying of exobiology that it is "'a branch of science so far without content'" (p. 9). Exobiologist Richard S. Young, "Post-Viking Exobiology," *BioScience* 28 (1978), makes the essentially logical (and thus largely formal) point that "the absence of evidence of life [on Mars] should not necessarily be construed as evidence of the absence of life" (p. 502).

5. For a discussion of the shift of informed opinion toward skepticism regarding extraterrestrial life, see Paul M. Henig, "Exobiologists Continue to Search for Life on Other Planets."

6. These dimensions are supplied by V. A. Firsoff, *Life Beyond the Earth* (New York: Basic Books, 1963), p. xi.

7. Ibid.

8. Bernard M. Oliver, "Search Strategies," in john Billingham, ed. *Life in the Universe* (Cambridge: Massachusetts Institute of Technology Press, 1982), .p 352

9. Ibid. Oliver entertains the possibility of a search voyage spanning several generations requiring thus "nursery and educational facilities [which adds weight and increases energy requirements].... The longer time," he realistically reminds us, "also increases the risk of disaffection or actual mutiny by the crew: the parents were presumably screened for psychological stability; the children are not" (pp. 354-55). Incidentally, Oliver's calculations do not neglect the time-dilating effects of speeds approaching the speed of light in relativity theory; his time calculations are given in the ship-time reference frame.

10. Ibid. Oliver calculates the energy required to accelerate a starship of 1,000 tons to $\frac{1}{5}$ the speed of light in multiples of units of millennia of U.S. energy consumption—that is, in units equivalent to 1,000 years of total energy consumption by the United States (p. 354)!

11. See Norman Myers, *The Sinking Ark: A New Look at the Problem of Disappearing Species* (New York: Pergamon Press, 1979), for an authoritative scientific account. For a philosophical-ethical response, see Bryan Nortin, ed., *The Preservation of Species* (Princeton, N.J.: Princeton University Press, 1986).

12. Hartmann, in "Space Exploration and Environmental Issues," *Environmental Ethics* 6 (1984): 227-39, very nicely summarizes and documents this impact. Hartmann's central practical concern seems to be that environmentalists not add their opposition to that of socialists, fiscal conservatives, and others who hope to see space-exploration projects scrapped. Although I do not share Hartmann's mythic vision of space colonies and space resource development, I am not opposed to space exploration, since I think

that the more we explore space, the more deeply impressed we will be with our embeddedness in and dependency upon Earth.

13. Ibid. Hartmann agrees, "It is no concidence that the first Earth Day, in 1970, came soon after these pictures became available."

14. See, for example, J. Baird Callicott, "On the Intrinsic Value of Nonhuman Species," in Norton, *The Preservation of Species,* pp. 138–72.

15. The role of intuition in ethics is controversial. Tom Regan, *The Case for Animal Rights* (Berkeley: University of California Press, 1983), pp. 133ff., provides a recent summary, a sorting of the issues, and a defense for the utility of moral intuitions such as this one as a point of departure for further ethical analysis.

16. For a schematic analysis of the land ethic, see J. Baird Callicott, "Elements of an Environmental Ethic: Moral Considerability and the Biotic Community." *Environmental Ethics* 1 (1979): 71–81.

17. Aldo Leopold, *A Sand County Almanac and Sketches Here and There* (New York: Oxford University Press, 1949), p. 109. Lewis Thomas, *The Lives of a Cell: Notes of a Biology Watcher* (New York: Viking Press, 1974), p. 5, notes that there is a "high probability that we derived from some single cell, fertilized in a bolt of lightning as the Earth cooled."

18. See Leopold, "The Land Ethic," in *A Sand County Almanac,* and J. Baird Callicott, "Elements of an Environmental Ethics," and "The Search for an Environmental Ethic," in Tom Regan, ed., *Matters of Life and Death,* 2nd ed. (New York: Random House, 1986).

19. Leopold, "The Land Ethic," p. 204.

20. Joel Feinberg, "The Rights of Animals and Unborn Generations," in William T. Blackstone, ed., *Philosophy and Environmental Crisis* (Athens: University of Georgia Press, 1974); Kenneth Goodpaster, "On Being Morally Considerable," *Journal of Philosophy* 22 (1978): 308–25; Albert Schweitzer, "The Ethic of Reverence for Life" in Tom Regan and Peter Singer, eds., *Animal Rights and Human Obligations* (Englewood Cliffs, N.J.: Prentice-Hall, 1976): 133–38. For a discussion of the dialectic see Kenneth Goodpaster, "From Egosim to Environmentalism," in K. E. Goodpaster and K. M. Sayre, eds., *Ethics and Problems of the 21st Century* (Notre Dame, In.: University of Notre Dame Press, 1979): 21–35.

21. Peter Singer, *Animal Liberation,* p. 1ff.

22. Ibid.

23. Kenneth Goodpaster, "On Being Morally Considerable."

24. Ibid., p. 316.

25. J. Baird Callicott, "On the Intrinsic Value of Non-human Species."

26. Joel Feinberg, "The Rights of Animals and Unborn Generations," p. 49. Italics added.

27. Ibid., p. 50. Goodpaster, in "On Being Morally Considerable," wisely steers clear of the intellectual quagmire of the nature of rights and the qualifications of rights holders.

28. Albert Schweitzer, "The Ethic of Reverence for Life," p. 133.

29. Kenneth Goodpaster, in "From Egoism to Environmentalism," provides a very clear and illuminating discussion of the moral reasoning, the logic, of all ethics that rest on a criterion for moral standing/moral rights, such as rationality, sentiency, conativity, etc.

30. Both Schweitzer and Goodpaster admit the strict impracticability of their conation-centered ethics. Goodpaster, in "On Being Morally Considerable," writes, "the clearest and most decisive refutation of the principle of respect for life is that one cannot *live* according to it, nor is there any indication in nature that we were intended to." And Schweitzer, in "The Ethic of Reverence for Life," writes, "It remains a painful enigma how I am to live by the rule of reverence for life in a world ruled by creative will which is at the same time destructive will...." For a fuller discussion see J. Baird Callicott, "On the Intrinsic Value of Non-Human Species."

31. See Arthur Schopenhauer, *The World as Will and Idea*, trans. R. B. Haldane and J. Kemp (Garden City, N.Y.: Doubleday, 1961), pp. 297ff.

32. Bryan G. Norton, "Environmental Ethics and Weak Anthropocentrism," *Environmental Ethics* 6 (1984): 131–48.

33. Ibid., p. 136.

34. For a historical analysis see J. Baird Callicott, "Intrinsic Value, Quantum Theory, and Environmental Ethics," *Environmental Ethics* 7 (1985): 257–75.

7

Foundations of Wildlife Protection Attitudes

Eugene C. Hargrove

In "Animal Liberation: A Triangular Affair," J. Baird Callicott distinguishes among *humane moralism*, the ethical position held by proponents of animal rights or liberation; *ethical humanism*, the traditional ethical position opposed to animal rights; and the *land ethic*, an ecologically oriented position based on the writings of Aldo Leopold. He then argues that ethical humanism and humane moralism are merely extensions of "familiar historical positions [that] have simply been retrenched, applied, and exercised" and that only the land ethic, since it is derived from ecological science, represents any significant breakthrough in ethical theory.[1] While I am sympathetic to Callicott's analysis and have learned from it, I do not believe that he has succeeded in showing that the animal rights position, right or wrong, is nothing more than an extension of traditional ethical theory. Both the humane moralists and the ethical humanists, however much they may disagree, do accept that the proposal to replace rationality with sentience as the primary criterion for identifying rights-bearing entities, if accepted, would be a very radical break with traditional theory. It is only as it is seen from the outside, from the standpoint of the land ethic, that the proposal seems too insignificant to be a bold step beyond.

Callicott's claim that ethical humanism and humane moralism have something fundamentally in common in opposition to the land ethic is, however, an important one that can be made fairly easily, I believe, if one turns from theoretical to historical considerations. Both John Passmore, an opponent of animal rights, and Peter Singer, a

151

defender, present historical accounts of the evolution of our attitudes toward animals in support of their theoretical positions, and these accounts, for all practical purposes, are identical.[2] Both agree that in the nineteenth century, attitudes toward animals changed and that it became morally wrong to inflict unnecessary suffering on animals. They disagree only as to how the new moral practice associated with these attitudes should be interpreted theoretically: as a restriction of human rights over animals, as Passmore claims, or as an extension of moral rights to animals, as Singer claims. While these interpretations are, of course, radically different from one another theoretically, they are nonetheless attempts to analyze and justify the *same* moral change, the *same* moral behavior. This is something that not only links them closely but also distinguishes them from the land ethic. Since supporters of the land ethic are not concerned with the suffering of individual animals, they clearly are not trying to interpret the nineteenth-century change in moral practice and attitude on which Passmore and Singer have focused. According to Callicott, pain is neither good nor evil; it is "primarily information": "In animals, it informs the central nervous system of stress, irritation, or trauma in the outlying regions of the organism."[3]

This historical approach to Callicott's distinction among the three views, while effective, points toward a new and unanswered question: If the land ethic has nothing to do with the history of ideas that philosophers like Passmore and Singer are trying to analyze, just what is its historical foundation or background? Callicott is not very helpful here, for, of course, he is not trying to be historical in his approach. When Callicott speaks of history in his article, he is speaking of the history of traditional ethics, not the history of the land ethic. One might suppose that the history is a short one, since Callicott asserts frequently that the land ethic is derived from the science of ecology, which has had a name for only a little over a century and has been a distinct discipline for only a few decades at most. Such a supposition, however, seems to be false, for, as I show, the concern for wildlife protection, but without regard for the suffering of individual animals, predates ecology and even the theory of evolution by more than a half-century.

In making this claim, I am not concerned with undermining Callicott's position that ecology supports the land ethic theoretically. As can be seen in the conflicting interpretations of Passmore and Singer, a theory and the history of ideas associated with it can be independent. Thus even though it may well be that ecology supports the land ethic theoretically and the land ethic can somehow be derived from it, it is probable that our present wildlife protection attitudes would have developed even if ecology and evolution had not become part of biological science.

In this chapter, I show that a history of ideas supports of our modern attitudes toward wildlife, and I argue (1) that the history of ideas does not support the animal rights position or the rights positions occasionally advanced by biologists, naturalists, and environmentalists, (2) that the theory of evolution and the science of ecology did not contribute positively to the establishment of our modern attitudes, and (3) that our attitudes actually emerged from an aesthetic interest in wildlife and nature generally that involved anthropocentric intrinsic value and treated animals as if they were exemplifications of an unusual kind of art.

I do not claim that the account I give is complete. There is, for example, also a legal tradition toward wildlife that is in some ways related and in some ways not. I am concerned with the history of the primary intuitions on which our modern attitudes toward wildlife are based, not the legal history of efforts to protect wild animals. The legal history begins in Europe with the establishment of royal forests and in the United States with a legal dispute, *Martin v. Waddell* (1842), over the right to take oysters out of the Raritan River in New Jersey.[4] My account begins with the American West just after Lewis and Clark's journey across North America and focuses on the attitudes of naturalists studying wildlife on the Upper Missouri River and in the Rocky Mountains. The wildlife of this area was studied and trapped extensively for nearly half a century before significant settlement began, and during this long period of time, significant disagreement over the treatment of wildlife developed between naturalists and trappers.[5] This dispute was made known to the general public in the eastern United States and in Europe by the travel accounts of the naturalists themselves and, I argue, formed the basis for our modern wildlife protection attitudes.

The people discussed in the account that follows were simply expressing attitudes, feelings, or sentiments without any philosophical pretension. They were not trying to formulate or articulate new ethical principles. This presentation, therefore, is intended merely as the starting point for a rational reconstruction that bridges the gap between our nineteenth-century attitudes toward wildlife and our contemporary ones. That reconstruction is the subject of all subsequent sections of this chapter.

The History of Ideas

Primitive tribes often had customs according to which they asked the forgiveness and understanding of wild animals that they killed for food. Such customs or traditions, however, did not survive in Western civilization, in which a tradition of sport killing of wildlife for pleasure, not food, developed instead. The hunter, according to this tradition, derives enjoyment from the killing animals without any feeling of guilt. Although naturalists of the eighteenth and nineteenth centuries did not consider themselves sport hunters, they all seem to have shared with sport hunters a complete lack of remorse when killing animals, an activity that they undertook with even greater frequency than sport hunters, since killing was the standard way to get close enough to an animal to study its properties. This lack of moral concern about the killing of individual animals continued throughout the period in which wildlife protection attitudes developed and continues for the most part among naturalists even today, although killing to study animals is no longer the normal practice in the field.

Occasionally naturalists were moved to sympathy under special circumstances, but these remained exceptions to normal practice. William Bartram, for example, was afflicted by pangs of moral conscience in the eighteenth century while accompanying a hunter who had just killed a bear with a cub.[6] Bartram was not, in principle, opposed to the killing of the adult bear; it was only the cries of the infant that stirred his moral sentiments. Had there been no cub present, Bartram would in all probability have derived some pleasure from the killing of the bear and afterward would have congratulated the hunter on his good marksmanship, not charged him with murder.

The journey of Lewis and Clark in 1804 up the Missouri River and across to the west coast of North America marked a new beginning in the scientific study of wildlife. Virtually any new animal encountered on the trip was shot immediately if Lewis and Clark or their guides and assistants could get within range. Although some of the accounts of these killings, especially the killings of the first grizzly bears, are exciting, there is nothing anywhere in the journals to suggest that Lewis and Clark harbored even the most latent wildlife protection attitudes. Perhaps had they encountered a bear cub, they might have felt a few moral qualms, but they did not and therefore simply had a good time killing and studying animals.

While Lewis and Clark were still on their journey, circumstances on the Upper Missouri changed in a way that affected the attitudes of nearly all subsequent naturalists traveling in the West. Shortly after

Lewis and Clark departed, Manwell Lisa of St. Louis established a fur-trapping company and started up the Missouri, leading the first group of American fur trappers west of the Mississippi. The Lewis and Clark expedition met them as it was returning, and one of the men on the expedition, John Colter, left the party and was hired by Lisa right on the spot.[7] From that time on until after the Civil War, fur trappers were scattered over the Rocky Mountains and up and down the Missouri River. Naturalists encountered them everywhere, and since they used these men as guides and for logistic support, they were almost never out of sight of four or five of them for more than a few minutes. These fur trappers were uneducated people who could neither read nor write and who seldom had any cultured sensitivities. As Osborne Russell, one of the few who could write, notes, "My comrades were men who never troubled themselves about vain and frivolous notions as they called them[;] with them every country was pretty when there was weather and as to beauty of nature or arts it was all 'humbug.'"[8] In general, the lack of scientific and aesthetic appreciation of nature in their guides did not bother the naturalists, except for one bad habit that they all possessed—that of shooting animals indiscriminately for target practice.

The first naturalist to visit the Upper Missouri after the Lewis and Clark expedition was John Bradbury of London, a corresponding member of the Liverpool Philosophical Society and an honorary member of the literary and philosophical societies of New York. Bradbury traveled in the western interior of North America with fur trappers from 1809 to 1811 and published a diary account of his journeys in 1817. Initially Bradbury's moral sentiments about animals seem to be much like those of Bartram. He too is striken with moral trauma when killing a mother bear.[9] Soon, however, Bradbury starts protesting repeatedly the unnecessary shooting of wild animals in general, and his diary begins to express moral indignation independent of any concern for the suffering of the individual animals.

Bradbury's disapproval of the fur trappers' behavior first appears in the following passage:

> Soon after we set out, we saw a great number of buffaloe on both sides of the river, over which several herds were swimming. Notwithstanding all the efforts made by these poor animals, the rapidity of the current brought numbers of them within a few yards of our boats, and three were killed. We might have obtained a great many more, but for once we did not kill *because* it was in our power to do so; but several were killed from Lisa's boat.[10]

Although this is the first mention of the subject in the account, it is clear that Bradbury had been upset about indiscriminate shooting for some time, judging by the use of the words "for once." Other passages of criticism follow: "Mr. Brackenridge joined me in preventing a volley being fired, as it would have been useless, and therefore wanton." And again: "The morning of the next day was very fine: we saw some buffaloe swimming, at which the men fired, contrary to our wishes, as we did not intend to stop for them." By the end of the journey, Bradbury has become so irritated that he is passing judgment over every shot fired by his guides.[11] Bradbury is clearly opposed to the killing of any wild animals on his trip unless the body can be recovered and used. To him, killing animals under any other circumstances is useless or *wanton*—done simply "*because* it was in our power to do so."

One might intuitively expect after Bradbury's trip to find a series of other naturalists lamenting the wanton destruction of wildlife with a gradual but growing awareness that something ought to be done to protect wildlife; in fact, however, the very scientific expedition into the West formally proposed such protection in its official government report. Dr. Edwin James of the Long expedition to the Rocky Mountains (1819–1820) urged in his part of the report that the entire area not be opened to settlement and that it be protected instead as a wildlife preserve. In the introduction to the report James writes: "The traveller who shall at any time have traversed its desolate sands, will, we think, join us in the wish that this region may forever remain the unmolested haunt of the native hunter, the bison, and the jackall." Later, in the main body of the report, he makes the proposed more specifically, in terms that reflect the attitudes of Bradbury:

> It would be highly desirable that some law for preservation of game might be extended to, and rigidly enforced in the country where the bison is still met with; that the wanton destruction of these valuable animals by white hunters might be checked.[12]

James' concern about the "country where the bison is still met with" comes at a point in history when only a handful of fur trappers had as yet gone west and when buffalo hides were of little value in the fur market in the East. Thus his conclusions could not have been based on concern about the actual numbers of buffalo being killed—as would be possible a few years later—and had to be based instead on a general displeasure at seeing the "wanton" destruction of individual animals.

Within ten years, it was possible for naturalists to make calculations about the enormous waste of wildlife through wanton destruction by white and Indian fur trappers. George Catlin, an artist studying Indians on the Upper Missouri during the early 1830s who had some interest in wildlife study (and protection), was one of the first to do so. Catlin is known today as the first American to call for a *"Nation's Park*, containing man and beast, in all the wild and freshness of their nature's beauty." Like Bradbury and James, Catlin too is concerned about the wanton destruction of wildlife, and his call for a national park—acutally echoing James' earlier call—arises out of his desire to protect wildlife from fur trappers:

> This profligate waste of the lives of these noble and useful animals, when from all that I could learn, not a skin or pound of the meat (except the tongue), was brought in, fully supports me in the seemingly extravagant predictions that I have made as to their extinction, which I am certain is near at hand.[13]

As other naturalists ventured into the American West, they too spoke out against the abuse of wildlife. In 1835, Prince Maximilian of Neu-Wied cited statistics similar to Catlin's and accused both the Indians and the fur trappers of endangering the buffalo. In 1839, John K. Townsend, traveling to Oregon, echoed the remarks of all the others, declaring the killing of wildlife by the fur trappers to be "a useless and unwarranted waste of the goods of Providence." As late as 1860, Captain Raynolds of the Raynolds expedition, the last to be guided by fur trappers, reported to Congress "that the wholesale destruction of the buffalo is a matter that should receive the attention of proper authorities" and predicted that "it is more than probable that another generation will witness almost the entire extinction of this noble animal."[14]

The lack of concern for the suffering of individual animals was conveyed in part by the silence of most naturalists about it. In some cases, however, naturalists blaringly omitted mention of it. George Catlin, for example, on one occasion wounded a buffalo and studied its suffering. In a long passage recounting the event, Catlin describes the immense aesthetic pleasure he experienced while admiring the death of the buffalo.[15] Without any feeling of guilt or twinge of conscience, he baits the bull so as to increase the sublimity of its expressions. He finally puts the animal out of its misery, not out of concern for its unnecessary suffering but simply because it is time to go. To Catlin, the death agony was not wanton, since it provided him with an opportunity for making valuable sketches.

Even when naturalists were moved emotionally by the killing of wildlife, the concern usually had nothing to do with the suffering of the individual animal. For example, when Townsend, overcome by his "evil genius and love of sport," committed an act of wanton destruction of his own, putting a ball through the side of a curious antelope following his party, he declared it an "unfeeling, heartless murder" for reasons completely different from those given by Bartram in the case of the bear with cubs.[16] As Townsend stresses, the killing of the antelope would have involved no cruelty if the animal had been needed for food. It was murder only because the act was wanton—that is, because it served no useful purpose. Presumably, had the travelers been in need of food, the antelope would have had no grounds for upbraiding Townsend and could have died satisfied that its death had not been in vain.

In 1872, at a time when the slaughter of the buffalo was at last at its height and the continued existence of the species was finally seriously endangered, Congress passed a bill to establish Yellowstone National Park. Although the purpose of the park was not to protect wildlife, the bill contained a passage directing the Secretary of the Interior to "provide against the wanton destruction of the fish and game for the purpose of merchandise and profit." As the discussion in the *Congressional Globe* indicates, there was strong sentiment in the Senate that the wording was not strong enough, and one Senator offered an amendment that the words "for merchandise or profit" be deleted, thereby prohibiting any killing of wildlife in the park for any purpose. The amendment was withdrawn, but only after the Senator proposing the amendment was reassured that the park was not intended as a "preserve for sporting" and that the powers given to the secretary of the interior would allow him to protect against this possibility as well as Congress could. Killing of animals was to be permitted only for the subsistence of parties traveling through the park.[17]

The inclusion of this passage in the Yellowstone park bill is not considered a legal milestone in the protection of wildlife because it provided no penalties for wanton destruction other than being escorted out of the park.[18] Whatever its legal failings, however, it signifies the existence of widespread public attitudes in favor of the preservation of wildlife in a fairly modern sense. Moreover, the phrase "wanton destruction" leaves no doubt that the introduction of the passage was intended as a partial response to the concerns about wildlife expressed by naturalists over the previous half-century. The naturalists cited in this section were appalled at what they considered the wanton slaughter of wildlife, particularly the buffalo. When they returned to civilization, all of them published reports of their adventures, just as naturalists do today, and these accounts spoke out against the useless slaughter of wildlife. Through these books, the complaints of the naturalists became the basis for a change in public attitude.

Reconstructing the Nineteenth-Century View

While it is clear that a favorable public attitude toward the preservation of wildlife had formed early in the second half of the nineteenth century and that this attitude is traceable directly to the expressed attitudes of naturalists earlier in the century, the justification of this new public attitude was not clear, for in the writings of these naturalists and in the legislation, no justification was given. The situation is comparable to the one faced by philosophers like Passmore and Singer with the other animal protection tradition: A change in attitude took place, but its significance remains a matter of interpretation. Possible foundations for the new attitude include the rights theories of the humane moralists, the ethical humanists, and even the land ethicists; the theory of evolution; and the science of ecology. In this section I show that none of these can account for the early nineteenth-century attitude toward wildlife, and I discuss three other possibilities: a scientific-aesthetic tradition in natural history, the theory of geological uniformitarianism, and the new system of biological and botanical classification developed by Linnaeus in the eighteenth century.

That the naturalist tradition is independent of the rights traditions cited by Passmore and Singer is obvious from the fact that the naturalists are never consistently concerned about the pain and suffering of animals, only about unnecessary (or wanton) killing of animals. If there was a good reason for a particular animal to be killed, the naturalists were indifferent, if not insensitive, to its suffering.

Even in contemporary form, the situation remains the same. For instance, Leopold's reservations about hunting emerged not from a belief that it was wrong to inflict unnecessary suffering on wildlife or that hunting in itself was in any way wrong but rather from a belief that predators killed prey animals more efficiently and kept them under better control ecologically than hunters did.[19] According to contemporary naturalists, people who worry about the pain and suffering of wildlife are victims of what has sometimes been called the "Bambi syndrome." Concern about pain and suffering, in fact, seems to become an issue among naturalists only when they wish to defend predators that kill their victims inefficiently.[20] In many cases, contemporary naturalists and the general public today take immense pleasure in the deaths of prey by predators—finding, for example, the film depiction of these kills a fascinating and aesthetically pleasing presentation appropriate for family viewing any evening on the television sets in their homes.

The naturalist tradition also does not support the claims of some contemporary biologists, such as Norman Myers, David Ehrenfeld, and Paul and Anne Ehrlich (or even Leopold), that animals have a right to exist.[21] As has been noted by a number of ethicists, rights theory focuses on individuals and their interests.[22] In contrast, nineteenth-century and contemporary concern for wildlife among naturalists is centered on the preservation of species and ecosystems, not the interests of the individual animals that make up those species and ecosystems.

I have argued elsewhere that nineteenth-century natural history scientists acquired preservationist attitudes toward nature on aesthetic grounds because of their close association with landscape artists and poets.[23] Briefly, my argument was as follows: In landscape landscape painting and poetry, the general desire that things of beauty be preserved was extended to include objects of beauty in nature, either actually represented in paintings and poetry or capable of being so represented. Natural history scientists—who were in fact studying the properties of nature of special interest to the painters, poets, and landscape gardeners of the time; secondary properties of rationalistic philosophy—developed a common aesthetic attitude toward nature with painters and poets as a result of the artistic training they routinely undertook in order to be able to illustrate their fieldwork. Among scientists with such artistic training, the desire to preserve objectives of beauty in nature was extended to include objects of scientific interest.

Although this position is correct as the general framework within which modern preservationist attitudes arose in the nineteenth century, it cannot explain an important feature of the naturalists' attitude toward wildlife—the concern for preservation of the species without equal concern for the preservation of the lives of the individual animals making up those species. In actuality, my account helps to explain a growing concern for the preservation of material objects of unusual beauty or scientific interest, such as Yosemite and Yellowstone, but does not do justice to the more complex (and peculiar) concern for animals and plants.

It is important to note that concern for the preservation of wildlife did not arise among all natural history scientists, only among those specifically studying living organisms. Although nineteenth-century geologists certainly did develop strong preservationist attitudes, they did not necessarily follow the naturalists in their aversion to the wanton destruction of wildlife. William H. Holmes, for example, both a geologist and an artist who was deeply involved in the exploration and preservation of Yellowstone and the Grand Canyon, despite showing great sensitivity to the wonders of Yellowstone in his field notebooks, is completely casual in his attitude toward the animals living there. As his notes make clear, Holmes automatically attempted to kill any animal that came within range of his rifle. In one passage, written while working in Yellowstone, Holmes writes:

> Aiming at him near as possible at his heart I fired, but the animal turned and disappeared. Following up in the same direction with caution, hoping for still another shot I heard a thumping in the pine bushes and hurrying on was delighted to find the magnificent creature in his death throes.

Preservationist-oriented though he was, Holmes' tendencies toward wanton destruction of wildlife far exceeded those of the fur trappers, whom the naturalists had come to despise. Holmes took positive delight in the deaths of animals, especially bears and, judging by his personal papers, did not improve his attitudes until the 1920s, fifty years later.[24]

One way to account for the enormous difference between geologists and naturalists with regard to animal protection is to conclude that natural history scientists were primarily concerned with preserving the objects of their particular studies—rocks or animals, respectively—but did not generalize this concern beyond their own narrow professional interests. Geologists, not being professionally interested in animals except as decoration along with vegetation on their beloved rocks, failed to become sensitive to the wanton destruction that naturalists saw all around them and sometimes remained insensitive enough to continue as active contributors to that destruction when opportunities arose.

While this explanation has much to commend it, it is possible that theoretical differences in scientific outlook may have had some influence as well. The scientific world view of the natural history scientist in the early nineteenth century, however, does not appear on the surface at least to offer any basis for preservationist attitudes, since the theory of evolution and the science of ecology, both of which are considered central to modern preservationist thought, had not yet appeared on the scene. The places where naturalists studied animals were not ecological units. They were merely, as James put it, "the country where the bison is still met with" or "the unmolested haunt of the native hunter, the bison, and the jackall." The animals that the naturalists studied were simply natural objects that happened contingently to be where they were (probably because that is where God wanted them) and were not elements in a greater natural whole. The animals themselves, moreover, were representatives of species that were fixed and immutable. Thus, with ecology and evolution still largely unthought and unaccepted, there were really only two innovations in natural history science that could possibly have any relevance to preservationist attitudes: uniformitarianism in geology and the standardization of biological classification, following Linnaeus, among naturalists. Unlikely as these may seem as bases for preservationist arguments, the first is, I contend, the initial scientific foundation for all preservationists thinking, and the second accounts for the special features for early wildlife protection attitudes, distinguishing them from the mainstream trends.

Uniformitarianism was a geological theory, first advanced by Hutton at the end of the eighteenth century, that geological changes in the Earth's surface take place slowly: The present is like the past. It is in opposition to an earlier theory, which it eventually replaced, called catastrophism, according to which geological changes take place suddenly and cataclysmically: The present is radically different from the past. Early modern work in geology in the seventeenth century, to the extent that it was not focused on locating mineral deposits, was a quest to find geological evidence to substantiate the biblical account of the creation of the Earth. This research naturally came to be centered on attempts to verify the flood of Noah, a major catastrophic event. Evidence, however, soon suggested not just one catastrophic event but many. Recognition of the fossil remains of extinct species in rock layers, moreover, provided a role for these events—bringing past ages to an end through divine intervention. It was concluded, therefore, that God exterminated all life periodically and unexpectedly and then replaced it with improved versions of the previous animal forms —for how else could the great changes in animal life be explained?

Stephen Jay Gould has pointed out that uniformitarianism transformed geology from a branch of theology into a branch of science.[25] The transformation, however, was not without controversy and debate. As Charles Coulston Gillispie has shown, opposition to uniformitarianism—in support of catastrophism and foreshadowing future controversies over evolution—was focused on the relationship of God, man, and nature:

> In the nineteenth century, unlike the eighteenth century, ortho-
> dox natural theology was more interested in control than design.
> It was chiefly on this account that Huttonian and uniformitarian
> theories were suspect. And on the popularizing level, Combe and
> Chambers were attacked, not because they impunged the divine
> character of the physical universe, which, in fact, they were at-
> tempting to illustrate, but because they held that God's Provi-
> dence, in the social and moral as well as in the organic and in-
> organic spheres, was a system of unvarying law, and that God
> never interfered in its workings.[26]

What uniformitarianism did religiously or theologically was to undermine the idea that God personally and consciously supervised and
carried out the catastrophes that geologists had been studying. The
history of early modern philosophy both illustrates and supports this
role of God. Beginning with Descartes, we find an account of physical
and mental existence that claims that God supervises the interaction
of incompatible kinds of matter, making our hands (physical substance) obey our mental commands (mental substance). Indeed,
Descartes even declares that God sustains everything from one individual moment to the next. Seemingly, if He became distracted for any
one of those moments, we and everything else would completely, if
only momentarily, disappear. This kind of intimacy with God is retained in catastrophism but rejected in uniformitarianism, in which
mindless physical processes are blindly transforming the Earth.

Because an all-powerful and benevolent divine being is the primary geological agent in theological catastrophism, preservationist
attitudes could not develop in connection with a scientific world view
associated with it. Given the immense amount of scientific evidence
that God periodically destroyed the Earth without advance notice, to
have tried to save parts of the Earth for all time would have been presumptuous to say the least, since God might have decided at any
moment to destroy everything, including all human life. Thus preserving the Earth was God's responsibility alone, carried out in accordance with His own plan. Human efforts to intervene were not only inappropriate but pointless.[27]

In terms of uniformitarian geology, however, the situation is very
different. God is not involved at all. The Earth has slowly taken its
current shape as a result of the slow working of uniform physical and
chemical processes over incredible spans of time, which were then

only barely beginning to be grasped. In this case, humans could change the world dramatically for the worse, and the Earth could not be expected to recover naturally in less time than it took for the damaged or destroyed objects to form to begin with, if at all. Thus, although theoretically those physical and chemical processes could reproduce what humans had destroyed, the time was so great that for all practical purposes the natural objects destroyed or damaged were irreplaceable. In this context, nature preservation now makes sense, since human action is significant, and responsible human action can prolong the existence of objects that are aesthetically or scientifically interesting or are needed to maintain human life on the Earth.

Although these connections were made by the middle of the nineteenth century, I do not believe that they had any direct effect on the preservation of wildlife at that time. From our standpoint in the twentieth century, arguments for the preservation of species could be made that are derived from the uniformitarian world view, but they would be in terms of the theory of evolution, which is the biological element of uniformitarianism. In terms of the theory of evolution, one could point out the length of time that was required to create this or that species and the extreme unlikelihood that this or that species could ever come into being again should we humans destroy it. Naturalists from the early nineteenth century, however, could not draw these conclusions for several reasons. First, they had probably never heard of evolution. Second, if they had heard of it, they had probably heard of it as a ridiculous consequence of uniformitarianism, which was supposed to reduce that geological theory to absurdity. Third, they undoubtedly all believed that the species were fixed and immutable.

Thus for lack of any substantive alternative, we are left with only one possibility: Naturalists were actually concerned with preserving the fixed and immutable species of preevolutionary biology. Though this may sound strange at first, it is not, for the species were fixed and immutable only in the sense that members of species could not acquire new properties. The immutability of the species, however, did not in any way guarantee that individual exemplifications of these species would continue to exist on Earth. In the late eighteenth and early nineteenth centuries, there was a growing awareness of the fact that species extinction could and did occur. American naturalists by that time had found dinosaur and mammoth fossil remains that confirmed that some very strange and large animals, which had once roamed the face of North America, had become extinct.[28] They also knew that large numbers of extinctions had occurred in Europe in recent historical times. It is in this context that the naturalists discussed earlier were voicing their objections to the wanton destruction of the buffalo: They do not want species to become extinct.

Today it is possible to express our concern for species protection in a way that is analogous to the concern for large natural objects. Just as natural objects like the Yosemite valley are gradually changing in accordance with the principles of uniformitarian geology, species are gradually changing in accordance with the principles of evolution. As a result, strictly speaking, we are not trying to preserve natural *things* so much as natural *processes*. In terms of fixed and immutable species, however, perhaps the best analogy is the periodic chart of chemistry. In the late nineteenth century, chemists found that chemical elements could be organized into a chart and that the chart could be so arranged that elements with similar properties were repeated throughout the chart in a regular or "periodic" manner. The naturalists were constructing a chart for species along similar lines. This chart was essentially the great chain of being, already obvious in the biological conceptions of Aristotle and used as the background structure for the worldwide species classification project that had been under way since Linnaeus standardized species classification methods in the early eighteenth century. In terms of the belief that species were fixed and immutable, the great chain of being was the periodic chart of elements for plants and animals. Most naturalists in the eighteenth century believed that God had created all possible creatures and that if they looked long and carefully enough, they would eventually find all of these animals and plants somewhere on the Earth's surface. Like the chemist, the naturalist could look forward to the day when all elements in his chart would be identified and studied. The realization that extinctions had occurred and would likely continue to occur, however, changed everything. The great chain of being was no longer a perfect listing of God's creation, for it was full of holes left by species that had ceased to exist on Earth. Moreover, the number of holes was likely to increase, perhaps even before the endangered species could be identified and adequately studied. It was the equivalent in chemistry of a discovery that, as some ancient Greek philosophers had suspected, matter did pop into and out of existence. In this context, the naturalists discovered that they were studying an idea, concept, or classificatory scheme exemplified in the natural world by individual entities that themselves were not very durable. If these individual entities all died, the object of their scientific research became nothing more than the object of memory and imagination. Species classifications became the equivalent of Platonic forms that were no longer formal causes and in which nothing in this world participated.

Seen in this way, the response of the early naturalists calling for wildlife protection was reasonable, even conservative. They understood that the creatures exemplifying the species they were studying also had instrumental value, sometimes even economic value. They therefore did not try to prevent all use of the individual animals, but rather tried to reduce wanton or useless destruction of them. Only in cases where *any* use of these creatures would clearly threaten the species with extinction did they try to prohibit all use. Consider the sequoias, for example. When word of their discovery first arrived and reports of wanton destruction soon followed, preservationist outcries began. When more trees at other locations were found, suggesting that the trees might not be rare at all, preservationist efforts stalled. When final appraisal confirmed that the trees were indeed reasonably rare, preservationist efforts were renewed, culminating in the inclusion of the Mariposa Grove in Yosemite.[29] In the case of the buffalo, rarity was not a factor, but the wanton destruction of the animals was so great that the naturalists became concerned anyway.

Curiously, unlike its geological counterpart, catastrophism, which provides no foundation for nature preservation, the biological concept of the great chain of being composed of fixed and immutable species—dependent, nevertheless, on the maintenance of exemplifications of each species on Earth—actually provides a better, stronger foundation for species preservation than our current concepts of evolution and ecology. In terms of the preevolutionary conception of species, extinction means a permanent gap in the great chain of being. Short of direct intervention by God, there is no way to reinstate individual exemplifications on the planet. In addition, extinction is the destruction by humans of God's work, going all the way back to the beginning of all creation. Thus extinction could be construed as a moral wrong against God. In terms of our evolutionary conception of species, however, there is no chain of being as such, only groups of individual entities, loosely classifiable under species designations, coming and going through time. Species are no longer Platonic, since the properties of a species are changing, evolving. Species may, for example, become extinct not only through evolutionary failure but also through evolutionary success as individual species evolve into new forms. In this conception of species, extinction is normal and natural. Since they are not the direct creations of God, we have not wronged Him if we extinguish all individuals of a species now and then. Moreover, in accordance with the evolutionary conception of species, unlike the preevolutionary one, there is the remote possibility that evolutionary processes could at some distant date reproduce a lost species or at least an adequate substitute.

With the introduction of ecology into the argument, the situation is no better. The loss of a species in an ecosystem is also natural and normal. When a species becomes extinct, the system simply adjusts. Some other creature comes forward and fills the ecological niche left vacant. Thus like evolutionary theory, ecological theory weakens the preservationist case. Since extinctions are natural, they are in principle morally neutral events. Claims that current rates of extinction are unnatural and therefore immoral are also unconvincing, since massive extinctions over short periods of geological time have occurred many times in the past.

In actual practice, however, the move from a fixed to an ecological and evolutionary conception of species has had no such weakening influence on our wildlife protection attitudes. There are apparently two reasons for this: First, a Platonic conception of the species/ individual relation continues to dominate our aesthetic appreciation of wildlife. Second, the new theories did not require any reassessment of value in wildlife preservation.

The Aesthetics of Wildlife Preservation

Nature aesthetics evolved directly out of art aesthetics. Two main lines of development were landscape painting and landscape gardening. The parallel developments in these areas may be characterized as follows: In painting, there was a movement from the appreciation of composed paintings representing imaginary places to an appreciation of paintings accurately representing real places and finally to an appreciation of natural landscapes resembling picturesque paintings.[30] In gardening, there was a movement from improved, composed gardens to ones closely resembling natural landscapes and from plants viewed as building material to entities worthy of study and appreciation in a natural, unimproved state. In both cases, the movement was from the ideal to the actual or real, from the general or universal to the particular or individual, and from the artificial to the natural in such a way that aesthetic appreciation became focused on natural objects and living organisms as objects of interest for their own sake.

To a degree, these aesthetic developments also involved wildlife, since wild animals and plants often found their way into landscape paintings, and wild foreign plants routinely found their way into informal and botanical gardens. As noted earlier, naturalists, as part of their professional training, took art lessons, which provided them with the same general aesthetic perceptions of the artists with whom they trained. Moreover, the properties that they used to classify and identify animals and plants were the same secondary properties that were of special interest to artists and poets: colors, textures, shapes, smells, and the like. Nevertheless, there was no comparable movement aesthetically from the ideal to the real and particular, for the species classification system was composed of ideals in a very straightforward Platonic sense—they were *life* forms, to be sure, but *forms* nonetheless.

To illustrate this point, we do not need to reconstruct the wildlife perceptions of the early naturalists, for the contemporary perceptions of a tourist visiting a natural area or even a zoo are quite sufficient. A person who sees a wild animal for the first time will try to discern the properties that are characteristic of the species the animal represents. Because of the great diversity of appearance among animals of each species, the first sighting of a new animal may be misleading. Only after having seen many specimens will the tourist have an adequately generalized conception of what a member of that particular species should look like. The tourist may decide, upon reflection, that the first animal sighted was a good example, an outstanding one, or a poor one. This is an aesthetic judgment made in terms of a generalized, even idealized listing of essential properties for the species in question.

Phenomenologically, this activity is in most respects identical to the account that Locke, for example, gives concerning the creation of abstract ideas. Indeed, that is exactly what the tourist is doing—finding the properties in individual animals which are essential and putting them together as an idea by which animals encountered in the future can be identified and aesthetically evaluated (a good representative, a poor one, and so on). Once the "abstraction" is complete, the tourist's conception of the species is functionally a Platonic form. Any aesthetic judgment concerning a particular animal involves three elements: the perceiver, the object perceived, and the perceiver's conception of the particular species, the form. The animal is treated aesthetically as if it is supposed to "participate" in the perceiver's conception of the species. Individual differences or irregularities are considered "imperfections": The animal in question may be too large, too small, not quite the right color; there may be something unusual about part of its body, for example, peculiarly shaped ears or horns.

This kind of appreciation is very different from all other nature appreciation, which places great value on diversity and uniqueness. A tourist looking at mountains does not expect all mountains to look alike or judge their beauty in terms of a Platonic ideal for all mountains. The observer wants each mountain to be different, to be an individual, to offer something which he or she has not seen before. To be sure, it is eventually possible for the tourist to adopt a similar view with regard to wild animals with which he or she has become familiar so as to savor the unique qualities of each specimen encountered. In terms of the theory of evolution, for example, the observer may come to see each individual as an attempt in the natural history of the species at innovation and change. In terms of ecology, he or she may see each individual as an attempt to adapt to particular natural conditions. However, I submit, the Platonic idea continues in the background as the framework within which this diversity is appreciated in a way that it does not for natural objects such as mountains.

Value in Wildlife Preservation

The focus on the species, rather than the individual, in both nature appreciation and nature preservation creates interesting problems concerning the value of wildlife. Two kinds of value must be considered. The first is instrumental value. An entity is instrumentally valuable if its existence or use benefits another entity, usually a human being. The second is intrinsic value. An entity has intrinsic value if it is (1) valuable for its own sake or (2) valuable without regard to its use. These kinds of value may, moreover, be either anthropocentric or nonanthropocentric. An anthropocentric value is basically a human value. It is often customary to assume that all anthropocentric values are also instrumental, that is, valuable because they benefit human beings. It is nevertheless possible for values to be anthropocentric and intrinsic. An art object, for example, is appreciated and preserved in terms of human aesthetic values but is not regarded as being valuable instrumentally. Most environmental ethicists, however, have been critical of anthropocentric values of any kind and have attempted to develop some kind of nonanthropocentric value theory that can be used to establish environmental or ecological value independent of human judgment. It is within this framework—instrumental versus intrinsic and anthropocentric verses nonanthropocentric—that the value of wildlife must be sought.

In terms of preuniformitarian geology, in which natural objects are the work of God, nature appreciation, to the degree it existed, could be justified on completely traditional grounds. God could be viewed as an artist and natural objects, even species, as art objects in accordance with divine design. Such objects could be construed as having intrinsic value, since they were beautiful independent of human use, and as being nonanthropocentric, since the standards of beauty were obviously established by God at the time of creation. In terms of uniformitarian geology, nature appreciation could still be regarded as intrinsically valuable, but since appreciation was obviously an acquired taste that was developing with growing scientific interest in nature, it was also anthropocentric, dependent on the way that humans in Western civilization had (very recently) come to value natural objects.

There seem to be two possible ways to ground nature appreciation and nature preservation in nonanthropocentric value. First, in terms of a historical critique of the impact of the primary and secondary distinction of Descartes and Galileo on value theory, one may wish to propose a radical revision of the way in which we perceive the world so that we come to think of values existing in the world as facts do, not just in our heads as a secondary reaction to factual perception. Second, one may wish to ground value in nonhuman entities in terms of their interests and perceptions. In this way, we could conceivably come to speak of the instrumental value of objects to a creature such as a squirrel as well as the intrinsic value of various objects in terms of the squirrel's aesthetic experience. Neither of these approaches, however, can be grounded in a history of ideas connected with wildlife, for in reality they are contemporary criticism, indeed, rejection of the attitudes that form the basis of our wildlife intuitions.[31]

There is, furthermore, a great deal of confusion caused by the two conflicting meanings of *anthropocentric* used in environmental ethics. As already noted, the word is often used to mean "instrumental" and just as often to mean "human" or "conceived in terms of human consciousness." Nonanthropocentrists, on the one hand, thus frequently call for the recognition, or discovery, of nonanthropocentric value so that natural things will no longer be treated in a purely instrumental manner. Anthropocentrists, on the other hand, who do not wish to treat all natural things instrumentally and define the term in the second sense, respond that even if we attribute nonanthropocentric value to nonhuman animals and natural objects, the values will still be anthropocentric or "human," since they are still values created by human valuers.[32]

Bryan Norton has developed what he calls a weak anthropocentric position, which avoids the metaphysical issues involved in nonan-thropocentrism, the search for value independent of the human mind, while also avoiding the perils of strong anthropocentrism, according to which all anthropocentric value is instrumental. In particular, Norton's discussion of societal ideals as the basis for environmental decision making leaves plenty of room for anthropocentric value—human values cherished without regard to their instrumental value or use in terms of human interests.[33] This conception of intrinsic value provides the easiest and most straightforward foundation for nineteenth- and twentieth-century aesthetic interest in wildlife. Although it may eventually be possible to develop a nonanthropocentric conception of intrinsic value that conforms better to current twentieth-century in-stitutions, such a conception would probably still be in conflict with nineteenth-century institutions, since aesthetic values at that time were generally thought of as matters of taste.

Viewed as a matter of taste, our aesthetic appreciation of art object requires anthropocentric intrinsic value of some kind. There are three possibilities: (1) that the anthropocentric intrinsic value is in the object itself, (2) that it is in the aesthetic experience of the ob-ject, or (3) that it is in both the experience and the object itself. The third possibility seems to be the one that best fits our basic aesthetic intuitions and practice. Anthropocentrically, it seems to be correct to say that the value is in the object as long as we do not make a meta-physical claim that the value exists as a property of the object itself. Such an attribution of value to an object does not rule out the possibil-ity that it may also possess intrinsic value nonanthropocentrically. It only means that humans aesthetically consider the object to be valu-able without regard to its use or instrumental value. Whereas an object might be instrumentally valuable as a paperweight, an object intrinsically valued is valuable without regard to such use—that is, its intrinsic value is considered more important than and overrides its instrumental value. (For example, a tool of unusual beauty might be considered too beautiful or "good" to use.) It is also possible for humans to consider the aesthetic contemplation of an art object to be intrinsically valuable. There is nothing wrong with this position either unless it requires that we reject the first position—for example, that we conclude that the art object is merely instrumentally valuable as a trigger for the aesthetic experience. To attribute intrinsic value ex-clusively to the experience demeans the object of the experience by converting it into something that is merely instrumentally valuable. Likewise, it leads to the equally counterintuitive conclusion that the mind itself is merely instrumental to the creation of the intrinsically valuable experience.

The writings of most nature preservationists in the nineteenth century strongly imply that nature is intrinsically valuable aesthetically in this double sense. In the later part of the century, however, another kind of environmentalism, resource conservation, also developed, which tended to treat nature instrumentally. A forest, for example, in accordance with this view of nature, was primarily valuable as a source of wood for various human purposes, not simply as a place for wild animals to roam or for nature lovers to wander. By the turn of the century, many preservationists, following the conservationists, had come to see the aesthetic value of natural objects as an instrumental trigger for the aesthetic experiences of humans. Yosemite, in this value scheme, is not intrinsically valuable as such but rather is instrumentally valuable insofar as it aids in the creation of aesthetic experiences, position two above.

This conversion of natural objects into aesthetic instruments for the production of aesthetic experiences has created a dilemma for policymakers that would not have occurred had the intrinsic/instrumental distinction been retained for both objects and experiences of them. If the object, viewed instrumentally, is damaged by tourists trying to create aesthetic experiences in their minds by exposing themselves to the object, the object becomes expendable and is consumed by the efforts to create these mental states or feelings. For example, cave formations and prehistoric cave paintings can be damaged and destroyed by fungus that grows using the light required for tourist viewing. When such objects are protected by turning out the lights and discontinuing the tours, they are considered to be of intrinsic value. If the tours are continued until the objects are destroyed and the tours are no longer profitable, the value of the objects is instrumental only, as a trigger for intrinsically valuable aesthetic experiences in humans.

The misguided efforts to establish rights for natural objects in this century is a reaction against this conversion of intrinsic value into instrumental value. The best way to resolve the problem, however, is simply to reinstate the intrinsic/instrumental distinction. Such confusion does not occur with art, since art objects are routinely removed from public viewing whenever such viewing starts to damage them. They are not, as our practice demonstrates, simply instrumental triggers to aesthetic experience. If natural objects are once again treated like art objects, as intrinsically valuable entities, the dilemma of whether or not to consume natural beauty disappears. If the direct generation of intrinsically valuable aesthetic experiences threatens to destroy, damage, or consume the natural object, we take whatever steps are necessary to preserve the object, including limiting or terminating visitation. Usually these experiences can be generated indirectly through the contemplation of artistic or photographic reproductions or through the exercise of the imagination without external aid.

If the value is perceived (anthropocentrically or nonanthropocentrically) as being in the object, as in the case of mountains, one preserves the value by preserving the object. While it is true that natural objects are gradually changing in accordance with the principles of uniformitarianism, there is enough permanence or durability in the objects for long-term preservationist efforts (in human time scales) to make sense. This element of impermanence, moreover, is not unique to objects of natural beauty, for art objects are also subject to deterioration over time. If, however, the value of the nature object is in its *use*, as in the case of trees to be used for lumber and paper pulp, the idea of preserving the trees as individuals is inappropriate. Since in such cases the instrumental value takes precedence over whatever intrinsic value the object may have, the practice is to consume the object and, if possible, take steps to ensure that there will be more objects of the same kind to consume in the future on a regular basis.

When one tries to assess the value of wildlife within the context of nature preservation and conservation, difficulties immediately appear, for the protection of species seems to be a problem of nature preservation, while the protection of the animals making up those species is a conservation problem. Just as the mountains are gradually changing in accordance with the principles of uniformitarian geology, the various forms of life are evolving in accordance with the principles of evolution. In this context, long-term preservation efforts make sense, since specific actions can be taken with a high expectation of success. Provided that human beings cooperate, natural catastrophe is the only major threat. Individual wild animals, by contrast, do not endure long enough in terms of preservationist time scales for any efforts at this level to be of much consequence. Their lives are extremely hazardous: Under natural conditions, they may be killed or eaten at almost any time. The only way to be reasonably sure that any particular animals will have an opportunity to live out a full life span is to remove them from their natural habitat and place them in an artifical environment—such as a zoo or a park—where they are safe from predation and other hazards. Medical care, comparable to that provided for human beings, is also a must.

In terms of the intrinsic/instrumental distinction, there are also serious problems. Species, like mountains, seem to be valuable for their own sake, without regard (primarily) to their use. Unlike mountains, however, which do have some instrumental value, species have none at all. As a concept, a species does not really do anything for its member exemplifications, the environment, or human beings. Indeed, as a concept, it certainly does nothing to cause its exemplifications to be or to continue in existence in any Platonic sense. Yet when we look at individual animals from almost any standpoint, they have both intrinsic and instrumental value, and the instrumental value predominates over the intrinsic. This is the case not only from the standpoint of the hunter and the commercial trapper but also from the standpoint of the naturalist, the environmentalist, the ecologist, and the ordinary person seeking aesthetic experience in nature. In each case, there is something of value beyond the individual that it contributes to instrumentally—income, the ecosystem, the species. To think in terms of the intrinsic value of the animal, one must take the position of an animal liberationist of some kind and start worrying about the welfare, interests, and rights of the individual organism, which is contrary to our basic practice as it has evolved over the past several centuries. By common consent among most of those concerned about wildlife, this last position, the only one based on the intrinsic worth of the individual, is the abandonment of proper attitudes toward wildlife in favor of improper sentimentalism. Thus, although the preservation of the species as a life form conforms with the intrinsic value perspective of nature preservation, the preservation of the member animals of the species conforms best with the instrumentalist perspective of nature conservation.

Because the individual animal is valued primarily as a representation of something beyond and distinct from it, the species, we value it in much the same way that we value a reproduction of a painting. However, since we are still much more protective of prints than individual wild animals, perhaps the best analogy is a mass-produced toy, such as a *Star Wars* action figure. The child's interest in the figure is primarily as an exemplification of the design, just as our natural (or cultural) interest in the individual animal is as an exemplification of the species. The child is not interested in preserving the figure for all times, only in using it in various ways in acting out imaginary stories. This use is not necessarily in the best "interest" of the figure, for the child may do things with the figure that eventually cause its head or arm to fall off or completely destroy it—for example, dropping it from a great height, crushing it with a brick, or throwing it in a fire. Likewise, we are interested in using wildlife in ways that are not necessarily in the best interests of the individual animals—hunting them, letting them be eaten by other animals, or letting them starve to death so as to preserve the natural character of the landscape. If the factory stops making *Star Wars* figures or it becomes difficult to obtain them, the child may tend to be more careful during play. If animals belonging to a particular species become rare, more difficult to find or obtain, we may also tend to be more careful in the way we use these particular animals. The analogy seems to break down only in one respect: The animals produce their own replacements in most cases, whereas the figures are produced in a factory. Even this distinction, however, is not absolute, since various species of birds and fish are factory-farm raised and released into the wild to be caught or shot for sport.

Ecology and Evolution Reconsidered

I noted at the beginning of this chapter that the history of ideas out of which an attitude develops may not necessarily have much to do with the justifications that eventually arise to explain it. This is certainly the case with wildlife protection attitudes, which are routinely justified in terms of ecology and evolution even though (1) they developed in terms of a preevolutionary and ecological conception of species as fixed and immutable and (2) were little affected by the new ecological and evolutionary perspectives that replaced that conception. Even today, in fact, the practical influence of the theory of evolution and the science of ecology on our behavior appears to be marginal at best. For example, if we look closely at our own intuitions, we will find, I believe, that we do care more strongly than evolution and ecology really allow. If a species faces extinction, even naturally, it is likely that there will be attempts to preserve the species in some way—for example, in zoos. Even if it is impractical to preserve a large enough population to maintain a healthy gene pool, there will be interest in preserving groups of individuals with an inadequate gene pool. Even if preservation efforts eliminate the natural behavior of the animals, considered by many to be properties of the species, the preservation of individuals lacking natural behavior will still be considered valuable by many people.

The conflict between these intuitions and the demands of the science of ecology or the theory of evolution is brought out rather dramatically in a paper by Callicott on the value of extraterrestrial life.

Extraterrestrial life forms, assuming that they were not of Earthy origin and inoculated somehow on some foreign body, or *vice versa*, would not be our kin—that is, descendants of a common paleontological parent stock—nor would they be participants in Earth's economy of nature or biotic community. Hence, they would lie outside the scope of Leopold's land ethic.

While admitting that in terms of such reflections "the land ethic seems almost parochial in extent and even tribal in nature," Callicott is not especially distrubed, for this parochialism, "Earth chauvinism," "reveals at once its strength for Earth-oriented environmental ethics— which is of course the only variety of environmental ethics with any genuine practical interest or application." But, Callicott asks with some reluctance, what if we do want to attribute some moral significance or status to life forms beyond the ecosystems and evolutionary splendor of the Earth? To muddle through, Callicott recommends a life-principle or reverence-for-life ethics, following Goodpaster or Schweitzer and in terms of the weak anthropocentrism of Norton: "In other words, the life-principle/reverence-for-life ethics are serviceable as extraterrestrial environmental ethics, but, ironically, fail miserably as terrestrial environmental ethics."[34]

To find out just how we behave toward extraterrestrial life, if it exists, we will probably have to wait until we locate some. But certain human reactions seem likely, even predictable. The discovery of creatures not part of our evolutionary history or our ecosystems would be sensationally exciting, provided, of course, that the organism or organisms had some adequate level of internal complexity, some propperties worthy of scientific and aesthetic interest. Assuming a rarity similar to that of sequoias or tube worms in volcanic vents on the floor of the ocean, endangerment of these creatures would certainly bring forth strong preservationist outcries. Contrary to Callicott's intuitions, I suspect that the organisms would be considered more valuable because they were not part of our system or our history than if they were. In this regard, the land ethic, if it could not embrace such creatures, would simply become irrelevant, truly parochial. If evolution and ecology could not support our desire to preserve such creatures, we would revert not to a life-principle or reverence-for-life ethic, but a reverence-for-life-*forms* ethic, the ethic of the naturalists of the early nineteenth century, who sought to preserve species classification, not promote the interests, welfare, or continued existence of individual exemplifications. Eventually, of course, if we looked hard enough and attended properly to subtle observations, we would undoubtedly uncover evolutionary and ecological data on these creatures that would permit the creation of an extraterrestrial land ethic. Should such an ethic come to be formulated, however, it would be very unlikely to displace the older life form ethic, which remains the foundation of concern for species even today, despite the demise of the fixed species theory.

This thought experiment does not mean, of course, that Callicott's position is completely wrong. It is possible, as already noted in the case of animal liberation, for the theoretical justification of culturally evolved intuitions, beliefs, and behavior to be distinct from the history of ideas that produced those intuitions, beliefs, and practices. It is even possible for them to persist without any justification at all. Moreover, it is not necessary that there be just one reason, one justification, to ground these intuitions, beliefs, and practices. There could be several, none of which is sufficient on its own. Each justification could be useful in limited or special contexts. It is even possible for this set of justifications to change dramatically over time. Thus it is remotely possible that we could someday ground our concern for species in terms of some sort of animal liberationist position, assuming that our intuitions, beliefs, and practices change appropriately, perhaps through the persuasion of the animal liberation movement. It is much more likely, however, that we may come to ground them in an ecological perspective. Nevertheless, even this possibility is reasonably remote, for concern for wildlife in terms of its value to ecosystems fails to account for all aspects of our basic contemporary behavior. Thus, as I see it, to adopt an exclusively ecological perspective would require almost as intense a campaign as the animal liberationists would have to undertake for their position. The limitations of a purely ecological justification are evident not only in speculations about our treatment of extraterrestrial life but also, as already noted, in our behavior toward wildlife that has lost its habitat—that is, its ecosystem. If wild animals were valuable only as parts of ecosystems, we would not spend so much time and money preserving them in zoological gardens and parks under artificial and seminatural conditions.

Curiously, the history of ideas that shaped our basic intuitions about wildlife protection has been a movement not through a series of incompatible foundations but rather through a series that has sustained a basic set of intuitions. Although the fixed species theory is incompatible with the evolutionary view of species and perhaps with their role in ecological systems, all three of these supported a common view of wildlife as instrumentally valuable entities serving as a means to some greater intrinsically valuable end—maintaining the great chain of being, continuing the natural evolution of species, or preserving the health and natural functioning of various ecosystems. Moving from the fixed species perspective to the evolutionary to the ecological, wildlife has been consistently regarded as something instrumentally valuable in a sense that is independent of the specific value of the individual animals living at any given moment. This instrumentalist approach to wildlife, moreover, has been remarkably compatible with non-environmental uses of wildlife. Since wild animals are entities that have instrumental status from the standpoints of both environmentalists and their opponents, wildlife preservation and conservation have been able to coexist with sport and subsistence hunting, even with trapping to a large degree. As long as there are enough of each kind to support the needs of the given ecosystems and the needs of trappers and hunters, on the one hand, and to preserve the life form classifications in such a way that many exemplifications are able to exhibit natural behavior and lead natural lives, on the other, serious problems do not arise. What we end up with is a layering of perspectives that all have a role in producing and justifying our basic ethical beliefs and behavior toward wild animals.

What ties all these perspectives together and reduces the conflict between them is the aesthetic element in both the concern for and the appreciation of wild animals. Aside from subsistence hunting and commercial trapping, human interest in wildlife is fundamentally aesthetic. Although, as I argue, wild animals are not straightforwardly regarded as aesthetic objects analogous to art objects, they are a key ingredient in various kinds of human experiences that are aesthetic in a broad sense. As I have already noted, aesthetic and scientific interests in nature overlap significantly. Scientists and nature lovers frequently have aesthetic experiences through the study of nature—and wildlife is a fundamental element in such study. Sport hunting, like other forms of outdoor recreation, likewise has its aesthetic component. These various perspectives provide additional dimensions, almost a kind of depth. From the standpoint of these perspectives, it is possible to admire wildlife in terms of their evolutionary history, as exemplifications of unique life forms, as worthy opponents and/or trophies, and as fundamental elements in healthy ecosystems—without having to choose between these viewpoints. Given that none of these perspectives allows for the intrinsic value of individual animals to outweigh their instrumental value to something else, thereby nearly closing the door on the animal liberationist, grounding our wildlife intuitions, beliefs, and practices in such (anthropocentric) aesthetic experience seems to be the best approach—one that takes into account not only those intuitions, beliefs, and practices as they are now understood by most people but also the history of ideas that produced them.

Notes

1. J. Baird Callicott, "Animal Liberation: A Triangular Affair," *Environmental Ethics* 2 (1980): 319-21. Chapter 2, this volume.

2. John Passmore, "The Treatment of Animals," *Journal of the History of Ideas* 36 (1975): 195-218; Peter Singer, *Animal Liberation: A New Ethics for Our Treatment of Animals* (New York: Avon Books, 1977), ch. 5.

3. Callicott, "Animal Liberation." p. 332 (p. 55, this volume).

4. Michael J. Bean, *The Evolution of National Wildlife Law* (Washington, D.C.: U.S. Government Printing Office, 1977), pp. 8-10.

5. For detailed accounts of the scientific exploration of the American West and its settlement, see William H. Goetzmann, *Exploration and Empire: The Explorer and the Scientist in the Winning of the American West* (New York: Knopf, 1966), and Richard A. Bartlett, *The New Country: A Social History of the American Frontier, 1776–1890* (London: Oxford University Press, 1974).

6. William Bartram, *Travels of William Bartram*, ed. Mark Van Doren (New York: Dover Publications, 1955), p. 22.

7. Goetzmann, *Exploration and Empire*, pp. 17-19.

8. Osborne Russell, *Journal of a Trapper*, ed. Aubrey L. Haines (Lincoln: University of Nebraska Press), p. 63.

9. John Bradbury, *Travels in the Interior of America* (Ann Arbor: University of Michigan Microfilms, 1966), p. 35.

10. Ibid., p. 108.

11. Ibid., pp. 182, 183, 198.

12. Edwin James, "James' Account of S. H. Long's Expedition, 1819-20," in *Early Western Travels, 1748–1864*, ed., Reuben G. Thwaites (Cleveland: Arthur H. Clark Co., 1904-06), vol. 14, p. 20; vol. 15, pp. 256-57.

13. George Catlin, *Letters and Notes on the Manners, Customs, and Conditions of the North American Indians* (New York: Dover Publications), vol. 1, pp. 262, 256-57.

14. Prince Maximilian of Neu-Wied, *Travels in the Interior of North America*, in *Early Western Travels*, vol. 22, p. 379; John K. Townsend, "Narra-

tive of a Journey across the Rocky Mountains to the Columbia River," in *Early Western Travels*, vol. 21, p. 170; William F. Raynolds, "Report on the Exploration of the Yellowstone and the Country Drained by That River," U.S. Congress, Senate, 40th Cong., 2nd Sess., *Senate Executive Document*, No. 77 (1868), p. 11.

15. Catlin, *Letters and Notes*, p. 26-27.

16. Townsend, "Narrative," in *Early Western Travels*, vol. 21, p. 178.

17. U.S., *Statutes at Large*, vol. 17 (1871-1872), ch. 24, pp. 32-33; U.S. Congress, Senate, *Congressional Globe*, 42d Cong., 2d Sess., 1 (January 30, 1872), p. 697.

18. Penalties for hunting and poaching were not provided until 1894. See U.S., *Statutes at Large*, vol. 28 (1893-1894), ch. 72, p. 73. Congress did not act until a poaching incident in the park was publicized in an issue of *Forest and Stream* magazine. See Hiram Martin Chittenden, *The Yellowstone National Park*, ed. Richard A. Bartlett (Norman: University of Oklahoma Press, 1964), pp. 121-125; Aubrey L. Haines, *The Yellowstone Story* (Yellowstone, Wyo.: Yellowstone Library and Museum Association and Colorado Associated University Press, 1977), vol. 2, pp. 54-64.

19. This is the main point of Susan L. Flader's book, *Thinking like a Mountain: Aldo Leopold and the Evolution of an Ecological Attitude toward Deer, Wolves, and Forests* (Columbia: University of Missouri Press, 1974).

20. For example, in Africa, hyenas, wild dogs, and jackals eat their prey alive using a method called "rapid disembowelment" rather than the method of suffocation used by larger predators. Since the victim displays a great deal more pain behavior in the former than in the latter, these smaller predators frequently develop bad reputations. In their defense, Jane Goodall writes:

> We still hate to watch it and yet, though it seems longer at the time, the victim is usually dead within a couple of minutes and undoubtedly in such a severe state of shock that it cannot feel much pain. Indeed, lions, leopards and cheetahs, which have the reputation of being "clean killers," often take ten minutes or more to suffocate their victims, and who are we to judge which is the more painful way to die? And so we do not join the ranks of those who condemn hyenas and wild dogs as vicious brutes that should be ruthlessly exterminated, for they kill in order to eat and to live in the only way for which evolution has fitted them.

Hugo and Jane van Lawick-Goodall, *Innocent Killers* (New York: Ballantine Books, 1970), pp. 17-18.

21. Norman Myers, *The Sinking Ark* (Oxford: Pergamon Press, 1979), p. 46; David Ehrenfeld, *The Arrogance of Humanism* (New York: Oxford University Press, 1978), pp. 207-9; Paul and Anne Ehrlich, *Extinction* (New York:

Random House, 1981), p. 48; Aldo Leopold, "The Land Ethic," in *A Sand County Almanac, and Sketches Here and There* (New York: Oxford University Press, 1949), p. 204. In *A Wealth of Wild Species: Storehouse for Human Welfare* (Boulder, Colo.: Westview Press, 1983), Myers, seeing the practical weaknesses of his rights position, retracted it, replacing it with radical instrumentalist argumentation stressing the value of wildlife to the production of toothpaste and other commercial household products.

22. See Richard A. Watson, "Self-consciousness and the Rights of Nonhuman Animals and Nature," *Environmental Ethics* 1 (1979): 99–129; Bryan G. Norton, "Environmental Ethics and Nonhuman Rights," *Environmental Ethics* 4 (1982): 17–36. Chapters 1 and 3 this volume.

23. Eugene C. Hargrove, *Foundations of Environmental Ethics* (Englewood Cliffs: Prentice-Hall 1989), ch. 3.

24. William H. Holmes, Random Records, Smithsonian Institution, vol. 3, "Survey of the Yellowstone, Part 2, 1878," random note 101, p. 19; "Survey of the Yellowstone Park in Two Parts, Part I, 1872," r.n. 28, p. 17, and r.n. 27, 16; vol. 2, sec. 3, "Episodes and Adventures: 1872-1930": "The Bear Story," r.n. 16-17, and "Bear Adventure in Yellowstone Park—1872," r.n. 34.

25. Stephen Jay Gould, "Is Uniformitarianism Necessary?" *American Journal of Science* 263 (1965): 223-28.

26. Charles Coulston Gillispie, *Genesis and Geology* (New York: Harper & Row, 1959), p. 226.

27. I came to realize the importance of catatastrophism as an inhibition to preservationist concern while studying the attitudes of Clarence King, the first head of the U.S. Geological Survey. Although King had an appropriate asethetic and scientific interest in nature and was influential in promoting landscape painting and photography, his concern for the preservation of nature was lackluster. In the chapter on Yosemite in his book, *Mountaineering in the Sierra Nevada* (Lincoln: University of Nebraska Press, 1970), King has very little to say in praise of the decision to preserve the Yosemite valley: "By Act of Congress the Yosmite Valley had been segregated from the public domain, and given—'donated,' as they call it—to the State of California, to be held inalienable for all time as a public pleasure-ground" (p. 134). The reason for his lack of enthusiasm, it turns out, was his belief in catastrophism. King simply could not accept the idea that land could be held "inalienable for all time" by "Act of Congress." While working for the California Geological Survey, King wrote:

I have read in revelations of the passing away of the earth and all the beauty and grandeur of it. I read too of a new Heaven and a new earth beautiful in type. Well, then, if this is transitory why study so hard into all the intricate mazes of facts, which will be swept away and known no more. I have looked for lessons. I have believed that God created all with design[,] that all was a lesson [and] that lessons were taught in nature which were not elsewhere.

(Clarence King Papers, Huntington Library, D23, "Journal of Trip in Northern Sierras, Grass Valley, Northern Survey," p. 26). Since King does not believe that scientific principles will continue to hold true beyond the next catastrophe, there is even less chance from his point of view of Yosemite's enduring inalienably "for all time" by act of Congress. Thus his comment in *Mountaineering* is properly read with sarcasm, not just with regard to the idea that the United States could "donate" the valley but that the nation could preserve it for all time.

28. See Loren Eisely, *Darwin's Century* (Garden City, N.Y.: Anchor Books/Doubleday, 1961), pp. 5–10.

29. In August 1958, the American Association for the Advancement of Science met in Albany, New York, and took an official stand on the preservation of the "famous fir-trees of California, the *Abils donglassei*." According to Chester Dewey, who spoke on behalf of the trees, "The attention of the Association is called to the fact that these trees are being exterminated as the settlement of the country advances. But twenty-five of them, we are informed, are now left standing in the States, and they are not to be found but in one place." The AAAS resolved that "this matter be referred to Professor Henry, of the Smithsonian Institution, with the request that he correspond, in behalf of this Association, with the authorities of California or at Washington, in relation to the preservation of these trees; or take such other course as may seem more effective." See *Proceedings of the American Association for the Advancement of Science*, Tenth Meeting (New York: Putnam, 1857), pt. 2, p. 239. Although there appears to be no record of the action Henry took, the resolution was well known in California only a few months later. J. E. Clayton, a mining engineer for John Frémont, immediately thereafter made known his discovery of three other groves of trees, promising to count the trees the next time he visited them. See *California Farmer*, 7 (November 1856): 1. The original letter, dated October 30, 1856, is preserved in the Huntington Library.

30. The connection with painted landscapes still remains. A scenic view, for example, is a point from which a tourist may view a collection of natural objects in a way that would most closely approximate the composition of a painting. The tourist at the scenic view will often pace back and forth so as to "get a better view"—that is, to compose the objects better.

31. As Birch and Cobb have noted, nonanthropocentric value in nonhumans actually calls for a position very similar to the one according to which animals have rights: "The intrinsic value of experience confers rights." See Charles Birch and John Cobb, Jr., *The Liberation of Life* (Cambridge: Cambridge University Press, 1981), p. 205. Matters are not much improved if we reject the view that the animals have rights but nevertheless conclude that

they have interests that we *ought* to respect, for we still treat animals in a manner that is counterintuitive to our current practice. For example, see Robin Attfield, *The Ethics of Environmental Concern* (New York: Columbia University Press, 1983), pp. 150–51, 156–60, where he argues that "the class of things with moral standing does not extend beyond that of individuals with a good of their own. Thus when species count it is because of their individual members" (p. 156).

32. See J. Baird Callicott, "Non-anthropocentric Value Theory and Environmental Ethics," *American Philosophical Quarterly* 21 (1984): 299–309. Callicott writes (p. 299):

> An anthropocentric value theory (or axiology), by common consensus, confers intrinsic value on human beings and regards all other things, including other forms of life, as being only instrumentally valuable, i.e., valuable only to the extent that they are means of instruments which may serve human beings. A non-anthropocentric value theory (or axiology), on the other hand, would confer intrinsic value on some non-human beings.

33. Bryan G. Norton, "Environmental Ethics and Weak Anthropocentrism," *Environmental Ethics* 6 (1984): 131–48. Norton himself creates some confusion by insisting that his weak anthropocentrism allows one to forgo the search for intrinsic value altogether. This is potentially confusing, since, of course, Norton cannot reject anthropocentric (noninstrumental) intrinsic value, as conceived by a human valuer, without collapsing into the strong position, according to which all anthropocentric value is instrumental. For a similar approach involving standards of moral character, see Thomas E. Hill, Jr., "Ideals of Human Excellence and Preserving Natural Environments," *Environmental Ethics* 5 (1983): 211–24.

34. J. Baird Callicott, "Moral Considerability and Extraterrestrial Life," in *Beyond Spaceship Earth: Environmental Ethics and the Solar System*, ed. Eugene C. Hargrove (San Francisco: Sierra Club Books, 1986), pp. 246–53 (pp. 143–46, this volume).

8

The Rights of the Nonhuman World

Mary Anne Warren

Western philosophers have typically held that human beings are the only proper objects of human moral concern. Those who speak of *duties* generally hold that we have duties only to human beings (or perhaps to God), and that our apparent duties towards animals, plants and other nonhuman entities in nature are in fact indirect duties to human beings.[1] Those who speak of moral *rights* generally ascribe such rights to human beings.

This strictly homocentric (human-centered) view of morality is currently challenged from two seemingly disparate directions. On the one hand, environmentalists argue that because humanity is only one part of the natural world, an organic species in the total, interdependent, planetary biosystem, it is necessary for consistency to view all of the elements of that system, and not just its human elements, as worthy of moral concern—in themselves, and not only because of their usefulness to us. The ecologist Aldo Leopold was one of the first and most influential exponents of the view that not only human beings, but plants, animals and natural habitats, have moral rights. We need, Leopold argued, a new ethical system that will deal with our relationships not only with other human individuals and with human society, but also with the land, and its nonhuman inhabitants. Such a "land ethic" would seek to change "the role of *Homo sapiens* from conqueror of the land community to plain member and citizen of it".[2] It would judge our interaction with the nonhuman world as "right when it tends to preserve the integrity, stability, and beauty of the biotic community", and "wrong when it tends otherwise."[3]

On the other hand, homocentric morality is attacked by the

185

so-called animal liberationists, who have argued, at least as early as the eighteenth century (in the Western tradition), that insofar as (some) nonhuman animals are sentient beings, capable of experiencing pleasure and pain,[4] they are worthy in their own right of our moral concern.[5] On the surface at least, the animal liberationist ethic appears to be quite different from that of ecologists such as Leopold. The land ethic is *wholistic* in its emphasis: it treats the good of the biotic *community* as the ultimate measure of the value of individual organisms or species, and of the rightness or wrongness of human actions. In contrast, the animal-liberationist ethic is largely inspired by the utilitarianism of Jeremy Bentham and John Stuart Mill.[6] The latter tradition is individualist in its moral focus, in that it treats the needs and interests of individual sentient beings as the ultimate basis for conclusions about right and wrong.

These differences in moral perspective predictably result in differences in the emphasis given to specific moral issues. Thus, environmentalists treat the protection of endangered species and habitats as matters for utmost concern, while, unlike many of the animal liberationists,[7] they generally do not object to hunting, fishing or rearing animals for food, so long as these practices do not endanger the survival of certain species or otherwise damage the natural environment. Animal liberationists, on the other hand, regard the inhumane treatment or killing of animals which are raised for meat, used in scientific experimentation and the like, as just as objectionable as the killing or mistreatment of "wild" animals.[8] They oppose such practices not only because they may sometimes lead to environmental damage, but because they cause suffering or death to sentient beings.

Contrasts such as these have led some philosophers to conclude that the theoretical foundations of the Leopoldian land ethic and those of the animal-liberationist movement are fundamentally incompatible,[9] or that there are "intractable practical differences" between them.[10] I shall argue on the contrary, that a harmonious marriage between these two approaches is possible, provided that each side is prepared to make certain compromises. In brief, the animal liberationists must recognize that although animals do have significant moral rights, these rights are not precisely the same as those of human beings; and that part of the difference is that the rights of animals may sometimes be overriden, for example, for environmental or utilitarian reasons, in situations where it would not be morally acceptable to override human rights for similar reasons. For their part, the environmentalists must recognize that while it may be acceptable, as a legal or rhetorical tactic, to speak of the rights of trees or mountains,[11] the logical foundations of such rights are quite different from those of the rights of human and other sentient beings. The issue is of enormous importance for moral philosophy, for it centres upon the theoretical basis for the ascription of moral rights, and hence bears directly upon such disputed cases as the rights of (human) foetuses, children, the comatose, the insane, etc. Another interesting feature is the way in which utilitarians and deontologists often seem to exchange sides in the battle—the former insist upon the universal application of the principle that to cause unnecessary pain is wrong, while the latter refuse to apply that principle to other than human beings, unless there are utilitarian reasons for doing so.

In section I I will examine the primary line of argument presented by the contemporary animal-rights advocates, and suggest that their conclusions must be amended in the way mentioned above. In section II I will present two arguments for distinguishing between the rights of human beings and those of (some) nonhuman animals. In section III I will consider the animal liberationists' objection that any such distinction will endanger the rights of certain "nonparadigm" human beings, for example, infants and the mentally incapacitated. In section IV I will reply to several current objections to the attempt to found basic moral rights upon the sentience, or other psychological capacities, of the entity involved. Finally, in section V, I will examine the moral theory implicit in the land ethic, and argue that it may be formulated and put into practice in a manner which is consistent with the concerns of the animal liberationists.

1. Why (Some) Animals Have (Some) Moral Rights

Peter Singer is the best known contemporary proponent of animal liberation. Singer maintains that all sentient animals, human or otherwise, should be regarded as morally equal; that is, that their interests should be given equal consideration. He argues that sentience, the capacity to have conscious experiences such as pain or pleasure, is "the only defensible boundary of concern for the interests of others".[12] In Bentham's often-quoted words, "the question is not, Can they reason? nor, Can they talk? but Can they suffer?"[13] To suppose that the interests of animals are outside the scope of moral concern is to commit a moral fallacy analagous to sexism or racism, a fallacy which Singer calls *speciesism*. True, women and members of "minority" races are more *intelligent* than (most) animals—and almost certainly no less so than white males—but that is not the point. The point does not concern these complex capabilities at all. For, Singer says, "The claim to equality does not depend on intelligence, moral capacity, physical strength, or similar matters of fact."[14]

As a utilitarian, Singer prefers to avoid speaking of moral *rights*, at least insofar as these are construed as claims which may sometimes override purely utilitarian considerations.[15] There are, however, many other advocates of animal liberation who do maintain that animals have moral rights, rights which place limitations upon the use of utilitarian justifications for killing animals or causing them to suffer.[16] Tom Regan, for example, argues that if all or most human beings have a right to life, then so do at least some animals.[17] Regan points out that unless we hold that animals have a right to life, we may not be able to adequately support many of the conclusions that most animal liberationists think are important, for example, that it is wrong to kill animals painlessly to provide human beings with relatively trivial forms of pleasure.[18]

This disagreement between Singer and Regan demonstrates that there is no single well-defined theory of the moral status of animals which can be identified as *the* animal liberationist position. It is clear, however, that neither philosopher is committed to the claim that the moral status of animals is completely identical to that of humans. Singer points out that his basic principle of equal *consideration* does not imply identical *treatment*.[19] Regan holds only that animals have *some* of the same moral rights as do human beings, not that *all* of their rights are necessarily the same.[20]

Nevertheless, none of the animal liberationists have thus far provided a clear explanation of how and why the moral status of (most) animals differs from that of (most) human beings; and this is a point which must be clarified if their position is to be made fully persuasive. That there is such a difference seems to follow from some very strong moral intuitions which most of us share. A man who shoots squirrels for sport may nor may not be acting reprehensibly; but it is difficult to believe that his actions should be placed in *exactly* the same moral category as those of a man who shoots women, or black children, for sport. So too it is doubtful that the Japanese fishermen who slaughtered dolphins because the latter were thought to be depleting the local fish populations were acting quite *as* wrongly as if they had slaughtered an equal number of their human neighbours for the same reason.

Can anything persuasive be said in support of these intuitive judgments? Or are they merely evidence of unreconstructed speciesism? To answer these questions we must consider both certain similarities and certain differences between ourselves and other animals, and then decide which of these are relevant to the assignment of moral rights. To do this we must first ask just what it means to say that an entity possesses a certain moral right.

There are two elements of the concept of a moral which are crucial for our present purposes. To say that an entity, X, has a moral right to Y (some activity, benefit or satisfaction) is to imply at least the following:

1. that it would be morally wrong for any moral agent to intentionally deprive X of Y without some sufficient justification;

2. that this would be wrong, at least in part, *because of the (actual or potential) harm which it would do to the interests of X.*

On this (partial) definition of a moral right, to ask whether animals have such rights is to ask whether there are some ways of treating them which are morally objectionable because of the harm done to the animals themselves, and not merely because of some *other* undesirable results, such as damaging the environment or undermining the moral character of human beings. As Regan and other animal liberationists have pointed out, the arguments for ascribing at least some moral rights to sentient nonhuman animals are very similar to the arguments for ascribing those same rights to sentient human beings.[21] If we argue that human beings have rights not to be tortured, starved or confined under inhumane conditions, it is usually by appealing to our knowledge that they will suffer in much the same ways that we would under like circumstances. A child must learn that other persons (and animals) can experience, for example, pain, fear or anger, on the one hand; pleasure or satisfaction, on the other, in order to even begin to comprehend why some ways of behaving towards them are morally preferable to others.

If these facts are morally significant in the case of human beings, it is attractive to suppose that they should have similar significance in the case of animals. Everything that we know about the behaviour, biology and neurophysiology of, for instance, nonhuman mammals, indicates that they are capable of experiencing the same basic types of physical suffering and discomfort as we are, and it is reasonable to suppose that their pleasures are equally real and approximately as various. Doubts about the sentience of other animals are no more plausible than doubts about that of other human beings. True, most animals cannot use human language to *report* that they are in pain, but the vocalizations and "body language" through which they *express* pain, and many other psychological states, are similar enough to our own that their significance is generally clear.

But to say this is not yet to establish that animals have moral rights. We need a connecting link between the premise that certain ways of treating animals cause them to suffer, and the conclusion that such actions are *prima facie* morally wrong, that is, wrong unless proven otherwise. One way to make this connection is to hold that it is a *self-evident truth* that the unnecessary infliction of suffering upon any sentient being is wrong. Those who doubt this claim may be accused (perhaps with some justice) of lacking empathy, the ability to "feel with" other sentient beings, to comprehend the reality of their experience. It may be held that it is possible to regard the suffering of animals as morally insignificant only to the extent that one suffers from blindness to "the ontology of animal reality";[22] that is, from a failure to grasp the fact that they are centres of conscious experience, as we are.

This argument is inadequate, however, since there may be those who fully comprehend the fact that animals are sentient beings, but who still deny that their pains and pleasures have any direct moral significance. For them, a more persuasive consideration may be that our moral reasoning will gain in clarity and coherence if we recognize that the suffering of a nonhuman being is an evil of the same general sort as that of a human being. For if we do not recognize that suffering is an intrinsic evil, something which ought not to be inflicted deliberately without just cause, then we will not be able to fully understand why treating *human beings* in certain ways is immoral.

Toturing human beings, for example, is not wrong merely because it is illegal (where it is illegal), or merely because it violates some implicit agreement amongst human beings (though it may). Such legalistic or contractualistic reasons leave us in the dark as to why we *ought* to have, and enforce, laws and agreements against torture. The essential reason for regarding torture as wrong is that it *hurts*, and that people greatly prefer to avoid such pain—as do animals. I am not arguing, as does Kant, that cruelty to animals is wrong because it causes cruelty to human beings, a position which consequentalists often endorse. The point, rather, is that unless we view the deliberate infliction of needless pain as inherently wrong we will not be able to understand the moral objection to cruelty of *either* kind.

It seems we must conclude, therefore, that sentient nonhuman animals have certain basic moral rights, rights which they share with all beings that are psychologically organized around the pleasure/

pain axis. Their capacity for pain gives them the right that pain not be intentionally and needlessly inflicted upon them. Their capacity for pleasure gives them the right not to be prevented from pursuing whatever pleasures and fulfillments are natural to creatures of their kind. Like human rights, the rights of animals may be overriden if there is a morally sufficient reason for doing so. What *counts* as a morally significant reason, however, may be different in the two cases.

2. Human and Animal Rights Compared

There are two dimensions in which we may find differences between the rights of human beings and those of animals. The first involves the *content* of those rights, while the second involves their strength; that is, the strength of the reasons which are required to override them.

Consider, for instance, the right to liberty. The *human* right to liberty precludes imprisonment without due process of law, even if the prison is spacious and the conditions of confinement cause no obvious physical suffering. But it is not so obviously wrong to imprison animals, especially when the area to which they are confined provides a fair approximation of the conditions of their natural habitat, and a reasonable opportunity to pursue the satisfactions natural to their kind. Such conditions, which often result in an increased lifespan, and which may exist in wildlife sanctuaries or even well-designed zoos, need not frustrate the needs or interests of animals in any significant way, and thus do not clearly violate their rights. Similarly treated human beings, on the other hand (e.g., native peoples confined to prison-like reservations), do tend to suffer from their loss of freedom. Human dignity and the fulfillment of the sorts of plans, hopes and desires which appear (thus far) to be uniquely human, require a more extensive freedom of movement than is the case with at least many nonhuman animals. Furthermore, there are aspects of human freedom, such as freedom of thought, freedom of speech and freedom of political association, which simply do not apply in the case of animals.

Thus, it seems that the human right to freedom is more extensive; that is, it precludes a wider range of specific ways of treating human beings than does the corresponding right on the part of animals. The argument cuts both ways, of course. *Some* animals, for example, great whales and migratory birds, may require at least as much physical freedom as do human beings if they are to pursue the satisfactions natural to their kind, and this fact provides a moral argument against keeping such creatures imprisoned.[23] And even chickens may suffer from the extreme and unnatural confinement to which they are subjected on modern "factory farms." Yet it seems unnecessary to claim for *most* animals a right to a freedom quite as broad as that which we claim for ourselves.

Similar points may be made with respect to the right to life. Animals, it may be argued, lack the cognitive equipment to value their lives in the way that human beings do. Ruth Cigman argues that animals have *no* right to life because death is no misfortune for them.[24] In her view, the death of an animal is not a misfortune, because animals have no desires which are *categorical;* that is which do not "merely presuppose being alive (like the desire to eat when one is hungry), but rather answer the question whether one wants to remain alive."[25] In other words, animals appear to lack the sorts of long-range hopes, plans, ambitions and the like, whhich give human beings such a powerful interest in continued life. Animals, it seems, take life as it comes and do not specifically desire that it go on. True, squirrels store nuts for the winter and deer run from wolves; but these may be seen as instinctive or conditioned responses to present circumstances, rather than evidence that they value life as such.

These reflections probably help to explain why the death of a sparrow seems less tragic than that of a human being. Human lives, one might say, have greater intrinsic value, because they are worth more *to their possessors*. But this does not demonstrate that no nonhuman animal has *any* right to life. Premature death may be a less *severe* misfortune for sentient nonhuman animals than for human beings, but it is a misfortune nevertheless. In the first place, it is a misfortune in that it deprives them of whatever pleasures the future might have held for them, regardless of whether or not they ever *consciously anticipated* those pleasures. The fact that they are not here afterwards, to *experience* their loss, no more shows that they have not lost anything than it does in the case of humans. In the second place, it is (possibly) a misfortune in that it frustrates whatever future-oriented desires animals *may* have, unbeknownst to us. Even now, in an age in which apes have been taught to use simplified human languages and attempts have been made to communicate with dolphins and whales, we still know very little about the operation of nonhuman minds. We know much too little to assume that nonhuman animals never consciously pursue relatively distant future goals. To the extent that they do, the question of whether such desires provide them with *reasons for living* or merely *presuppose* continued life, has no satisfactory answer, since they cannot contemplate these alternatives—or, if they can, we have no way of knowing what their conclusions are. All we know is that the more intelligent and psychologically complex an animal is, the more *likely* it is that it possesses specifically future-oriented desires, which would be frustrated even by *painless* death.

For these reasons, it is premature to conclude from the apparent intellectual inferiority of nonhuman animals that they have no right to life. A more plausible conclusion is that animals do have a right to life but that it is generally somewhat weaker than that of human beings. It is, perhaps, weak enough to enable us to justify killing animals when we have no other ways of achieving such vital goals as feeding or clothing ourselves, or obtaining knowledge which is necessary to save human lives. Weakening their right to life in this way does not render meaningless the assertion that they have such a right. For the point remains that *some* serious justification for the killing of sentient nonhuman animals is always necessary; they may not be killed merely to provide amusement or minor gains in convenience.

If animals' rights to liberty and life are somewhat weaker than those of human beings, may we say the same about their right to *happiness;* that is, their right not to be made to suffer needlessly or to be deprived of the pleasures natural to their kind? If so, it is not immediately clear why. There is little reason to suppose that pain or suffering are any less unpleasant for the higher animals (at least) than they are for us. Our large brains *may* cause us to experience pain more intensely than do most animals, and *probably* cause us to suffer more from the anticipation or remembrance of pain. These facts might tend to suggest that pain is, on the whole, a worse experience for us than for them. But it may also be argued that pain may be *worse* in some respects for nonhuman animals, who are presumably less able to distract themselves from it by thinking of something else, or to comfort themselves with the knowledge that it is temporary. Brigid Brophy points out that "pain is likely to fill the sheep's whole capacity for experience in a way it seldom does in us, whose intellect and imagination can create breaks for us in the immediacy of our sensations."[26]

The net result of such contrasting considerations is that we cannot possibly claim to know whether pain is, on the whole, worse for us than for animals, or whether their pleasures are any more or any less intense than ours. Thus, while we may justify assigning them a somewhat weaker right to life or liberty, on the grounds that they desire these goods less intensely than we do, we cannot discount their rights to freedom from needlessly inflicted pain or unnatural frustration on the same basis. There may, however, be *other* reasons for regarding all of the moral rights of animals as somewhat less stringent than the corresponding human rights.

A number of philosophers who deny that animals have moral rights point to the fact that nonhuman animals evidently lack the capacity for moral autonomy. Moral autonomy is the ability to act as a moral agent; that is, to act on the basis of an understanding of, and adherence to, moral rules or principles. H. J. McCloskey, for example, holds that "it is the capacity for moral autonomy... that is basic to the possibility of possessing a right."[27] McCloskey argues that it is inappropriate to ascribe moral rights to any entity which is not a moral agent, or *potentially* a moral agent, because a right is essentially an entitlement granted to a moral agent, licensing him or her to *act* in certain ways and to *demand* that other moral agents refrain from interference. For this reason, he says, "Where there is no possibility of [morally autonomous] action, potentially or actually... and where the being is not a member of a kind which is normally capable of [such] action, we withhold talk of rights."[28]

If moral autonomy—or being *potentially* autonomous, or a member of a kind which is *normally* capable of autonomy—is a necessary condition for having moral rights, then probably no nonhuman animal can qualify. For moral autonomy requires such probably uniquely human traits as "the capacity to be critically self-aware, manipulate concepts, use a sophisticated language, reflect, plan, deliberate, choose, and accept responsibility for acting."[29]

But why, we must ask, should the capacity for autonomy be regarded as a precondition for possessing moral rights? Autonomy is clearly crucial for the *exercise* of many human moral or legal rights, such as the right to vote or to run for public office. It is less clearly relevant, however, to the more basic human rights, such as the right to life or to freedom from unnecessary suffering. The fact that animals, like many human beings, cannot *demand* their moral rights (at least not in the words of any conventional human language) seems irrelevant. For, as Joel Feinberg points out, the interests of non-morally autonomous human beings may be defended by others, for example, in legal proceedings; and it is not clear why the interests of animals might not be represented in a similar fashion.[30]

It is implausible, therefore, to conclude that because animals lack moral autonomy they should be accorded *no moral rights whatsoever*. Nevertheless, it may be argued that the moral autonomy of (most) human beings provides a second reason, in addition to their more extensive interests and desires, for according somewhat *stronger* moral rights to human beings. The fundamental insight behind contractualist theories of morality[31] is that, for morally autonomous beings such as ourselves, there is enormous mutual advantage in the adoption of a moral system designed to protect each of us from the harms that might otherwise be visited upon us by others. Each of us ought to accept and promote such a system because, to the extent that others also accept it, we will all be safer from attack by our fellows, more likely to receive assistance when we need it, and freer to engage in individual as well as cooperative endeavours of all kinds.

Thus, it is the possibility of *reciprocity* which motivates moral agents to extend *full and equal* moral rights, in the first instance, only to other moral agents. I respect your rights to life, liberty and the pursuit of happiness in part because you are a sentient being, whose interests have intrinsic moral significance. But I respect them as *fully equal to my own* because I hope and expect that you will do the same for me. Animals, insofar as they lack the degree of rationality necessary for moral autonomy, cannot agree to respect our interests as equal in moral importance to their own, and neither do they expect or demand such respect from us. Of course, domestic animals may expect to be fed, etc. But they do not, and cannot, expect to be treated as moral equals, for they do not understand that moral concept or what it implies. Consequently, it is neither pragmatically feasible nor morally obligatory to extend to them the same *full and equal* rights which we extend to human beings.

Is this a speciesist conclusion? Defenders of a more extreme animal-rights position may point out that this argument, from the lack of moral autonomy, has exactly the same form as that which has been used for thousands of years to rationalize denying equal moral rights to women and members of "inferior" races. Aristotle, for example, argued that women and slaves are naturally subordinate beings, because they lack the capacity for moral autonomy and self-direction;[32] and contemporary versions of this argument, used to support racist or sexist conclusions, are easy to find. Are we simply repeating Aristotle's mistake, in a different context?

The reply to this objection is very simple: animals, unlike women and slaves, really *are* incapable of moral autonomy, at least to the best of our knowledge. Aristotle certainly *ought* to have known that women and slaves are capable of morally autonomous action; their capacity to use moral language alone ought to have alerted him to this likelihood. If comparable evidence exists that (some) nonhuman animals are moral agents we have not yet found it. The fact that some apes (and, possibly, some cetaceans) are capable of learning radically simplified human languages, the terms of which refer primarily to objects and events in their immediate environment, in no way demonstrates that they can understand abstract moral concepts, rules or principles, or use this understanding to regulate their own behaviour.

On the other hand, this argument implies that if we *do* discover that certain nonhuman animals are capable of moral autonomy (which is certainly not impossible), then we ought to extend full and equal moral rights to those animals. Furthermore, if we someday encounter extraterrestrial beings, or build robots, androids or supercomputers which function as self-aware moral agents, then we must extend full and equal moral rights to these as well. Being a member of the human species is not a necessary condition for the possession of full "human" rights. Whether it is nevertheless a *sufficient* condition is the question to which we now turn.

3. The Moral Rights of Nonparadigm Humans

If we are justified in ascribing somewhat different, and also somewhat stronger, moral rights to human beings than to sentient but non-morally autonomous animals, then what are we to say of the rights of human beings who happen not to be capable of moral autonomy, perhaps not even potentially? Both Singer and Regan have argued that if any of the superior intellectual capacities of normal and mature human beings are used to support a distinction between the moral status of *typical*, or paradigm, human beings, and that of animals, then consistency will require us to place certain "nonparadigm" humans, such as infants, small children and the severely retarded or incurably brain damaged, in the same inferior moral category.[33] Such a result is, of course, highly counterintuitive.

Fortunately, no such conclusion follows from the autonomy argument. There are many reasons for extending strong moral rights to nonparadigm humans; reasons which do not apply to most nonhuman animals. Infants and small children are granted strong moral rights in part because of their *potential* autonomy. But *potential* autonomy, as I have argued elsewhere,[34] is not in itself a sufficient reason for the ascription of full moral rights; if it were, then not only human foetuses (from conception onwards) but even ununited human sperm-egg pairs would have to be regarded as entities with a right to life the equivalent of our own—thus making not only abortion, but any intentional failure to procreate, the moral equivalent of murder. Those who do not find this extreme conclusion acceptable must appeal to reasons other than the *potential* moral autonomy of infants and small children tc explain the strength of the latter's moral rights.

One reason for assigning strong moral rights to infants and children is that they possess not just *potential* but *partial* autonomy, and it is not clear how much of it they have at any given moment. The fact that, unlike baby chimpanzees, they are already learning the things which will enable them to *become* morally autonomous, makes it likely that their minds have more subtleties than their speech (or the lack of it) proclaims. Another reason is simply that most of us tend to place a very high value on the lives and well-being of infants. Perhaps we are to some degree "programmed" by nature to love and protect them; perhaps our reasons are somewhat egocentric; or perhaps we value them for their potential. Whatever the explanation, the fact that we do feel this way about them is in itself a valid reason for extending to them stronger moral and legal protections than we extend to nonhuman animals, even those which may have just as well or better-developed psychological capacities.[35] A third, and perhaps the most important, reason is that if we did *not* extend strong moral rights to infants, far too few of them would ever *become* responsible, morally autonomous adults; too many would be treated "like animals" (i.e., in ways that it is generally wrong to treat even animals), and would consequently become socially crippled, antisocial or just very unhappy people. If any part of our moral code is to remain intact, it seems that infants and small children *must* be protected and cared for.[36]

Analagous arguments explain why strong moral rights should also be accorded to other nonparadigm humans. The severely retarded or incurably senile, for instance, may have no potential for moral autonomy, but there are apt to be friends, relatives or other people who care what happens to them. Like children, such individuals may have more mental capacities than are readily apparent. Like children, they are more apt to achieve, or return to moral autonomy if they are valued and well cared for. Furthermore, any one of us may someday become mentally incapacitated to one degree or another, and we would all have reason to be anxious about our own futures if such incapacitation were made the basis for denying strong moral rights.[37]

There are, then, sound reasons for assigning strong moral rights even to human beings who lack the mental capacities which justify the general distinction between human and animal rights. Their rights are based not only on the value which they themselves place upon their lives and well-being, but also on the value which other human beings place upon them.

But is this a valid basis for the assignment of moral rights? Is it consistent with the definition presented earlier, according to which X may be said to have a moral right to Y only if depriving X of Y is *prima facie* wrong *because of the harm done to the interests of X*, and not merely because of any further consequences? Regan argues that we cannot justify the ascription of stronger rights to nonparadigm humans than to nonhuman animals in the way suggested, because "what underlies the ascription of rights to any given X is that X has value independently of anyone's valuing X."[38] After all, we do not speak of expensive paintings or gemstones as having rights, although many people value them and have good reasons for wanting them protected.

There is, however, a crucial difference between a rare painting and a severely retarded or senile human being; the latter not only has (or may have) value for other human beings but *also* has his or her own needs and interests. It may be this which leads us to say that such individuals have intrinsic value. The sentience of nonparadigm humans, like that of sentient nonhuman animals, gives them a place in the sphere of rights holders. So long as the moral rights of all sentient beings are given due recognition, there should be no objection to providing some of them with *additional* protections, on the basis of our interests as well as their own. Some philosophers speak of such additional protections, which are accorded to X on the basis of interests other than X's own, as *conferred* rights, in contrast to *natural* rights, which are entirely based upon the properties of X itself.[39] But such "conferred" rights are not necessarily any weaker or less binding upon moral agents than are "natural" rights. Infants, and most other nonparadigm humans have the *same* basic moral rights that the rest of us do, even though the reasons for ascribing those rights are somewhat different in the two cases.

4. Other Objections to Animal Rights

We have already dealt with the primary objection to assigning *any* moral rights to nonhuman animals; that is, that they lack moral autonomy, and various other psychological capacities which paradigm humans possess. We have also answered the animal liberationists' primary objection to assigning somewhat *weaker*, or less-extensive rights to animals; that is, that this will force us to assign similarly inferior rights to nonparadigm humans. There are two other objections to animal rights which need to be considered. The first is that the claim that animals have a right to life, or other moral rights, has absurd consequences with respect to the natural relationship *among* animals. The second is that to accord rights to animals on the basis of their (differing degrees of) sentience will introduce intolerable difficulties and complexities into our moral reasoning.

Opponents of animal rights often accuse the animal liberationists of ignoring the realities of nature, in which many animals survive only by killing others. Callicott, for example, maintains that, whereas environmentally aware persons realize that natural predators are a vital part of the biotic community, those who believe that animals have a right to life are forced to regard all predators as "merciless, wanton, and incorrigible murderers of their fellow creatures."[40] Similarly, Ritchie asks whether, if animals have rights, we are not morally obligated to "protect the weak among them against the strong? Must we not put to death blackbirds and thrushes because they feed n worms, or (if capital punishment offends our humanitarianism) starve them slowly by permanent captivity and vegetarian diet?"[41]

Such a conclusion would of course be ridiculous, as well as wholly inconsistent with the environmental ethic. However, nothing of the sort follows from the claim that animals have moral rights. There are two independently sufficient reasons why it does not. In the first place, nonhuman predators are not moral agents, so it is absurd to think of them as wicked, or as *murdering* their prey. But this is not the most important point. Even if wolves and the like *were* moral agents, their predation would still be morally acceptable, given that they generally kill only to feed themselves, and generally do so without inflicting prolonged or unnecessary suffering. If we have the right to eat animals in order to avoid starvation, then why shouldn't animals have the right to eat one another for the same reason?

This conclusion is fully consistent with the lesson taught by the ecologists, that natural predation is essential to the stability of biological communities. Deer need wolves, or other predators, as much as the latter need them; without predation they become too numerous and fall victim to hunger and disease, while their overgrazing damages the entire ecosystem.[42] Too often we have learned (or failed to learn) this lesson the hard way, as when the killing of hawks and other predators produces exploding rodent populations—which must be controlled, often in ways which cause further ecological damage. The control of natural predators may *sometimes* be necessary, for example, when human pressures upon the populations of certain species become so intense that the latter cannot endure continued *natural* predation. (The controversial case of the wolves and caribou in Alaska and Canada may or may not be one of this sort.) But even in such cases it is preferable, from a environmentalist perspective, to reduce human predation enough to leave room for natural predators as well.

Another objection to assigning moral rights to sentient nonhuman animals is that it will not only complicate our own moral system, but introduce seemingly insoluble dilemmas. As Ritchie points out, "Very difficult questions of casuistry will ... arise because of the difference in grades of sentience."[43] For instance, is it morally worse to kill and eat a dozen oysters (which are at most minimally sentient) or one (much more highly sentient) rabbit? Questions of this kind, considered in isolation from any of the practical circumstances in which they might arise, are virtually unanswerable. But this ought not to surprise us, since similarly abstract questions about the treatment of human beings are often equally unanswerable. (For instance, would it be worse to kill one child or to cause a hundred to suffer from severe malnutrition?)

The reason such questions are so difficult to answer is not just that we lack the skill and knowledge to make such precise comparisons of interpersonal or interspecies utility, but also that these questions are posed in entirely unrealistic terms. Real moral choices rarely depend entirely upon the comparison of two abstract quantities of pain or pleasure deprivation. In deciding whether to eat molluscs or mammals (or neither or both) a human society must consider *all* of the predictable consequences of each option, for example, their respective impacts on the ecology or the economy, and not merely the individual interests of the animals involved.

Of course, other things being equal, it would be morally preferable to refrain from killing *any* sentient animal. But other things are never equal. Questions about human diet involve not only the rights of individual animals, but also vital environmental and human concerns. On the one hand, as Singer points out, more people might be better fed if food suitable for human consumption were not fed to meat-producing animals.[44] On the other hand, a mass conversion of humanity to vegetarianism would represent "an increase in the efficiency of the conversion of solar energy from plant to human biomass,"[45] with the likely result that the human population would continue to expand and, in the process, to cause greater environmental destruction than might occur otherwise. The issue is an enormously complex one, and cannot be solved by any simple appeal to the claim that animals have (or lack) certain moral rights.

In short, the ascription of moral rights to animals does not have the absurd or environmentally damaging consequences that some philosophers have feared. It does not require us to exterminate predatory species, or to lose ourselves in abstruse speculations about the relative degrees of sentience of different sorts of animals. It merely requires us to recognize the interests of animals as having intrinsic moral significance; as demanding some consideration, regardless of whether or not human or environmental concerns are also involved. We must now consider the question of how well the animal rights theory meshes with the environmental ethic, which treats not only animals but plants, rivers and other nonsentient elements of nature as entities which may demand moral consideration.

5. Animal Liberation and the Land Ethic

The fundamental message of Leopold's land ethic, and of the environmentalist movement in general, is that the terrestrial biosphere is an integrated whole, and that humanity is a part of that natural order, wholly dependent upon it and morally responsible for maintaining its integrity.[46] Because of the wholistic nature of biotic systems, it is impossible to determine the value of an organism simply by considering its individual moral rights: we must also consider its relationship to other parts of the system. For this reason, some philosophers have concluded that the theoretical foundations of the environmentalist and animal liberation movements are mutually contradictory.[47] Alastair Gunn states: "Environmentalism seems incompatible with the Western obsession with individualism, which leads us to resolve questions about our treatment of animals by appealing to the essentially atomistic, competitive notion of rights."[48]

As an example of the apparent clash between the land ethic and the ascription of rights to animals, Gunn points to the situation on certain islands off the coast of New Zealand, where feral goats, pigs and cats have had to be exterminated in order to protect indigenous species and habitats, which were threatened by the introduced species. "Considered purely in terms of rights," he says, "it is hard to see how this could be justified. [For,] if the goats, etc. are held to have rights, then we are violating these rights in order perhaps to save or increase a rare species."[49]

I maintain, on the contrary, that the appearance of fundamental contradiction between the land ethic and the claim that sentient nonhuman animals have moral rights is illusory. If we were to hold that the rights of animals are *identical to those of human beings*, then we would indeed be forced to conclude that it is wrong to eliminate harmful introduced species for the good of the indigenous ones or of the ecosystem as a whole—just as wrong as it would be to exterminate all of the human inhabitants of North America who are immigrants, however greatly this might benefit the native Americans and the natural ecology. There is no inconsistency, however, in the view that animals have a significant right to life, but one which is somewhat more easily overriden by certain kinds of utilitarian or environmental considerations than is the human right to life. On this view, it is wrong to kill animals for trivial reasons, but not wrong to do so when there is no other way of achieving a vital goal, such as the preservation of threatened species.

Another apparent point of inconsistency between the land ethic and the animal liberation movement involves the issue of whether sentience is a *necessary*, as well as *sufficient*, condition for the possessions of moral rights. Animal liberationists sometimes maintain that it is, and that consequently plants, rivers, mountains and other elements of nature which are not themselves sentient (though they may *contain* sentient life forms) cannot have moral rights.[50] Environmentalists, on the other hand, sometimes argue for the ascription of moral rights to even the nonsentient elements of the biosphere.[51] Does this difference represent a genuine contradiction between the two approaches?

One argument that it does not is that the fact that a particular entity is not accorded moral rights does not imply that there are no sound reasons for protecting it from harm. Human health and survival alone requires that we place a high value on clean air, unpolluted land, water and crops, and on the maintenance of stable and diverse natural ecosystems. Furthermore, there are vital scientific, spiritual, aesthetic and recreational values associated with the conservation of the natural world, values which cannot be dismissed as luxuries which benefit only the affluent portion of humanity.[52] Once we realize how *valuable* nature is, it may seem immaterial whether or not we also wish to speak of its nonsentient elements as possessing moral *rights*.

But there is a deeper issue here than the precise definition of the term "moral rights." The issue is whether trees, rivers and the like ought to be protected *only* because of their value to us (and to other sentient animals), or whether they also have *intrinsic* value. That is, are they to be valued and protected because of what they are, or only because of what they are good for? Most environmentalists think that the natural world is intrinsically valuable, and that it is therefore wrong to wantonly destroy forests, streams, marshes and so on, even where doing so is not *obviously* inconsistent with the welfare of human beings. It is this conviction which finds expression in the claim that even nonsentient elements of nature have moral rights. Critics of the environmental movement, on the other hand, often insist that the value of the nonhuman world is purely instrumental, and that it is only sentimentalists who hold otherwise.

John Passmore, for instance, deplores "the cry... for a new morality, a new religion, which would transform man's attitude to nature, which would lead us to believe that it is *intrinsically* wrong to destroy a species, cut down a tree, clear a wilderness."[53] Passmore refers to such a call for a nonhomocentric morality as "mystical rubbish."[54] In his view, nothing in the nonhuman world has *either* intrinsic value or moral rights. He would evidently agree with William F. Baxter, who says that "damage to penguins, or to sugar pines, or geological marvels is, without more, simply irrelevant.... Penguins are important [only] because people enjoy seeing them walk about the rocks."[55]

This strictly instrumentalist view of the value of the nonhuman world is rejected by animal liberationists and environmentalists alike. The animal liberationists maintain that the sentience of many nonhuman animals constitutes a sufficient reason for regarding their needs and interests as worthy of our moral concern, and for assigning them certain moral rights. Sentience is, in this sense, a sufficient condition for the possession of intrinsic value. It does not follow from this that it is also a *necessary* condition for having intrinsic value. It may be a necessary condition for having individual moral *rights;* certainly it is necessary for *some* rights, such as the right not to be subjected to unnecessary pain. But there is room to argue that even though mountains and trees are not subject to pleasure or pain, and hence do not have rights of the sort we ascribe to sentient beings, nevertheless they have intrinsic value of another sort, or for another reason.

What sort of intrinsic value might they have? The environmentalists' answer is that they are valuable as organic parts of the natural whole. But this answer is incomplete, in that it does not explain why we ought to value the natural world *as a whole*, except insofar as it serves our own interests to do so. No clear and persuasive answer to this more basic question has yet been given. Perhaps, as Thomas Auxter has suggested, the answer is to be found in a teleological ethic of the same general sort of that of Plato or Aristotle, an ethic which urges us "to seek the highest good, which is generally understood as the most perfect or complete state of affairs possible."[56] This most perfect or complete state of affairs would include "a natural order which encompasses the most developed and diverse types of beings,"[57] one in which "every species finds a place... and... the existence and functioning of any one species is not a threat to the existence and functioning of any other species".[58]

It is not my purpose to endorse this or any other philosophical explanation of why even the nonsentient elements of nature should be regarded as having intrinsic value. I want only to suggest that better answers to this question can and should be developed, and that there is no reason to presume that these answers will consist entirely of "mystical rubbish." Furthermore, I would suggest that the claim that mountains and forests have intrinsic value of *some* sort is intuitively much more plausible than its denial.

One way to test your own intuitions, or unformulated convictions, about this claim is to consider a hypothetical case of the following sort. Suppose that a virilent virus, developed by some unwise researcher, has escaped into the environment and will inevitably extinguish all animal life (ourselves included) within a few weeks. Suppose further that this or some other scientist has developed another virus which, if released, would destroy all plant life as well, but more slowly, such that the effects of the second virus would not be felt until after the last animal was gone. If the second virus were released *secretly*, its release would do no further damage to the well-being of any sentient creature; no one would suffer, even from the knowledge that the plant kingdom is as doomed as we are. Finally, suppose that it is known with certainty that sentient life forms would never re-evolve on the earth (this time from plants), and that no sentient aliens will ever visit the planet and grieve over its lifeless condition. The question is would it be morally preferable, in such a case, *not* to release the second virus, even secretly? If we tend to think it would be, that it would certainly be better to allow the plants to survive us than to render the earth utterly lifeless (except perhaps for the viruses), then we do not really believe that it is only sentient—let alone only human—beings which have intrinsic value.

This being the case, it is relatively unimportant whether we say that even nonsentient natural entities may have moral *rights*, or whether we say only that, because of their intrinsic value, they ought to be protected, even at some cost to certain interests. Nevertheless, there is an argument for preferring the latter way of speaking. It is that nonsentient entities, not being subject to pleasure or pain, and lacking any preferences with respect to what happens to them, cannot sensibly be said to have *interests*. The Gulf Stream or the south wind may have value because of their role in the natural order, but if they were to be somehow altered or destroyed, *they* would not experience suffering, or lose anything which it is in *their* interest to have. Thus, "harming" them would not be wrong *in and of itself*, but rather because of the kinds of environmental efforts which the land ethic stresses. In contrast, harm done to a sentient being has moral significance even if it has no further consequences whatsoever.

The position at which we have arrived represents a compromise between those animal liberationists who hold that only sentient beings have *either* intrinsic value or moral rights, and those environmentalists who ascribe *both* intrinsic value and moral rights to even the nonsentient elements of nature. Mountains and trees should be protected not because they have moral rights, but because they are intrinsically—as well as instrumentally—valuable.

So stated, the land ethic is fully compatible with the claim that individual sentient animals have moral rights. Indeed, the two positions are complementary; each helps to remedy some of the apparent defects of the other. The animal liberation theory, for instance, does not in itself explain why we ought to protect not only *individual* animals, but also threatened *species* of plants as well as animals. The land ethic, on the other hand, fails to explain why it is wrong to inflict needless suffering or death even upon domestic animals, which may play little or no role in the maintenance of natural ecosystems, or only a negative role. Practices such as rearing animals in conditions of severe confinement and discomfort, or subjecting them to painful experiments which have no *significant* scientific purpose, are wrong primarily because of the suffering inflicted upon individual sentient beings, and only secondarily because of any social environmental damage they may incidentally cause.

Thus, it is clear that as we learn to extend our moral concern beyond the boundaries of our own species we shall have to take account of both the rights of individual animals *and* the value of those elements of the natural world which are not themselves sentient. Respecting the interests of creatures who, like ourselves, are subject to pleasure and pain is in no way inconsistent with valuing and protecting the richness, diversity and stability of natural ecosystems. In many cases, such as the commercial slaughter of whales, there are both environmental and humane reasons for altering current practices. In other cases, in which humane and environmental considerations appear to point in opposite directions (e.g., the case of the feral goats on the New Zealand islands) these factors must be weighed against each other, much as the rights of individual human beings must often be weighed against larger social needs. In no case does a concern for the environment preclude *also* considering the rights of individual animals; it may, for instance, be possible to trap and deport the goats alive, rather than killing them.

6. Summary and Conclusion

I have argued that the environmentalist and animal liberationist perspectives are complementary, rather than essentially competitive or
mutually inconsistent approaches towards a nonhomocentric moral
theory. The claim that animals have certain rights, by virtue of their
sentience, does not negate the fact that ecosystems are complexly
unified wholes, in which one element generally cannot be damaged
without causing repercussions elsewhere in the system. If sentience is
a necessary, as well as sufficient, condition for having moral rights,
then we cannot ascribe such rights to oceans, mountains and the like;
yet we have a moral obligation to protect such natural resources from
excessive damage at human hands, both because of their value to us
and to future generations, and because they are intrinsically valuable
as elements of the planetary biosystem. It is not necessary to choose
between regarding biological communities as unified systems, analagous to organisms, and regarding them as containing many individual
sentient creatures, each with its own separate needs and interests; for
it is clearly both of these things at once. Only by *combining* the
environmentalist and animal rights perspectives can we take account
of the full range of moral considerations which ought to guide our
interactions with the nonhuman world.

Notes

1. See, for instance, Immanuel Kant, "Duties to Animals and Spirits," in
Lectures on Ethics, trans. Louis Infield (New York: Harper and Row, 1964),
excerpted in *Animal Rights and Human Obligations*, ed. Tom Regan and
Peter Singer (Englewood Cliffs, N.J.: Prentice-Hall, 1976), pp. 122-23.

2. Aldo Leopold, *A Sand County Almanac* (New York: Oxford University Press, 1949), p. 204.

3. Ibid., p. 225.

4. Here, as elsewhere in this paper, the terms "pleasure" and "pain"
should not be understood in the narrow sense in which they refer only to particular sorts of *sensation*, but rather as an abbreviated way of referring to the
fulfillment or frustration, respectively, of the needs, interests and desires of
sentient beings.

5. See, for example, the selections by Jeremy Bentham, "A Utilitarian
View"; John Stuart Mill, "A Defence of Bentham"; and Henry S. Salt, "The
Humanities of Diet," "Animal Rights," and "The Logic of the Larder," in *Animal*

Rights, ed. Regan and Singer.

6. Ibid.

7. See, Maureen Duffy, "Beasts for Pleasure," in *Animals, Men and Morals,* ed. Stanley and Rosalind Godlovitch (New York: Taplinger Publishing Co., 1972), pp. 111-24.

8. See, Stephen R. L. Clark, *The Moral Status of Animals* (Oxford: Clarendon Press, 1977); Tom Regan, "Animal Rights, Human Wrongs," *Environmental Ethics* 2, no. 2 (Summer 1980): 99-120; Richard Ryder, "Experiments on Animals," in *Animal Rights,* ed. Regan and Singer, pp. 33-47; and Peter Singer, *Animal Liberation: A New Ethics for Our Treatment of Animals* (New York: Avon, 1975), especially chaps. 2 and 3.

9. J. Baird Callicott, "Animal Liberation: A Triangular Affair", *Environmental Ethics* 2, no. 4 (Winter 1980): 315 (p. 40, this volume).

10. Ibid., p. 337.

11. See Christopher D. Stone, *Should Trees Have Standing? Toward Legal Rights for Natural Objects* (Los Altos, Calif.: William Kaufman, 1974).

12. Singer, *Animal Liberation,* p. 9.

13. Jeremy Bentham, *The Principles of Morals and Legislation* (1789), chap. 18, sec. 1; cited by Singer, *Animal Liberation,* p. 8.

14. Singer, *Animal Liberation,* p. 5.

15. Peter Singer, "The Fable of the Fox," *Ethics* 88, no. 2 (January 1978): 122.

16. See, for instance, Brigid Brophy, "In Pursuit of a Fantasy," in *Animals, Men and Morals,* pp. 125-45; Joel Feinberg, "The Rights of Animals and Unborn Generations," in *Philosophy and Environmental Crisis,* ed. William T. Blackstone (Athens, Ga.: University of Georgia Press, 1974), pp. 43-68; Roslind Godlovitch, "Animals and Morals," in *Animals, Men and Morals,* pp. 156-71; Lawrence Haworth, "Rights, Wrongs and Animals," *Ethics* 88, no. 2 (January 1978): 95-105; Anthony J. Povilitis, "On Assigning Rights to Animals and Nature," *Environmental Ethics* 2 (Spring 1980): 67-71; and Tom Regan, "Do Animals Have a Right to Life?" in *Animal Rights,* ed. Regan and Singer, pp. 197-204.

17. Regan, "Right to Life?"

18. Ibid., p. 203.

19. Singer, *Animal Liberation,* p. 3.

20. Regan, "Right to Life?"; see also, idem, "An Examination and Defence of One Argument Concerning Animal Rights," *Inquiry* 22, nos. 1-2 (1979):

189–217.

21. Regan, "Right to Life?" p. 197.

22. T. L. S. Sprigge, "Metaphysics, Physicalism, and Animal Rights", *Inquiry* 22, nos. 1–2 (1979): 101.

23. See John C. Lilly, *Lilly on Dolphins* (New York: Anchor Books, Garden City, 1975), p. 210. Lilly, after years of experimenting with dolphins and attempting to communicate with them, concluded that keeping them captive was wrong because they, like us, suffer from such confinement.

24. Ruth Cigman, "Death, Misfortune, and Species Inequality," *Philosophy and Public Affairs* 10, no. 1 (Winter 1981): p. 48.

25. Ibid., pp. 57–58. The concept of a categorical desire is introduced by Bernard Williams, "The Makropoulous Case," in his *Problem of the Self* (Cambridge: Cambridge University Press, 1973).

26. Brophy, "Pursuit of Fantasy," p. 129.

27. H. J. McCloskey, "Moral Rights and Animals," *Inquiry* 22, nos. 1–2 (1979): 31.

28. Ibid., p. 29.

29. Michael Fox, "Animal Liberation: A Critique," *Ethics* 88, no. 2 (January 1978): 111.

30. Feinberg, "Rights," pp. 46–47.

31. Such as that presented by John Rawls, *A Theory of Justice* (Oxford: Oxford University Press, 1972).

32. Aristotle *Politics* 1. 1254, 1260, and 1264.

33. Singer, *Animal Liberation*, pp. 75–76; Regan, "One Argument Concerning Animal Rights".

34. Mary Anne Warren, "Do Potential People Have Moral Rights," *Canadian Journal of Philosophy* 7, no. 2 (June 1977): 275–89.

35. This argument does not, as one might suppose, justify placing restrictions upon (early) abortions which are as severe as the restrictions upon infanticide or murder, although there are certainly many people who place a high value upon the lives of foetuses. The reason it does not is that such restrictions, unlike restrictions upon infanticide (given the possibility of adoption), violate all of the most basic moral rights of women, who are not morally obligated to waive their own rights to life, liberty and happiness, in order to protect the sensibilities of human observers who are not directly affected.

36. Anthropological evidence for this claim may be found in Margaret

Mead's study of the Mundugumor, a Papuan tribe in New Guinea which placed little value on infants and abused them casually; adult Mundugumors, men and women alike, appear to be hostile, aggressive and generally amoral, to a degree barely compatible with social existence (Margaret Mead, *Sex and Temperament in Three Primitive Societies* [New York: William Morrow, 1963]).

37. One exception to the rule that mental incapacitation does not justify the denial of basic human rights is *total and permanent* incapacitation, such that there is no possibility of any future return to sentience. Once a person has entered a state of terminal coma, he or she has nothing to gain from continued biological life, and nothing to lose by dying. Where there is any doubt about the possibility of full or partial recovery, every benefit of the doubt should be given; but where there is clearly no such possibility, the best course is usually to allow death to occur naturally, provided that this is consistent with the wishes of the individual's family or friends. (To sanction *active* euthanasia, i.e., the deliberate *killing* of such terminally comatose persons might be unwise, in that it might lead all of us to fear [somewhat more] for our lives when we are forced to place them in the hands of medical personnel; but that is an issue which we need not settle here.)

38. Regan, "One Argument Concerning Animal Rights", p. 189.

39. See, for example, Edward A. Langerak, "Abortion, Potentiality, and Conferred Claims," (Paper delivered at the Eastern Division of the American Philosophical Association, December 1979).

40. Callicott, "Animal Liberation", p. 320 (p. 43, this volume).

41. D. G. Ritchie, "Why Animals Do Not Have Rights," in *Animal Rights*, ed. Regan and Singer, p. 183.

42. See Aldo Leopold, *Sand County Almanac*, pp. 129-33.

43. Ritchie, "Why Animals Do Not Have Rights."

44. Singer, *Animal Liberation*, pp. 169-74.

45. Callicott, "Animal Liberation," p. 335 (p. 57, this volume).

46. For exposition of this holistic message, see, William T. Blackstone, "Ethics and Ecology", in *Philosophy and Environmental Crisis*, pp. 16-42; Thomas Auxter, "The Right Not To Be Eaten," *Inquiry* 22, nos. 1-2 (Spring 1979): 221-30; Robert Cahn, *Footprints on the Planet: The Search for an Environmental Ethic* (New York: Universe Books, 1978); Albert A. Fritsch, *Environmental Ethics* (New York: Anchor Press, Doubleday, 1980), p. 3; Alastair S. Gunn, "Why Should We Care About Rare Species," *Environmental Ethics* 2, no. 1 (Spring 1980): 17-37, Eugene P. Odum, "Environmental Ethics and the Attitude Revolution", in *Philosophy and Environmental Crisis* pp. 10-15; and, of course, Leopold, *Sand County Almanac*.

47. See Callicott, "Animal Liberation," p. 315 (p. 40, this volume).

48. Gunn, "Rare Species," p. 36.

49. Ibid., p. 37.

50. See Feinberg, "Rights," pp. 52-53.

51. See Stone, *Should Trees Have Standing?*

52. For example, Baxter maintains that "environmental amenities... fall in the category of a luxury good" (William F. Baxter, *People or Penguins: The Case for Optimal Pollution* [New York and London: Columbia University Press, 1974], p. 105).

53. John Passmore, *Man's Responsibility for Nature* (London: Duckworth, 1974), p. 111.

54. Ibid., p. 173.

55. Baxter, *People or Penguins*, p. 5.

56. Thomas Auxter, "The Right Not To Be Eaten," *Inquiry* 22, nos. 1-2 (1979): 222.

57. Ibid., p. 225.

58. Ibid., p. 226.

9

The Mixed Community

Mary Midgley

1. The Well-Filled Stage

All human communities have involved animals. Those present in them always include, for a start, some dogs, with whom our association seems to be an incredibly ancient one, amounting to symbiosis. But besides them an enormous variety of other creatures, ranging from reindeer to weasels and from elephants to shags, has for ages also been domesticated. Of course they were largely there for use—for draught and riding, for meat, milk, wool and hides, for feathers and eggs, as vermin-catchers or as aids to fishing and hunting. In principle, it might seem reasonable to expect that these forms of exploitation would have produced no personal or emotional involvement at all. From a position of ignorance, we might have expected that people would view their animals simply as machines. If we impose the sharp Kantian dichotomy between *persons* and *things*, subjects and objects, and insist that everything must be considered as simply one or the other, we might have expected that they would be viewed unambiguously as things. But in fact, if people had viewed them like this, the domestication could probably never have worked. The animals, with the best will in the world, could not have reacted like machines. They became tame, not just through the fear of violence, but because they were able to form individual bonds with those who tamed them by coming to understand the social signals addressed to them. They learned to obey human beings personally. They were able to do this, not only because the people taming them were social beings, but because they themselves were so as well.

211

All creatures which have been successfully domesticated are ones which were originally social. They have transferred to human beings the trust and docility which, in a wild state, they would have developed towards their parents, and in adult life towards the leaders of their pack or herd. There are other, and perhaps equally intelligent, creatures which it is quite impossible to tame, because they simply do not have the innate capacity to respond to social signals in their own species, and therefore cannot reach those which come from outside. The various kinds of wild cat are an impressive example. Even their youngest kittens are quite untamable. Egyptian cats, from which all our domestic moggies are descended, are unique among the small-cat group in their sociability. It is interesting that they do not seem to have been domesticated in Egypt before about 1600 BC, and after that time they quickly became extremely popular.[1] Unless they were only discovered then—which would be odd—it seems that there may have been an actual mutation at that point producing a more responsive constitution.

Cats, however, are notoriously still not sociable or docile in quite the same way as dogs. Circus people do not usually waste their time trying to train cats. Similarly, there are important differences between the social natures, as well as the physiques, of horses, mules, donkeys, camels and the like. Both as species and as individuals they react variously to training; they cannot be treated just as standard-issue physical machines. People who succeed well with them do not do so just by some abstract, magical human superiority, but by interacting socially with them—by attending to them and coming to understand how various things appear from each animal's point of view. To ignore or disbelieve in the existence of that point of view would be fatal to the attempt. The traditional assumption behind the domestication of animals has been that, as Thomas Nagel has put it, there is something which it is to be a bat,[2] and similarly there is something which it is to be a horse or donkey, and to be this horse or donkey. There is not, by contrast, any such experience as *being* a stone, or a model-T Ford, or even a jet-plane. There is no being which could have that experience, so mechanics do not have to attend to it.

2. Exploitation Requires Sympathy

I am saying that this has been the traditional assumption. Modern Behaviourists who think it a false one can of course argue against it. My present point is simply that their opinion is a recent and sophisticated one. It is not the view which has been taken for granted during the long centuries in which animals have been domesticated. If we ask an Indian farmer whether he supposes that the ox which he is beating can feel, he is likely to answer, 'Certainly it can, otherwise why would I bother?' A skilled horseman needs to respond to his horse as an individual, to follow the workings of its feelings, to use his imagination in understanding how things are likely to affect it, what frightens it and what attracts it, as much as someone who wants to control human beings needs to do the same thing. Horses and dogs are addressed by name, and are expected to understand what is said to them. Nobody tries this with stones or hammers or jet-planes. The treatment of domestic animals has never been impersonal. We can say that they are not 'persons', because (apart from the Trinity) that word does generally signify *Homo sapiens*. But they are certainly not viewed just as things. They are animals, a category which, for purposes of having a point of view belongs, not with things, but with people.

This point is important because it shows what may seem rather surprising—a direct capacity in man for attending to, and to some extent understanding, the moods and reactions of other species. No doubt this capacity is limited. Human callousness makes some of its limitations obvious. But then, similar callousness is also often found in our dealings with other human beings. The question whether somebody knows what suffering he is causing may be a hard one to answer in either case. The callous person may not positively *know*, because he does not want to; he does not attend. But he could know if he chose to scan the evidence. This seems to be equally true in either case. The reason for overworking an ox or horse is usually much the same as that for overworking a human slave—not that one does not believe that they mind it, or supposes that they cannot even notice it, but that one is putting one's own interest first. The treatment of domestic animals resembles that of slaves in being extremely patchy and variable. There is not normally a steady, unvarying disregard, such as should follow if one genuinely supposed that the creature was not sentient at all, or if one was quite unable to guess what its feelings might be. Disregard is varied by partial spasmodic kindness, and also by spasmodic cruelty. And cruelty is something which could have no point for a person who really did not believe the victim to have definite feelings. (There is very little comfort in working off ill-temper on a cushion.) Family pigs are often treated with real pride and affection during their lives, they may even be genuinely mourned—only this will not protect them from being eaten. Horses, bell-wethers, Lapp reindeer and the cattle of the Masai can similarly receive real regard, can be treated as dear companions and personally cherished, can form part of human households in a different way from any machine or inanimate treassure[3]—only they will still on suitable occasions be killed or otherwise ill-treated if human purposes demand it. But we should notice too a similar arbitrariness often appearing in the treatment of human dependants, so that we can scarcely argue that there is no real capacity for sympathy towards the animals. In the treatment of other people, of course, our natural caprice is constantly disciplined by the deliberate interference of morality. We know that we must not eat our grandmothers or our children merely because they annoy us. Over animals this restraint is usually much less active; caprice has much freer play. That does not mean that they are taken not to be conscious. Belief in their sentience is essential even for exploiting them successfully.

3. The Implausibility of Scepticism

This point matters because it tells strongly against the Behaviourist idea that the subjective feelings of animals are all, equally, quite hidden from us, cannot concern us and may well not even exist. This idea is often expressed by saying that belief in them is illicitly *anthropomorphic.* The notion of anthropomorphism is a very interesting one; we must look at it shortly. But straight away I want to point out how odd it would be if those who, over many centuries, have depended on working with animals, turned out to have been relying on a sentimental and pointless error in doing so, an error which could be corrected at a stroke by metaphysicians who may never have encountered those animals at all. For instance—working elephants can still only be successfully handled by mahouts who live in close and life-long one-to-one relations with them. Each mahout treats his elephant, not like a tractor, but like a basically benevolent if often tiresome uncle, whose moods must be understood and handled very much like those of a human colleague. If there were any less expensive and time-consuming way of getting work out of elephants, the Sri Lankan timber trade would by now certainly have discovered it. Obviously the mahouts may have many beliefs about the elephants which are false because they are 'anthropomorphis'—that is, they misinterpret some outlying aspects of elephant behaviour by relying on a human pattern which is inappropriate. But if they were doing this about the basic everyday feelings—about whether their elephant is pleased, annoyed, frightened, excited, tired, sore, suspicious or angry—they would not only be out of business, they would often simply be dead. And to describe and understand such moods, they use the same general vocabulary which is used for describing humans.

Nearer home, here is an example from the memoirs of a blind woman being taught to walk with a guide-dog. The dog-trainer says,

> 'Don't stop talking, or Emma'll think you've fallen asleep... You've got to keep her interest. She's a dog, and there are lots of nice, interesting smells all round, and things passing which you can't see. So unless you talk to her, she'll get distracted, and stop to sniff a lamp-post.'[4]

This is a particularly good example, because it makes so clear the point that there is no question of illicitly attributing human sensibility. The trainer—whose interest is of course purely practical—is at pains to point out just what is distinctive about the dog's own sensibilities, simply because they must be allowed for if it is to do its work. But to make this point, he necessarily and properly uses the same words (interest, distract, she'll think you've fallen asleep) which would be used in a comparable human case. The wide difference between the two species does not affect the correctness of this language at all.

This is not, of course, the only context where a Behaviourist approach runs into difficulties. It encounters grave problems about the possibility of attributing subjective feelings to other humans, as well as to animals. I do not think that this problem will turn out very different for animals, certainly not in cases where either the feeling is very strong or the species is very familiar. The charge of 'anthropomorphism' as a general objection to attributing *any* feelings to animals, rather than to attributing the wrong feelings, is probably a red herring.

4. What Are Pets?

Before we come to this larger point, however, we need to go into an aspect of the matter which might seem still more remarkable and unexpected to an observer who was totally ignorant of human affairs. This is the real individual affection, rather than exploitation, which can arise between animals and people. Since pet-keeping is sometimes denounced as a gratuitous perversion produced by modern affluence, I take a respectably ancient example from the prophet Nathan:

> The poor man had nothing save one little ewe lamb, which he had bought and nourished up; and it grew up together with

him, and with his children; it did eat of his own morsel, and drank of his own cup, and lay in his bosom, and was to him as a daughter.[5]

Several things should be noticed here.

1. The man is *poor*. We are not dealing with the follies of the idle rich.

2. He is not childless; his children share the lamb's company with him.

3. The relation is regarded as a perfectly natural one.

Nathan chooses this story confidently to enlist King David's sympathy for the lamb-keeper. When he goes on to tell how the rich man killed this lamb for a feast, David breaks out in horror, 'As the Lord liveth, the man that has done this is worthy to die.' This makes it possible for Nathan to say 'Thou art the man!' and to apply the fable to David's treatment of Uriah the Hittite. But what would Nathan have said if David had replied that of course poor men can expect that sort of thing to happen if they will go in for sentimental pet-keeping instead of adopting human orphans? Clearly no such answer was on the cards. David knows as well as Nathan does what the lamb meant to the poor man, and both understand clearly how this strong individual relation was possible, even in a society where lambs were being killed all the time. This paradoxical ambivalence of pastoral and hunting peoples comes out very often in the metaphors of Christ. The good shepherd lays down his life for his sheep, he searches out every single lost sheep and cherishes it—yet the Passover Lamb is eaten at the last supper, and in general this must be the destiny of nearly all Hebrew sheep. It is, to an economic eye, the main reason why they are kept at all.

5. The Flexibility of Parent-Child Behaviour

It is hopeless trying to understand this situation if we keep pressing the crude Kantian question, 'but are lambs people or things?' If we want to grasp it, we must wake up to a much wider range of possibilities. Our conceptual map needs revising. In extending it, our first guiding light should be the thought that the poor man's lamb 'was to him as a daughter'. His love for it was the kind of love suited to a child.

He loved it in this way, *not* because he had no children and was so undiscriminating that he was ready to deceive himself and cuddle a cushion, but because the lamb really was a live creature needing love, and it was able to respond to parental cherishing. This is not fetishism, but a perfectly normal feeling. The appeal of small and helpless creatures is not limited by species. Animals in the wild certainly do not normally notice young outside their own kind, but if they are thrown together with them, as they are in captivity, they often respond in a remarkable way: they can adopt. Full-scale adoption is sometimes possible, even in the wild.[6] And it is striking how domestic animals will put up with rough treatment from small children, which they would certainly not tolerate from adults. How, we ask, does the cat know that a baby much larger than itself is a child—is, in effect, a kitten? What the signals are does not matter much—some of them may well be chemical. But if we ourselves were presented with a baby elephant, and had a chance to watch and take in its playful behaviour, we would be able to grasp the same point.

Play-signals penetrate species-barriers with perfect ease.[7] What is even more interesting is the startling set of emotional and practical consequences which the adult animal draws from the signals. The cat shows a mood of tolerance, playfulness and positive affection which would astonish us if we did not ourselves so readily share it. Of course it would be no use trying this kind of appeal on a codfish. Infantile signals work only with species which cherish their own young. And even there, the gap must not be too large if the message is to get across. Birds would in general be unlikely to decipher human infantile signals; if the ravens fed Elijah, it seems that he must have gaped like a young cuckoo. But where the message does get across, its power in producing fellowship is astonishing. It affects not only adults, but other young as well, releasing in them the hope of play. The human baby makes a beeline for the cat. The cat, if it is a kitten, returns the compliment with particular fervour. Both are inquisitive and playful. This attraction seems, again, to be common to all those relatively intelligent species which are capable of play. In wild conditions, it normally will not overcome the stronger tendency to species-imprinting unless playmates of one's own species are uncommonly scarce, as in the case which Jane Goodall describes. But in a mixed human community it can very well do so. None of the creatures present is getting a really exclusive imprinting. Accordingly, the species-barrier there, imposing though it may look, is rather like one of those tall wire fences whose impressiveness is confined to their upper reaches. To an adult in formal dress, engaged on his official statesmanly interactions, the fence is an insuperable barrier. Down below, where it is full of holes, it presents no obstacle at all. The young of *Homo sapiens*, like those of the other species present, scurry through it all the time. Since all human beings start life as children, this has the quite important consequence that hardly any of us, at heart, sees the social world as an exclusively human one.

6. The Child's Quest for Variety

To spell this out: The point is not just that most human beings have in fact been acquainted with other creatures early in life, and have therefore received some non-human imprinting. It is also that children who are not offered this experience often actively seek it. Animals, like song and dance, are an innate taste. Even those whose homes have contained none often seek them out and find them irresistible. The fact seems too obvious to need mentioning and does not usually attract much criticism. Even people who believe that there is something perverse and wrong about adults taking an interest in animals are often quite content that children should do so. Like some other interests which appeal to children it may, however, be considered as something which one ought to grow out of. Prolonged interest in it may seem a sign of emotional immaturity. Behind this thought lies the more general idea that animals are suitable only as practice material for the immature, because they are in effect nothing but simplified models of human beings. On this pattern, those who graduate past them to real human relationships are not expected to have any further interest in them, any more than a real golfer does in clock-golf in the park.

This way of thinking has a certain point, but beyond the crudest level it can be very misleading. No animal is just a simplified human being, nor do children take them to be so. However friendly they may be, their life is radically foreign, and it is just that foreignness which attracts a child. The point about them is that they are different. As for immaturity, it is of course true that we must all come to terms first and foremost with our own species. Those unwilling to do this can indeed seek refuge with animals, as they can in other activities. But the mere fact of taking an interest in animals does not show that kind of motive, any more than taking an interest in machines or music does. Experience of animals is not essentially a substitute for experience of people, but a supplement to it—something more which is needed for a full human life. The ewe lamb did not come between the poor man and his children. Instead it formed an extra delight which he could share with them, and so strengthened the family bond. (That, surely, is why Nathan mentions the children.) One sort of love does not need to block another, because love, like compassion, is not a rare fluid to be economized, but a capacity which grows by use. And if we ask (again impersonating an ignorant observer) whether the limits of its natural use in human beings coincide with the species-barrier, we see plainly that they do not. In early childhood that barrier scarcely operates. And even in later life it seldom becomes absolute.

7. Neoteny and Extended Sympathy

There are two likely reasons for this extra emotional porousness of the human species-barrier. The less interesting one is sheer security. Animal mothers are often nervous of letting their children play with outsiders, and this is not foolish; real dangers often do threaten. (Chimps, for instance, do occasionally eat baby baboons.) Human life by contrast is usually secure enough to allow some wider experiment. But the second and more profound reason is simply the much greater intensity of human sympathy and curiosity. That eager reaching-out to surrounding life and to every striking aspect of the physical world, which in other species belongs only to infancy, persists in human beings much longer, and may be present throughout their lives. Humans are *neotenous*—that is, they prolong certain infantile characteristics into maturity, develop them and continue to profit by them as adults. From an evolutionary point of view, this may be the main key to their exceptional development. People retain as adults a number of physical marks which in other primates are found only in infants or in embryos, the most notable of which is, of course, the great size and long-continued growth of the brain. They also retain some marked infantile patterns of behaviour, among which is a tendency to play of all sorts, including such things as imitating, singing, dancing and the making of objects for pleasure, habits on which the arts are based. Adults among other advanced species do indeed sometimes play together, and their doing so is rightly seen as a sign of intelligence. But they all do it far less than humans.[8] The real corner-stones of these prolonged and intensified infantile faculties, however, probably do not lie in play itself, but in the sympathy and curiosity which underly it. Man at his best is no longer satisfied to confine these two motives within the grooves of habit. He continually reaches out to further use of them. But this insatiability of interest is itself characteristic of childhood. Of course when it is extended into adult life it takes on a different meaning. But it is a faculty retained and put to use, not a faculty invented.

Neoteny raises the whole question of 'childishness'—of what can, and what cannot, rightly be kept and used from early life by an individual moving into maturity. To St Paul, this question looked very easy. As he said, 'When I was a child, I spoke as a child, I thought as a child, I understood as a child; but when I became a man, I put aside childish things.'[9] This position looks sensible. The trouble about it is that those who take it have often included among the 'childish things' on the rubbish-pile matters absolutely central to life. They have, indeed, sometimes lost all interest in life itself because they have parted with aspects of it without which it ceases to be worth living. Erik Berne suggests a deeper view—that the child in each of us is never lost, but remains active at the core of our being:

> The Child is in many ways the most valuable part of the personality, and can contribute to the individual's life exactly what an actual child can contribute to family life; charm, pleasure and creativity. If the Child in the individual is confused and unhealthy, then the consequences may be unfortunate, but something can and should be done about it.[10]

The capacity for widely extended sympathy, for social horizons not limited to one's familiar group, is certainly a part of this childish spontaneity. It is also the window through which interest in creatures of other species enters our lives, both in childhood and—if we do not firmly close the window—in later life as well. It is one aspect of that openness to new impressions, that relative freedom from constraining innate programmes, which makes us culturally malleable and enables us, through pseudo-speciation, to accept and build such varied ways of life. It carries with it, too, that still wider curiosity, that capacity for interest in other, inanimate surrounding objectives—plants and stones, stars, rocks and water—which extends our horizon beyond the social into the ecological, and makes us true citizens of the world. In theory we might, perhaps, have been creatures who enjoyed none of this liberty, who were programmed from birth to be capable only of interesting ourselves in the doings of our own species. But Fate has not been so mean.

A rather touching example of this wider power of human sympathy occurs when Jane Goodall describes the effect of a polio epidemic on the chimpanzees she was studying. One old animal, his legs wholly paralysed by the disease, was dragging himself around with his arms. He was suffering from loneliness, since he, like the other crippled individuals, was shunned and sometimes attacked by those who were still healthy. In the hope of inducing companions who were grooming each other to groom him as well, he dragged himself up into a tree:

> With a loud grunt of pleasure he reached a hand towards them in greeting—but even before he made contact they both swung quickly away and, without a backward glance, started grooming on the far side of the tree. For a full two minutes, old Gregor sat motionless, staring after them. And then he laboriously lowered himself to the ground. As I watched him sitting there alone, my vision blurred, ane when I looked up at the groomers in the tree *I came nearer to hating a chimpanzee than I have ever done before or since.*[11]

As she well knows, it would be unfair to hate them, since they are incapable of reacting otherwise. Their response is one which of course is perfectly possible for humans also, and indeed is often found among them. They are repelled by the damaged individual, and really do not see him as their old friend at all, but as something strange and alarming. Chimpanzees can only occasionally break through this barrier and cherish a sick comrade—wolves, elephants, dolphins and whales are known to do it rather more often. People, however, have, if they care to use it, a much wider capacity still, one which is perfectly able to function like this right across the species-barrier. Jane Goodall and her colleagues do not only get upset about Gregor's situation, they do everything they can to relieve it.

8. Evolutionary Considerations

Is this wider power of sympathy at all surprising, or is it what one would naturally expect for a species in our position? So far I have treated this as an open question, and said that 'in theory'—that is before investigation—an intelligent species might, for all we know, really be isolated emotionally from all surrounding species, might view them simply as moving objects and have no access to their moods. But this 'theoretical' isolated possibility is actually very obscure and may perhaps not make much sense. Biological questions often cannot be asked in isolation like this. To ask 'could there be an intelligent species with no senses?' or 'living in total solitude?' is scarcely comprehensible. If we say 'no' to these ideas, we are not ruling about the possibilities of forms of life totally unknown to us, but clarifying the meaning which concepts like 'intelligence' can have to us here and now. The difficulty about imagining a species cut off in this way from all its neighbours is in the first place a practical one. Apart from deliberate communication at close quarters (which is all we have mentioned so far) species make use of all kinds of unintended signals from each other, and to interpret these they need to grasp the moods that underly them. For hunting, and also for avoiding danger from predators and other threatening creatures, it is vitally necessary to recognize fear, anger, suspicion, territorial outrage and a dozen other moods. Warnings and hints can also be gained all the time from the conduct of creatures which are not interested in oneself at all. But it needs interpretation. This is the sort of thing in which people living in the wilds often excel, and they need to do so. What looks to the urban oik like a mere silly mob of excited birds means to the instructed local perhaps an indication of approaching predators—perhaps food available in the neighborhood, perhaps a sign of approaching migration, and therefore an unexpectedly early winter, perhaps a score of further important things which the townsman would never think of.

The local is able to interpret these, partly of course by sheer experience, but also (as we shall shortly see) probably because human neurological processes have not diverged far enough from those of the birds to make sympathetic interpretation impossible or even difficult. To get rid of that similarity, physical changes would be needed, and they would apparently be disadvantageous.

Evolutionarily speaking, then, it is likely that a species such as ours would find itself equipped for the position which some Old Testament texts give it,[12] of steward and guardian, under God, placed over a range of creatures which he is in principle able to care for and understand, rather than in the one often imagined in science fiction, of an invader exploiting an entirely alien planet.

Many of those who are anxious to distract human attention from animals would not, of course, want to deny that this is true; they would simply say that it is a pity.

9. The Stigma of Savagery

Critics who object to attempts at inter-species communication often do not take the theoretical Behaviourist line that these attempts are simply impossible. They do not doubt the success, but the desirability of the enterprise. They see themselves as standing for an adult, civilized attitude against goings-on which are primitive and childish. They recommend indifference to animals—and indeed to all non-human nature—as a condition of emotional maturity. Ought this advice to impress us? It is not obvious why it should. Emotional maturity is not necessarily achieved by limiting one's emotional commitments, nor by rejecting interests held in common with children. Increasing callousness is, on the whole, rather a bad sign for it. Children and 'primitives' need not always be wrong.

The view that an adult and civilized approach cannot fail to remove such interests is remarkably well expressed in the article on 'Animals' in that magisterial work, the *Encyclopaedia of Religion and Ethics*. Writing in 1908, before certain embarrassments descended on the human end of the argument, the author explains:

> Civilization, or perhaps rather education, has brought with it a sense of the great gulf that exists between man and the lower animals.... In the lower stages of culture, whether they be found in races which are, as a whole, below the European level, or in the uncultured portion of civilized communities, the distinction between men and animals is not adequately, if at all, recognized ... The savage ... attributes to the animal a vastly more complex set of thoughts and feelings, and a much greater range of knowledge and power, than it actually possesses.... It is therefore small wonder that his attitude towards the animal creation is one of reverence rather than superiority.

The author does not bring, as support for his more enlightened views, any evidence of a zoological kind to show that those who were familiar with the animals actually knew less about their capacities than those who were not. The locals have, of course, often been found to be mistaken, on particular points, but they can only be shown to be so by empirical inquiry. In fact, ethological investigation, once it was vigorously set on foot in this century, has shown that Western urban thought was (not surprisingly) often even more ill-informed than local superstition on many such questions, and that it had consistently attributed to animals a vastly *less* complex set of thoughts and feelings, and a much smaller range of knowledge and power, than they actually possessed. The only fact to which the author appeals is that animals do not talk. This is true, but he does not explain why language should be the only quality to deserve respect. He does, however, considerately account for the errors of the heathen, as follows:

> One of the main sources of the respect paid to animals is the belief that certain species are the embodiments of the souls of the dead.... Thus a kind of alliance springs up between certain human kins and certain species of animals, in which some writers have sought the germ of totemism.

In this way respect for animals is accounted for as a by-product of a false belief in reincarnation. That explanation seems to put the cart (or coffin) before the horse. Belief in reincarnation must surely be seen as an expression, or consequence, of a previous high opinion of those animals. In fact, apart from the point about speech, the grounds for correcting primitive views here scarcely seem to be factual at all.

They are moral, but they do not get the support of explicit moral argument. The reference to 'civilization, or perhaps rather education' as making this desirable change does not seem to be an appeal to any special scientific knowledge of animals, but rather to the general rationalistic European tradition which we have discussed earlier. From this point of view, the criticism made against both primitives and children is not that they are *ignorant*—that they credit animals with feelings which they actually do not have—but that they are frivolous, are occupying themselves with something unimportant.

In this chapter, we have looked at the natural, emotional preference for one's own species over others which seems to underlie much conduct attacked as 'speciesist', and have found reason to admit its existence and to treat it with considerable respect, but no reason to think it an impenetrable social barrier, cutting us off from other creatures in a way which makes them none of our proper concern. On the factual question whether, and how much, humans are naturally equipped to notice and respond to the moods of other species, we find that their equipment is quite good, rather better than that of other comparable creatures, though all have some gifts that way.

This has some rather interesting consequences. We have to consider...the sceptical position that the use of ordinary social and emotional language to refer to animals is illegitimate because it is 'anthropomorphic'. This attack assumes that human language is invented in the first place not only *by* humans, but exclusively *about* humans—to describe them and them alone. Any use of it to describe any other being would then be an 'extension'—a leap out into the unknown. But if language has, from the start, arisen in a mixed community and has been adapted to describe all beings whose moods etc.

might be of general importance and interest, then that is the proper use of the concepts from the start, and no leap is needed.

Notes

1. Muriel Beadle, *The Cat, its History, Biology and Behaviour* (Collins and Harvill Press, 1977), p. 66.

2. Thomas Nagel, *Mortal Questions* (Cambridge, 1979), essay 12, on 'What Is It Like to Be a Bat?'

3. See the very touching account of Polyphemus and his ram, *Odyssey IX*, 447–60. Polyphemus, it should be noticed, was not an outstandingly sentimental person.

4. Sheila Hocken, *Emma and I* (Sphere Books, 1978), p. 33.

5. II Samuel xii: 3.

6. For adoption by elephants, see Daphne Sheldrick, *The Tsavo Story* (Collins and Harvill Press, 1973).

7. See 'Play-Behaviour in Higher Primates, a Review' by Caroline Loizos, in *Primate Ethology*, ed. Desmond Morris (Weidenfeld & Nicolson, 1967).

8. The relation of play to the arts and other highly valued human activities has often been noticed. It is well treated in Johan Huizinga's classic book *Homo Ludens* (tr. the author and another, Paladin Books, 1970). I have dealt with it myself in a paper called 'The Game Game' (*Philosophy* 49, 1974), reprinted in abridged form in my *Heart and Mind* (Harvester Press, 1981).

9. I Corinthians xiii. 11.

10. *Games People Play* (Penguin Books, 1968), Chapter 1, pp. 23–24.

11. *In The Shadow of Man* (Collins, 1971), p. 202. Italics mine.

12. Collected by Passmore, *Man's Responsibility for Nature* Part 1, Chapter 2, 'Stewardship and Co-operation with Nature'.

——— 10 ———

Taking Sympathy Seriously:
A Defense of Our Moral Psychology
Toward Animals

John A. Fisher

> Is there a more mysterious idea for an artist than to imagine
> how nature is reflected in the eyes of an animal? How does a horse
> see the world, how does an eagle, a doe, or a dog?
>
> —Franc Marc[1]

1. The Trouble with Sympathy

The enormous growth in recent years of concern for the welfare of
animals is largely a function of the sympathy that very many people
feel for them, a sympathy that lies at the heart of our moral psychology
regarding animals. The animal liberation movement, in particular, has
been especially effective when it has educated people through films
and other media about the conditions under which many animals are
forced to lead their lives—in pounds, on factory farms, and in laboratories. Such demonstrations, either by creating sympathy or by engag-
ing previously existing sympathies, lead people to do a variety of
things: boycott pet shops, break into scientific labs to free the animals,
cease eating meat, and so on.

Perhaps because of its emotional power, sympathy arouses skepticism in moral theorists.[2] Certainly, sympathy toward animals is
widely regarded both by theorists and by practical people as inappropriate or weak-minded. Proponents of animal liberation, fearing this
criticism, construct their theories in such a way as to distance themselves from sentimental appeals to sympathy. Even some theorists of

227

environmental ethics have questioned the concern for animals generated by the advocates of animal liberation. In an influential article, J. Baird Callicott has argued that the animal liberation movement is incompatible with environmental ethics.[3] Insisting that environmental concern has principally to do with preserving unspoiled nature, Callicott attacks the animal liberationist concern for the plight of domesticated animals. Domesticated animals, for Callicott, "are living artifacts," and he implies that concern for *them* (as opposed to concern for the encroachment of technology into nature that the increase of the domesticated animal populations represents) is entirely misplaced (p. 330 [p. 52, this volume]).

Sympathy for animals, wild or domestic, is typically thought to be problematic because it rests upon a faulty analogy between human and nonhuman animals: we feel sympathy for animals because we mistakenly think of them as humans.[4] Yet animals are fundamentally unlike us. Therefore, the perception of them as appropriate objects of moral concern is incorrect.

This tough-minded claim strikes at the heart of concern for animals. The arguments that undermine the validity of our sympathies for animals also tend to undermine the moral claims made on behalf of animals. If our sympathies for animals are simply inappropriate, then our moral concern for their welfare stands in danger of losing much of its practical force.

One of the most important reasons why sympathy is of interest to moral theory lies in the way that it determines the range of application of our moral intuitions. Our sympathetic response to animals makes them a part of our moral community; that is, our moral concerns and our ideas of right and wrong action extend to animals as well as to fellow humans.[5]

This sympathetic extension of moral reasoning to animals leads most people to two basic moral intuitions concerning animals. The first is that it is wrong to kill an animal gratuitously. The second is that it is wrong to hurt an animal gratuitously. Although it might be claimed that these intuitions are based, not on sympathy for animals, but merely on a revulsion against these human actions, this is implausible. What is wrong with the human action? Why do we feel that killing an animal differs from picking a flower or turning off a computer? The most obvious hypothesis is that we feel a kinship with animals, just as we do with humans, and that we implicitly depend upon that feeling when we elicit our moral intuitions about these cases.

It is particularly difficult for any moral theorist to give an adequate account of the harm of death. This is because no individual (human or animal) exists after death to suffer the harm.[6] Nevertheless, even though we may lack a satisfactory theoretical account of the harm of death, our *intuitions* assure us that death is a harm to humans. We extend that intuition to animals on the basis of our felt sympathies, and we think of an animal's death as analogous to a person's death.

In this way, our intuitions about the rightness or wrongness of killing and hurting animals are conditioned by our sympathies. This is not to say that such intuitions cannot be countered by self-interest or by tough-minded attitudes. The tough-minded do not try to justify the routine killing of animals by claiming that it is necessary; rather, they argue that to give credence to sympathy in such cases is simply naive and intellectually mistaken.

Before we can determine the plausibility of the tough-minded position, however, we have to get clear about what sympathy is. In what follows I explore the character of sympathy and argue that it does constitute an appropriate mode of feeling toward animals. Moreover, far from incompatible with environmental concerns—as argued by Callicott—I argue that sympathy for animals, wild as well as domesticated, can provide a partial basis for environmental ethics.

2. Two Levels of Sympathy

We speak about sympathy in a variety of ways. We *give* sympathy to persons, we *feel* sympathy *for* someone, our sympathies are *engaged*, we *are* sympathetic *to* you, your plight, your line of thought. These are not just linguistic artifacts, but neither are they to be taken literally. Sympathy is, I believe, a real part of our psychology, but our linguistic expressions are not invariable guides as to how to theorize about it.

To begin with, we should contrast sympathy with mere concern. The threatened destruction of a valuable historical building might upset certain citizens, and even move them to do whatever they can to prevent its demolition. But unless they are mentally aberrant they will not literally feel *sympathy* for the building. By contrast, suppose that a family is to be evicted and their home destroyed. Here, too, our concerned citizens may try to prevent the destruction of the house, but they are likely also to feel sympathy for the family. Sympathy, then, is not merely caring about what happens. Nor, when we feel sympathy, are we merely intellectually drawing the conclusion of a practical syllogism that tells us what we *ought* to do given moral principles and the conditions true of the case in question. Sympathy is something we *feel* toward particular individuals—say, a dog in a pound or a child being abused—or toward groups of individual creatures—say, elk or cattle which are starving as a result of a blizzard, or humans who are starving as a result of a famine.

Some environmentalist thinkers (for example, Callicott) have implied that we have a very different relationship to wild animals than we do to domesticated species.[7] Do we in fact relate sympathetically to wild animals (elk) as well as to domesticated animals (cows)? I think we do. By definition we have a different *relationship* with wild animals, but it does not follow that we do not feel the same sympathetic concern for similar animals under similar conditions. Consider the case of animal experimentation. Animal liberationists have shown strong concern for the animals used in such experiments whether they are wild (chimps, baboons, apes) or domesticated (cats, dogs). Perhaps the claim is that animal lovers have a double standard concerning animals *in the wild:* we typically do not care about deer starving, but we do care about cattle starving. I do not think there is any reason to believe that this double standard exists. To be sure, most of us do not know the conditions under which most wild animals live their lives, but when misfortunes to wild animals are brought to public attention—e.g., extinction of species—it appears that people show just as much concern.[8] If anything, the more obvious problem is that people show an inappropriate concern for wild animals, a concern that fails to respect the nature of the animals and their lives. (I return to this matter in section three.)

Sympathy, as we see, involves empathy. To feel sympathetic toward someone, or to feel sympathy for some creature, involves being moved by that creature's condition. What is distinctive about sympathy is that this response is mediated by a recognition of a sort of kinship with the object of sympathy. We think of what it would be like to be in those circumstances, to have that happen, to suffer like that, to be like that. If we have no sympathy for the criminal who is to be executed, it is either because we will not put ourselves in his position —we reject him as an appropriate object of empathy—or because we can put ourselves in his position and think we would deserve to be executed.

We must, then, distinguish further between two senses of sympathy: sympathy *for* an individual in a certain condition and sympathy *with* that individual. The former occurs, for example, when we are sympathetic *to* someone's problems, or when we lack sympathy *for* the criminal who is executed. It occurs also in our response to animals, as when we feel great sympathy for the wildebeest calf that we see killed by wild dogs after a courageous defense by its mother. Such sympathy is frequently predicated on the attribution of value-laden human characteristics such as innocence, courage, cleverness, parental protectiveness, etc. Detecting these characteristics in the behavior of animals or humans, we are moved emotionally; we feel sorrow, anger, protectiveness. I call this sense "sympathy for."

There is a wider and more basic sort of sympathy that one being may have *with* another. To feel sympathy with another, in this sense, is to feel akin to the other and thus able to understand that being. This is what is happening when we detect "human" characteristics, such as innocence, courage, and anger, in animals. In this sense, other persons can often feel sympathy *with* a criminal; they know what it is like to be him. To have sympathy with an individual is to be able to project oneself in such a way as to partially encompass the inner life of the other. Hume's well-known conception of sympathy is, in fact, a conception of "sympathy with," expressed in extreme mechanistic terms:

> The minds of all men are similar in their feelings and operations, nor can anyone be actuated by an affection of which all others are not in some degree, susceptible. As in strings equally wound up, the motion of one communicates itself to the rest, so all the affections readily pass from one person to another, and beget correspondent movements in every human creature.[9]

The notion of sympathy with can be generalized plausibly to include animals. One can understand, i.e., explain, why the animal acts as it does because its behavior is similar to human behavior. In this way one projects oneself into the inner life of nonhuman animals. Although sympathy *for* beings presupposes some sympathy *with* them, it does not always work the other way around. Farmers must inevitably have a great deal of sympathy with their livestock, and trout fishermen with trout, but such persons may lack sympathy *for* their victims.

Sympathy with and sympathy for are both quasicognitive states in the sense that they can be more or less adequate to their object. Take sympathy for: if I feel sympathy for a victim of an accident, my emotions are engaged by a perception of someone as (say) innocent and harmed by the accident—surely a complex cognition.

The Humean model of sympathy I have sketched suggests that empathy, and in turn a sort of kinship, is central.[10] I have also implied that sympathy for depends upon first feeling sympathy with someone, and, finally, feeling sympathy with a wide variety of creatures. There is tension in this explanation. We must have some idea of what it would be like to be that creature, *W*. Moreover, our emotions are engaged, so I am hypothesizing, by an exercise in which we consider how *we* would feel in *W*'s circumstances. But if *W* is a different *kind* of creature, this exercise could go wrong or be impossible to perform.[11]

The solution to this difficulty is not to discount empathy, but to note two features of our ability to empathize with other creatures. The first is that our lives are part of a larger biological life full of common characteristics and needs. Animals have needs for nourishment, water, air; they have life cycles, a sort of family life, a sort of social life with other members of their species; they suffer and flourish; many of them engage in exploratory and playful behavior. While I think such characteristics of our common biological life support and explain sympathy *with* other creatures, they do not guarantee that we correctly put ourselves in the animal's place, that is, that we correctly perceive what we have in common with the other creature. We may very well go wrong, then, when we feel sympathy *for* the creature. If an emperor penguin sits on an egg for many months, never moving through the black Antarctic winter, we may feel empathy, comparing that sort of devotion to similar behavior by other animals, including humans, who make sacrifices for their offspring. But would I be justified in feeling sympathy *for* the emperor penguin because it has to sit so miserably on the egg in the cold? It is difficult to say; I must think of what is good for a penguin, and whether the penguin really suffers, and whether its suffering is avoidable.

This brings us to the second mitigating feature. We frequently feel sympathy for a creature when we believe it to be suffering. The obvious marks of suffering, and of flourishing, are widespread throughout the animal kingdom. Although I may have it wrong when I think that a penguin suffers to hatch its egg, I plausibly have it right when I think that a young ape is suffering if it appears to pine over its mother's death and dies a few days later. We can often detect the direct signs of suffering (and flourishing) even if we get their causes wrong, and even if we misperceive the contexts of suffering because we are ignorant of the nature of the animal.[12]

There are those who would reject all such cases, claiming that we feel sympathy for animals because we suppose that they are just like us: because I would feel cold at sub-zero temperatures, I assume that a penguin also feels cold. There is no reason, however, to believe that all, or even most, feelings of sympathy for animals involve such an obvious mistake. All we need suppose is that animals are like us in important ways, and this surely is true. Those who charge that sympathy is based on mistaken assumptions of similarity sometimes assume that there is a radical gulf between humans and other animals, and that humans cannot transcend that gulf intuitively. Thus, if we feel sympathy for animals it *must* be because we are illicitly projecting a thoroughly human psychology upon them. The assumption of an unbridgeable gulf is, however, implausible. Humans are members of a larger biological family, and the common life shared by members of that family enables us to respond intuitively to animals.

Our sympathy with various creatures does not necessarily entail projecting onto them specifically human characteristics. We often empathize with animals that we experience as very different from us. Animals have all sorts of forms and powers that humans do not have and though we have sympathy with them, we do not suppose that they resemble us closely. Consider such favorite animals as the large whales, the polar bear, the kangaroo, the lion, the elephant, and the eagle. We love, admire, or fear these animals because their special powers are so different from our own. Yet the sympathetic experience of these animals entails some understanding of what it is like to be them—for example, of what it is like to be huge and to walk on four legs, to have a large trunk, and so forth.

As a quasicognitive state, sympathy (both for and with) is subject to a sort of reflective equilibrium. It can be criticized and improved; it can be more or less appropriately grounded upon the empirical facts of the case. Moreover, being based on a perception of similarity, feelings of sympathy with can be a matter of degree. For example, having studied an octopus, I may begin to care for its well-being, developing a modest sympathy with its fears and interests, even though much about its mental life remains alien. Hypothesizing a particular psychology for the animal I am able to explain and understand its behavior; this hypothesis suggests further observations, which, of course, are themselves far from uninfected by my hypothesis of the animal's psychology. The observations will support the hypothesis and vice versa, until the explanation breaks down or until I find a simpler explanation that does not invoke a life (including a mental life) analogous to my own (e.g., involving consciousness, pleasure, pain, beliefs, and desires).[13]

3. Species, Character, and the Environment: Two Objections

Far from experiencing animals as approximating us, we experience them, from the sympathetic point of view, as in many ways larger than we are, as more purely embodying various character traits that have a moral dimension. This is particularly true of animals considered as members of a species. The polar bear, for instance, may appear to be extremely noble, powerful, and dangerous. More broadly, we find animals of many species apparently displaying such virtues as extreme courage, fortitude, patience, loyalty, self-sacrifice, and so forth. Sympathy with animals is thus typically correlated with the attribution of character traits to them. It may be possible to avoid such attrition, but this seems doubtful. Certainly, when we experience other persons we habitually attribute character traits to them.

The tendency to attribute character traits to animals elicits two objections to taking sympathy seriously. The first is that the traits that appear to us to accompany the object with which we sympathize, traits like innocence, courage, and patience, are illusory in the case of animals. Why? Two reasons might be offered for this claim. First, attributions of such traits cannot be objectively *demonstrated* to be appropriate. Innocence, for example, can never be established or refuted by a scientific description of animals and their behavior. But it is doubtful that such proof exists in the human case either. We think people exhibit virtues in their behavior, but we do not expect such virtues to be logically inferable from objective descriptions of that behavior.

The deeper reason for denying that animals have character traits is the claim that the presuppositions of attributing such traits to humans cannot be satisfied in the case of animals. I believe that this is a correct claim about many but not all human traits. Many character traits ascribed to humans—for example, fairness—may persuppose motivations, thoughts, and concepts that nonhuman animals cannot be thought to have. But even if we deny these "higher" traits to an animal, we might still value the animal because it exhibits an analogue of a valuable human trait or because it exhibits traits that strike us as valuable even though they are different from human traits. The penguin sitting on its egg through the dead of winter may be considered to show an analogue of patience, even though the penguin does not exhibit strictly human patience (the penguin is not as cold as a human would be, and it does not have the same mental life while sitting). It is also an exhibition of such extreme "self-sacrifice" as to go beyond human models. Thus, it is a trait that we may find valuable, though alien.

Indeed, for many people, it is the *difference* between animals and humans, the straightforwardness of animal character, that marks off animals as worthy objects of admiration. Montaigne has been described, for example, as regarding animals, as our moral superiors, in every significant way.... They seek only 'tangible' and 'attainable' goods, while we have only 'wind and smoke' as our portion. They have an unimpaired sense of reality, seeking only repose, security, health, and peace, while we pursue reason, knowledge, and renown, which brings us nothing but grief.[14]

The second major objection to taking sympathy seriously can be formulated as an implication about the relative worthiness of various species: because of the mental and character traits we discern through the eye of sympathy in various species of animals, we like or dislike or are neutral toward those species, and we rank them accordingly in a hierarchy. But, the objection continues, surely if all species of animals are equal in value, then such a hierarchy would be implausible, and it would have untoward consequences if applied to environmental issues. Our sympathies thus conflict with a larger environmental concern for *all* species of animals and plants. For example, the public controversy over preserving the snail darter fish clearly showed the conflict between environmentalism and normal, untutored sympathy, which finds nothing to mourn about the extinction of the snail darter.

Although sympathy for animals overlaps with environmentalism, there is a distinction between them. Environmental concern focuses on the integrity of an ecosystem, and may spring from a variety of sources, from aesthetics to self-interest. By contrast, sympathetic concern focuses on individuals (and derivatively on species), who are to some degree like us, and whom we therefore care about, and who therefore seem to us to deserve a good life.[15] The objection seeks to drive a wedge between these two points of view, and suggests that sympathy will give us the wrong answer about the value of species.

The objection loses some of its force if we distinguish "folk sympathy" from "enlightened sympathy." Folk sympathy is based on a culturally bound set of ideas about animals. Our own folk wisdom, for example, portrays some animals as noble, others as sneaky—the lion is kingly, the fox is full of tricks. Enlightened sympathy, on the other hand, is based on the far more adequate descriptions of animals by ethologists and biologists. Such descriptions are not going to lead us to think that the lion has traits like nobility and courage, whereas the African dog does not. Both lions and dogs will be treated neutrally, i.e., free from folk prejudices. Each species, for example, has an interesting, but different, large family structure—and to speak of "family structure" is to indicate how sympathy still finds a foothold within these more objective concepts.

Yet, to give substantive weight even to enlightened sympathy has implications for the value of species. On the assumption suggested above that sympathy generates a hierarchy of value, it seems reasonable to suggest the following two principles: first, with regard to *species value*, species are valuable if and only if they have valuable traits (character, mental, behavioral) that we discern through enlightened empathetic perception; second, with regard to the *hierarchy of value*, species are more valuable the more closely they approximate to human traits.[16]

This second principle captures the fact that sympathy with is a matter of degree, and if it yields value in our eyes, then it must yield less value as sympathy with lessens. The two principles together, however, do not appear adequate to ground concern for the environment as a whole, nor concern for important species within the environment. What of the snail darter and the shark, one a species we do not care about, the other a species we positively fear?

Sympathy for animals clearly plays an important role in generating concern for the environment. It is desirable, therefore, to show that the implications of sympathy are not anti-environmental. The first way to bring sympathy for animals into line with concern for the environment is to adjust the claim of the species value principle so that it states merely a *sufficient* condition of value. While sympathy is probably the most important source of value, it is not the only one. We might, for example, attribute aesthetic value both to unsympathetic kinds of creatures and to the total environment. In addition, we must allow that the ecosystem is an interactive whole in which unsympathetic species of animals and plants can have a instrumental value insofar as they support the ecosystem and in so doing directly or indirectly support the animals we especially care about. On this view, plankton are important because, among other reasons, they provide food for whales. The dung beetle has value, not only by virtue of the biological aesthetics of its design and function, but also because it supports the large animals and herds of the African plains. If there should be a species—the mosquito, for example—that has no positive characteristics from the point of view of sympathy, and that does the ecosystem no good, then its extinction would be no loss.

Sympathy for animals thus explains the harm of extinction for some species, and it also helps to explain the value of the larger ecosystems in which such species have their lives. Indeed, it is the existence of sympathetic animals that creates ecosystems that we care about. In this way sympathy with animals helps to resolve one of the central puzzles of environmental positions that favor the *whole* biotic community: why should we favor some wholes over other wholes?[17] As Johnson puts it: "Why isn't *whatever* happens integral, stable, and beautiful?"[18] The environments that we seek to protect, that we find beautiful, I suggest, are just those in which sympathetic creatures live.

Two further points temper the alleged conflict between sympathy and environmentalism. First, we have *some* sympathy even with snail darters and sharks, and they must therefore have *some* characteristics that have a slight value. All things being equal, the extinction even of very primitive creatures would then be a slight loss. Second, our antipathy for creatures like the shark is, I assume, compounded largely of ignorance and self-interest. Our sympathies, therefore, can be enlightened by further knowledge of the shark. Self-interest, on the other hand, always has the potential to rob sympathy of its psychological force. Whether sharks are totally unsympathetic could be truly determined only under conditions in which humans could interact safely with sharks.

Taking our animal sympathies seriously entails real consequences for environmental issues, but these consequences are not implausible. Far from being in conflict with a concern for the whole environment, our sympathies can help ground such a concern.

4. Further Objections: The Variability of Sympathy

Let us now turn to a further salient reason for skepticism about sympathy *for* animals. While natural, sympathy for animals is far from universal. Nor are we consistent in our sympathies; a hunter may love his dog, yet gleefully kill his game. Moreover, responses to animals are diverse and vary from culture to culture. This relativity of responses makes it appear that our sympathy for animals is not a cognitive state in the sense that it corresponds to any objective condition of the animal.[19]

A different explanation of these points is that sympathy is not a simple perception, but more like a *way* of perceiving some object. Sympathy is very strongly influenced by particular beliefs about the object, as well as by more general values and attitudes. The fact that people vary widely in their sympathy, or lack of sympathy, for animals can be explained as a result of a difference in background cognitive states. Moreover, sympathy can be cultivated or suppressed. These factors easily account for the fact that many people can be indifferent and even cruel to animals.

People are notoriously capable of great cruelty to other humans. But we do not take it to follow from the variability of human sympathy for humans that we are morally free to feel sympathy or not independently of the facts of the case. In war, soldiers sometimes commit atrocities; those soldiers who feel sympathy for the victims are displaying a sane and rational response. If one believes either that the individual in question is not suffering or that the individual deserves to suffer, it is not irrational to feel no sympathy for him or her. Barring these beliefs, it seems obvious that it is more rational to feel sympathy than to be indifferent. It is psychologically possible to be indifferent without these background beliefs, but such indifference borders on a psychological disorder.

This kind of example reminds us that we do not consider sympathy for people to be largely irrational, nor to be ungrounded in facts. Sympathy for animals is constructed, and can be justified, on a similar basis.[20] If the facts in a given case, facts about suffering and innocence, for example, are such as to justify a certain response toward humans, then they justify a similar response if the individuals involved are animals. For instance, the sympathy that an ethologist may develop for an old animal that is weak and losing its place in the family group may be informed by the best available knowledge of the mentality of the animals in question, knowledge that may make it just as appropriate to feel sad for this creature as for a human under roughly similar circumstances.

Indeed, on the minimal assumption that sympathy for humans is appropriate, we can argue that there is no way to logically limit such sympathy to humans. Other species of creatures are imaginable, even if none in fact exist, that would merit a sympathetic response. Imagine, for example, that we discover a previously unknown primate species that is approximately halfway between the orangutan and Homo sapiens in development (or imagine that we create such a species through gene splicing). Imagine that this species has the mental development of a very retarded human, and has a rudimentary language. Surely such creatures would merit a sympathetic response; it would be appropriate to be sad if they suffered, and impressed if they struggled and conquered some obstacle. Sympathetic responses, then, cannot be logically restricted to one species. The limits of appropriate sympathy are an open question. Once we see there is no species barrier, however, the empirical facts about animals appear to justify wide application of our sympathies to them.

5. Anthropomorphism and Animal Thought

At bottom, it is the traditional charge of anthropomorphism that undoubtedly underlies tough-minded claims that sympathy for animals is mistaken.[21] I have already rejected the claim that sympathy presupposes an assumption of close similarity between a given animal and humans. Even if people often do assume a false similarity between human mental life and that of animals, when these mistakes are corrected there still is a broad objective basis for feeling sympathy for animals. To justify the rejection of sympathy for animals, the charge of anthropomorphism has to be made in a more radical way. One way to do this would be to claim, as supporters of the traditional charge of anthropomorphism do, that animals simply lack any mental life that we can sympathize with. However, it is difficult to accept the argument once advanced for this: that animals are mere machines, and humans are not. Humans are, after all, a species of animal. We need some other grounds to show that our sympathy *with* animals is entirely mistaken.

Mary Midgley suggests that the worry about anthropomorphism rests on the skeptical problem of other minds.[22] Yet there appears to be no way to formulate the other minds problem so that it applies to animals but not to fellow humans. Indeed, some ways of formulating the problem apply to humans and *not* to animals. For instance, one classic way to generate the problem involves the possibility of deception.[23] People sometimes pretend to have mental states that in fact they do not have. They can pretend to be in pain when they are not, and vice versa; they can dissemble about their beliefs, and so forth. Hence, so the argument goes, there is always in every particular case a logical gap between behavior and mental state, and thus we cannot tell what mental state, if any, underlies a person's behavior. This way of formulating the other minds worry appears to have little application to animals. Skeptics about animals do not suppose that they are capable of this sort of deception, and to suppose that they are capable of deception would automatically undermine the charge of anthropomorphism. Creatures capable of higher order intentionally, such as the intention to deceive, would be comparable to humans in mentality.

The main mechanism for deception between humans is language. The lack of language has traditionally been used to deny animals a mental life; the same lack can also be turned in their favor. In lacking language animals lack that which makes other persons potentially alien.[24] In many respects the mind of another person is potentially more unknown to me than the mind of my dog.

Can more be made out of animals' lack of language? The most influential recent attempt to establish a Cartesian-like gap between humans and nonhuman animals on the basis of language has been made by Donald Davidson. In "Thought and Talk" Davidson argues for the thesis "that a creature cannot have thoughts unless it is an interpreter of the speech of another."[25] Having a language is a necessary condition for thoughts, by which Davidson means the whole array of propositional attitudes, both states and events, such as are reported by "believes," "wants," and "intends," on the one hand, and by "came to believe," "forgot," "noticed," on the other. Since as far as we know no animals have anything that Davidson would count as a true language, we may conclude that no animals have any thoughts.[26] Davidson's argument sounds devastating to the validity of sympathy for animals. Is it?

To answer this question we must first distinguish two stages of Davidson's skepticism about the thoughts of languageless creatures. The first stage follows from the plausible claim that it is inaccurate to attribute to creatures without language thoughts that contain the distinctions embodied in our linguistic expression:

> It is much harder to say, when speech is not present, how to distinguish universal thoughts from conjunctions of thoughts, or how to attribute conditional thoughts, or thoughts with, so to speak, mixed quantification.... unless there is behavior that can be interpreted as speech, the evidence will not be adequate to justify the fine distinctions we are used to making in the attribution of thoughts. (p. 163f)

It follows that we must be cautious when we attribute thoughts to animals, and that our attributions will always be fundamentally misleading. This caution comes as no surprise, for we typically block the usual implications of such attributions when we apply them to animals. We credit the dog who barks up the wrong tree with the belief that the squirrel he was chasing is in the tree, but we do not comfortably connect that belief attribution to other related beliefs that would require human concepts. What does not follow, even for Davidson, is that animals do not have thoughts, for he does not suppose that every thought can be correctly formulated in words.

Davidson's more controversial position goes well beyond this first stage of skepticism to deny thought entirely to nonlinguistic creatures. He argues that beliefs are required for thoughts of all sorts: "It is necessary that there be endless interlocked beliefs. The system of such beliefs identifies a thought by locating it in a logical and epistemic space" (p. 157). He then argues that languageless creatures cannot have beliefs. Hence, they cannot have thoughts. It is not that we cannot adequately formulate their beliefs, but that belief can arise only in the process of interpreting the utterances of a linguistic community.

The argument for these claims appears incomplete, however, because it moves from an analysis of beliefs that arise in connection, with assertion, to the claim that belief arises *only* in this connection. Davidson claims, "The concept of belief thus stands ready to take up the slack between objective truth and the held true, and we come to understand it *just* in this connection" (p. 170, my emphasis). His argument, however, best supports the weaker claim that this connection is one way we come to understand and attribute beliefs. To move from the claim that belief is required for the interpretation of speech to the conclusion that the interpretation of speech is required for belief does not appear to take seriously the possibility of languageless belief.

Davidson partially fills this gap by further arguing that languageless creatures cannot have the *concept of belief,* and hence cannot have beliefs:

> Someone cannot have a belief unless he understands the possibility of being mistaken, and this requires grasping the contrast between truth and error—true belief and false belief. But this contrast, I have argued, can emerge only in the context of interpretation, which alone forces us to the idea of an objective public truth. (p. 170)

This claim seems stronger than any argument Davidson explicitly presents. It is plausible that languageless creatures cannot have a self-conscious concept of error, but it is not self-evident that they cannot have some behavioral analogue of such a concept. At issue is what it is to "understand the possibility of being mistaken." If a polar bear mother searches for her cubs in one spot and then gives up and goes to another place, apparently continuing her search, is it mistaken to attribute to her in some sense the realization that her first thought was wrong? To take another example, it is very natural to attribute false beliefs, and some understanding of being mistaken, to primates in experiments in which they learn to solve puzzles by trial and error.

Even granting that languageless creatures cannot have beliefs, it can be argued that this has no damaging implications for sympathy with animals. Consider the claim that beliefs are central to other thoughts. Davidson argues persuasively that thoughts need to be located somehow: "Even to wonder whether the gun is loaded, or to speculate on the possibility that the gun is loaded, requires the belief, for example, that a gun is a weapon, that it is a more or less enduring physical object, and so on" (p. 157). What this shows is that for a creature to have thoughts it must have some conceptual scheme, some picture of the world. The dog that barks up the wrong tree must in some sense have a conception of squirrels, of trees, of objects being up in trees, and so on. No doubt a dog's conceptual scheme is extremely different from our own. Lacking language or other means of self-conscious analysis, the dog cannot scrutinize its own conceptual scheme, and it therefore lacks Davidsonian beliefs. But it is not clear that the dog thereby lacks a scheme to locate thoughts with respect to the world.

As Davidson admits, "Adverting to beliefs and desires to explain action is therefore a way of fitting an action into a pattern of behavior made coherent by the [common-sense theory of action]" (p. 159). It is far from clear that such appeal to beliefs, or something very like beliefs, to explain both human and animal action, even where no verbal expression of thought is in question, is any less fundamental to the concept of belief than is the use of belief to explain utterances. Furthermore, even if we are not to explain animal behavior within the strict terms of this model, it can be plausibly urged that we will be forced to appeal to a very similar model to explain why animals do what they do. If they do not strictly have beliefs, desires, and intentions, then they certainly appear to have cognitive states that are closely analogous to beliefs, desires, and intentions. When a pride of lions steals up on a herd of antelope they surely have something remarkably analogous to the intention to catch and kill one of the antelope, something very analogous to the desire to do so, and something very analogous to a set of beliefs about the location of the antelope.

More generally, it does not follow that animals do not have a mental life just because they do not have Davidsonian thoughts. They appear to "remember," to "identify" objects, to "recognize" individuals, and so on. Whales, lions, wolves, and many other social animals engage in flexible, interactive group behavior that does a good job of imitating consciously coordinated activity. All of this is cognitive behavior that is at least analogous to human cognitive behavior.[27]

This suggests that the presupposition of sympathy, namely a mental life analogous to our own, is not undermined by Davidson's thesis. We can support this conclusion further by noting that Davidson's thesis applies perfectly to nonlinguistic humans. If his argument is correct, a child learning language will have neither beliefs nor thoughts. Even if the child has "names" for objects, it will not yet have anything like a theory of interpretation, and so nothing like Davidsonian beliefs. Nor would feral children or the prelinguistic Mr. Ballard, reported by William James, have Davidsonian beliefs or thoughts. But surely all such individuals have a mental life of significant proportions. And just as we appropriately feel sympathy for prelinguistic children, similar grounds justify sympathy for animals that have an equal cognitive development. We can even imagine cases of highly intelligent humans, capable of solving complex problems, who might be languageless for one reason or another. We would surely attribute to such persons many mental states analogous to our own, even though it could not be said that they have Davidsonian thoughts.

I have been arguing in defense of sympathy *with* animals in the face of Davidson's thesis. Although earlier I claimed that sympathy *for* animals presupposes sympathy *with* them, it is not obvious that the requisite sympathy with amounts to requiring analogous *cognitive* states, such as belief. Suffering, for example, may require only the ability to feel pain, which Davidson has given us no reason to question in animals. If, quite implausibly, it is claimed that suffering worthy of sympathy requires more than this ability, then we can advert to the argument of the preceding paragraph. Whatever is required for real suffering, nonlinguistic humans can suffer, and so can animals in analogous situations.

6. Conclusion

I conclude that in spite of a bad press, sympathy for animals is as appropriate and justified as sympathy for humans. Although feelings of sympathy may sometimes be based on mistaken assumptions of similarity between humans and animals, sympathy does not logically require such misinformation and inappropriate projections. There appears to be no very cogent set of ideas underlying the frequent and casually made charge of anthropomorphism. There are no plausible grounds that establish the sort of gulf between humans and animals that is required to refute the application of our sympathies to animals. Moreover, it appears that the concept of sympathy for animals is coherent and its implications both substantive and not absurd.

Hence, it appears that something has to give way in our usual views about the difference between sympathy for fellow humans and sympathy for animals. One familiar aspect of sympathy is compassion.

Those who have compassion for persons who suffer are considered to be morally conscientious, especially if they act on that compassion. On the other hand, those who have compassion for animals who suffer are thought to be a bit eccentric, especially if they act on that compassion. Even if humans suffer much more than animals can, the difference does not appear to warrant praising one response while dismissing the other. The same moral psychology is being applied in both cases, and it is equally likely to be based on objective conditions of suffering in both cases. And just as people *ought* to respond sympathetically to the plight of certain humans, they *ought* to respond to the plight of certain animals. We can, of course, propose giving up compassion and other aspects of sympathy for humans; what we cannot do coherently is to draw a line sharply limiting sympathy to our fellow humans.

Notes

1. Herschell Chipp, *Theories of Modern Art* (Berkeley: University of California Press, 1971), p. 178.

2. Some moral theorists may doubt the relevance of sympathy to moral theory, claiming that the relevant moral factors in any situation are entirely determined by objective factors such as justice, fairness, or utility. But sympathy may play a role in determining these factors. Moreover, many accounts of morality take moral psychology seriously, and almost any moral theory will have to find some place for our moral feelings, connected as they are to our moral intuitions. See note 5.

3. J. Baird Callicott, "Animal Liberation: A Triangular Affair," *Environmental Ethics* 2 (1980): 311-38. (All page references in this section are to chapter 2, this volume.) More precisely, Callicott argues that the conceptual foundations of animal liberation are *incompatible* with the conceptual foundations of Leopold's land ethic, a philosophy that Callicott takes as the paradigm of environmental ethics. For a criticism of Callicott's interpretation of animal liberation see Edward Johnson, "Animal Liberation Versus the Land Ethic," *Environmental Ethics* 3 (1981): 265-73. In "Non-Anthropocentric Value Theory and Environmental Ethics," *American Philosophical Quarterly* 21 (1984): 299-309, Callicott argues for the slightly different position, that animal liberation is *inadequate* to ground a radical environmental ethics that takes the biosphere as the ultimate repository (or object) of value. Callicott is right about this, but wrong, I argue, to suggest that without such a radical break with traditional ethics, concern for the biosphere cannot be adequately grounded.

4. That *anthropomorphism* is something definite and inherently mistaken is commonly assumed without argument in discussions of animal thought. Davidson, for example, suggests that "Attributions of intentions and beliefs to dogs smack of anthropomorphism." Donald Davidson, "Thought and Talk," in *Inquiries into Truth and Interpretation* (Oxford: Oxford University Press, 1984), p. 155. John Bishop claims that "one can argue validly from the similarity between a dumb creature's and a human's behaviour to the conclusion that the former as well as the latter is the outcome of practical reasoning only if one can exclude the possibility that the similarity results from anthropomorphic projection." John Bishop, "More Thought on Thought and Talk," *Mind* 89 no. 353 (January 1980): 1–16.

5. Sympathy is fundamental to moral theory in that it determines the range of individuals to which moral principles apply. This is illustrated by Robert Elliot's argument that Rawls is wrong to exclude nonhuman animals from the principles of justice developed in *A Theory of Justice*. The issue turns on whether the participants in the original position could turn out to be nonhuman animals in the real world. To make sense out of this possibility, Elliot argues that "The idea of judging how things are from an animal's point of view makes sense. Indeed we do make such judgments. We are capable of empathetic understanding with regard to animals and we can make comparative judgments about different lifestyles based on our understanding of the propensities, desire, interests and preferences that they have." Robert Elliot, "Rawlsian Justice and Non-Human Animals," *Journal of Applied Philosophy* 1, no. 1 (1984): 103.

6. See Dale Jamieson, "Utilitarianism and the Morality of Killing," *Philosophical Studies* 45, (1984): 209–21.

7. Callicott, "Animal Liberation: A Triangular Affair." He repeats this claim without argument in "Non-Anthropocentric Value Theory and Environmental Ethics," where he criticizes animal liberation because "it makes no distinction between wild and domestic organisms. A Pekinese lap dog and a 'bobby calf' have the same moral status as a wild timber wolf and wild otter" (p. 300f). In my view, if we consider these animals independently of the conditions under which they may be living, it is perfectly appropriate that each can engage our sympathies. On the other hand, each of these animals makes a very different contribution to different ecosystems, and these systems may have nonequivalent worth. See sec. 3 below.

8. This only shows that animal liberationists, and many ordinary people, do not make a sharp distinction between wild and domesticated animals. Some environmentalists may hold that this is a mistake and that a sharp distinction *ought* to be made between the two classes of animals; we *ought* to care much more about wild creatures of all sorts than we do about domestic animals, and we *ought not* to feel "sympathy" for wild animals (because this is

merely sentimental), nor for domestic animals (because they interfere with the wild ecosystem). It is sufficient to note that this is a theoretically motivated position that follows from valuing "wild" ecosystems over mixed or human-altered ecosystems. In other words, this position expresses a commitment to an abstract set of values (the beauty, integrity, and stability of certain biosystems) and is not a report of our moral psychology toward animals. Our sympathies, I contend, appropriately extend to all sorts of creatures living in all sorts of conditions.

9. David Hume, *Treatise of Human Nature*, bk. 3, pt. 3, sec. 1. Hume's notion of a sentiment of humanity is a natural sympathy based on "common humanity." That which is the common basis of this sentiment seems clearly to be distributed more widely than just to our species.

10. J. Baird Callicott, "Hume's *Is/Ought* Dichotomy and the Relation of Ecology to Leopold's Land Ethic," *Environmental Ethics* 4 (1982): 163–74. According to Callicott, Leopold would concur in this extension of our sympathies to nonhuman animals: "Leopold tries to excite our sympathy and fellow feeling by portraying animal behaviour as in many ways similar to our own and as motivated by similar psychological experiences" (p. 172). The consequence of Leopold's argument is that "we should feel and thus behave... toward other living things in ways similar to the way we feel and thus behave toward our human kin" (ibid.). From Callicott's perspective, however, this extension of a feeling of kinship is not radical enough. He claims to find in Hume that we have "not only... sympathy for our fellows, we are also naturally endowed with a sentiment, the proper object of which is society itself" (p. 173). Then, arguing that ecology shows that the biotic community as a whole is a society of which humans are members, he attempts to derive a more radical holistic environmental ethics based on Humean sentiments. This argument is repeated in "Non-Anthropocentric Value Theory" and in "Intrinsic Value, Quantum Theory, and Environmental Ethics," *Environmental Ethics* 7 (1985): 257–75. However, I doubt: (a) that there really is a sentiment for society as a whole—as opposed to an interacting collection of individuals; (b) that it makes sense to extend the notion of society to include "soils and waters"; (c) that the existence of such an extendable sentiment could have any implications concerning the value of a wild biotic society over a tame one.

11. Nagel has argued that we cannot really understand the experience of alien creatures with very different bodies. I believe that he overstates the case. Moreover, a partial understanding will do for what I am arguing. See Thomas Nagel, "What Is It Like to Be a Bat?" *Philosophical Review* 83 (1974): 435–50.

12. For more details about the problems of detecting animal suffering see Marian Stamp Dawkins, *Animal Suffering: The Science of Animal Welfare* (London and New York: Chapman and Hall, 1980).

13. Thus, rational sympathy is closely related to Daniel Dennett's notion

that we explain (and understand) humans or computers by taking up the *intentional stance.* Cf. Daniel Dennett, *Brainstorms* (Montgomery, Vt.: Bradford, 1978).

14. Judith Shklar, "Putting Cruelty First," *Daedalus* 3 no. 3 (Summer 1982): 17–27, 20.

15. This is why we cannot literally have sympathy for an ecosystem. The kind of sympathy most people feel for cars, machines, and perhaps ecosystems is an as-if or pretend sympathy. We pretend, or perhaps cannot quite escape the idea, that the object, say a machine that is being dismantled, is suffering just as a living, conscious being would. But as far as we know this belief is false. For sympathy to be truly appropriate, the object I feel sympathy *with* must be at least a conscious being.

16. The notion of approximating to human traits should not be taken in the superficial sense of approximating to human physical appearance. What is involved is, rather, an approximation to the general features of human life, largely biological in nature, as well as to human mental life. An organism from outer space might look nothing like us and yet be very like us. Conversely, an organism might look like us but be so alien in its mental, biological and social life that it would be nothing like us in reality.

17. By contrast, Callicott's extension of Humean sentiments to the biosphere *per se* fails to give any clear answer to this central value question. Even accepting the idea that we have a sentiment for society as a whole, and that this sentiment endows society with value, nothing follows about *which* form of society is to be preferred from the many possible forms it has taken and could take. The extension of such a sentiment to the biosphere (see "Non-Anthropocentric Value Theory," p. 305) stumbles over the same logical point. Nothing follows from our "biophilia" *per se* about how we should prefer a wild biosphere to a domesticated biosphere.

18. Edward Johnson, "Animal Liberation," p. 270 (his emphasis).

19. The widespread use of animals in scientific experiments reinforces the idea that sympathy is mistaken from the scientific point of view. This conclusion, however, doesn't follow: (a) it is in scientists' self-interest to bracket the sympathy they might naturally feel for the animals they experiment upon; (b) most scientists undoubtedly accept the need for guidelines on the care and use of laboratory animals, and such need implies that animals should not be made to suffer gratuitously.

20. I believe that this claim for animals can be defended even in the face of the evidence from history of culturally validated cruelty to animals. For such an example, see Robert Darnton, *The Great Cat Massacre and Other Episodes in French Cultural History* (New York: Basic Books, 1984). The background beliefs and attitudes in other societies may be very different, especially concerning the two criteria just mentioned, harm and innocence.

Nor is it implausible to suggest that these societies were simply ignorant by our standards about the animals to which they were cruel.

21. Not the *original* charge of anthropomorphism, which was attributing human characteristics to God. Cf. Mary Midgley, *Animals and Why They Matter* (Athens, Ga.: University of Georgia Press, 1983), chap. 11.

22. Midgley, *Animals*, p. 129–38.

23. Cf. the well-known version of the other minds argument by V. C. Chappell in his introduction to *The Philosophy of Mind* (Englewood Cliffs, N.J.: Prentice-Hall, 1962).

24. This is denied by Jonathan Bennett in *Linguistic Behaviour* (Cambridge: Cambridge University Press, 1976): "On the face of it, a language seems to offer an extra way of revealing and disguising them" (p. 31).

25. Donald Davidson, *Inquiries into Truth and Interpretation*, p. 157. Subsequent parenthetical page references are to this edition.

26. The opposite position is vigorously defended by D. M. Armstrong, *Belief, Truth and Knowledge* (Cambridge: Cambridge University Press, 1973), chap. 3, and by Jonathan Bennett, *Linguistic Behaviour*, sec. 9.

27. I take for granted that we may properly attribute some sort of perceptual life and sensations to animals. If a Davidsonian held that seeing, hearing, etc., are propositional in nature, then it would follow that animals do not even see or hear things. This is so implausible that we ought to conclude either that perception is not a thought in Davidson's sense or that Davidson's argument against languageless thought must be wrong.

11

Animal Liberation and Environmental Ethics: Back Together Again

J. Baird Callicott

Probably more than any other one thing, my article "Animal Liberation: A Triangular Affair" has led to an increasingly acrimonious estrangement between advocates of individualistic animal welfare ethics and advocates of holistic ecocentric ethics.[1] I think this estrangement is regrettable because it is divisive. Animal welfare ethicists and environmental ethicists have overlapping concerns. From a practical point of view, it would be far wiser to make common cause against a common enemy—the destructive forces at work ravaging the nonhuman world—than to continue squabbling among ourselves.

Not long after the schism emerged, that is, not long after the appearance of "Triangular Affair," Mary Anne Warren took a positive step toward reconciliation. She insisted that ecocentric environmental ethics and animal welfare ethics were "complementary," not contradictory.[2]

Warren's approach is thoroughly pluralistic. She argues that animals, like human beings, have rights. But she also argues that animals do not enjoy the *same* rights as human beings and that the rights of animals are not *equal* to human rights. And she argues, further, that animal rights and human rights are grounded in different psychological capacities. A holistic environmental ethic, Warren suggests, rests upon still other foundations—the instrumental value of "natural resources" to us and to future generations and the "intrinsic value" we (or at least some of us) intuitively find in plants, species, "mountains,

249

oceans, and the like."[3]

Warren recommends, in short, a wholly reasonable ethical eclecticism. Human beings have strong rights because we are autonomous; animals have weaker rights because they are sentient; the environment should be used with respect—even though it may not have rights —because it is a whole and unified thing which we value in a variety of ways. Conflicts will certainly arise among all the foci of the human/ animal/environment triangle—an example cited by Warren concerns introduced feral goats which threaten native plant species on New Zealand—but well-meaning people can muddle through the moral wilderness, balancing and compromising the competing interests and incommensurable values. In general, Warren concludes, "Only by *combining* the environmentalist and animal rights perspectives can we take account of the full range of moral considerations which ought to guide our interactions with the nonhuman world."[4]

However reasonable, there is something philosophically unsatisfying in Warren's ethical eclecticism. Moral philosophy historically has striven for theoretical unity and closure—often at considerable sacrifice of moral common sense. Consider, for example, Kant's deontological dismissal of the moral value of actions tainted with "inclination," even when the inclination in question is wholly altruistic. Or consider the morally outrageous consequences that some utilitarians have been led to accept in order faithfully to adhere to the theoretical foundations of utilitarianism.

In striving for theoretical unity and consistency, moral philosophy is not unlike natural philosophy. When a variety of apparently disparate phenomena (e.g., falling bodies, planetary motions, and tides) can be embraced by a single idea (gravity), the natural philosopher feels that a deep (though perhaps not ultimate) truth about nature has been struck. Similarly in moral philosophy, we strive to explain the commonly held welter of practical precepts and moral intuitions by appeal to one (or at most very few theoretically related) imperative(s), principle(s), summary maxim(s), or Golden Rule(s). And if we succeed we feel that we have discovered something true and deep about morality.

The moral philosopher's love for theoretical unity, coherency, and self-consistency may represent more than a matter of mere intellectual taste. There is a practical reason to prefer theoretical unity in moral philosophy just as there is in natural philosophy. Probably more than anything else, the failure of the Ptolemaic system of astronomy— with its hodgepodge of ad hoc devices—accurately to predict the positions of the planets led Copernicus to unify the celestial phenomena by introducing a single radical assumption: that the sun, not the earth, is at the center of it all. In moral philosophy, when competing moral claims cannot be articulated in the same terms, they cannot be decisively compared and resolved. Ethical eclecticism leads, it would seem inevitably, to moral incommensurability in hard cases. So we are compelled to go back to the theoretical drawing board.

To achieve something more than a mere coalition of convenience —to achieve, rather, a lasting alliance—between animal welfare ethics and ecocentric environmental ethics will require the development of a moral theory that embraces both programs *and* that provides a framework for the adjudication of the very real conflicts between human welfare, animal welfare, and ecological integrity. It is the purpose of this essay to suggest such a theory on terms, shall we say, favorable to ecocentric environmental ethics, just as Tom Regan has suggested such a theory on terms favorable to animal welfare ethics.

Regan proposes a "rights-based environmental ethic" consistent with and, indeed, launched from his "rights view" version of animal welfare ethics. He himself has not worked out the grounds for the rights of individual trees and other non-"subjects-of-a-life," but he urges environmental ethicists seriously to take up the challenge. Writes Regan,

> The implications of the successful development of a rights-based environmental ethic, one that made the case that individual inanimate objects (e.g. *this* redwood) have inherent value and a basic moral right to treatment respectful of that value, should be welcomed by environmentalists....A rights-based environmental ethic remains a live option, one that, though far from being established, merits continued exploration....Were we to show proper respect for the rights of individuals who make up the biotic community, would not the *community* be preserved?[5]

To this (actually rhetorical) question Mark Sagoff replied, "I believe [that] this is an empirical question, the answer to which is 'no'. The environmentalist is concerned about preserving evolutionary processes, e.g., natural selection, whether these processes have deep enough respect for the rights of individuals..." or not.[6] Nature, as Sagoff points out, is not fair; it does not respect the rights of individuals. To attempt to safeguard the rights of each and every individual member of an ecosystem would, correspondingly, be to attempt to stop practically all trophic processes beyond photosynthesis—and

even then we would somehow have to deal ethically with the individual life-threatening and hence rights-violating competition among
plants for sunlight. An ethic for the preservation of nature, therefore,
could hardly get off on the right foot if, at the start, it condemns as
unjust and immoral the trophic asymmetries lying at the heart of evolutionary and ecological processes. An environmental ethic cannot be
generated, as it were by an invisible hand, from a further extension of
rights (on the basis of some yet-to-be-worked-out-theory) to "individual inanimate objects."

I have another, and I think better, proposal which was suggested
to me by the work of Mary Midgley.

Midgley, in her book *Animals and Why They Matter*, grounds the
mattering—that is, in more familiar contemporary philosophical
terminology, the moral considerability—of animals in what she calls
"the mixed community":

> All human communities have involved animals. The ani-
> mals...became tame, not just through fear of violence, but be-
> cause they were able to form individual bonds with those who
> tamed them by coming to understand the social signals ad-
> dressed to them.... They were able to do this, not only because
> the people taming them were social beings, but because they
> themselves were so as well.[7]

Midgley goes on to draw out a number of consequences from this
pregnant and profound observation. Since we and the animals who
belong to our mixed human-animal community are coevolved social
beings participating in a single society, we and they share certain
feelings that attend upon and enable sociability—sympathy, compassion, trust, love, and so on. Her main point is to show that it is preposterous to believe, with those whom she identifies as "Behaviourists,"
that animal members of our mixed community are mere automata,
devoid of a rich subjective life. And her subordinate point is to show
that the species-barrier to human-animal social interaction is both
artificial and unhistorical. We have enjoyed, and there is no good philosophical reason why we should not continue to enjoy, interspecies
social relationships and intimacy. Says Midgley, "the problem here is
not about anthropomorphism, but about Behaviourism, and it arises
already on the human scene. The barrier [between subjects] does not
fall between us and the dog. It falls between you and me.... Natural
sympathy, as Hume rightly said, has a basis in common humanity.
Does it therefore follow that it stops at the species-barrier?"[8]

Midgley, curiously, does not go on to elaborate a positive moral theory which incorporates to the best advantage the very thorough and convincing case she has made for the existence of a wide variety of animal consciousness—from that of dogs to that of work elephants —each with its species' peculiarities, but each broadly based in, shall we say, a common bio-sociality. Midgley certainly does not go on to argue, à la Peter Singer, that the "sentiency" ambient among animal members of the mixed community, which she has so fully and forcefully defended, should constitute a *criterion* for equal moral consideration; nor does she argue, à la Tom Regan, that having a rich subjective life entitles domestic animals to equal moral *rights*. Her approving mention of Hume, however, and her emphasis on social affections and sympathy suggest to me that, if pressed, Midgley would sketch a Humean ethical theory to make moral hay of her defense of the subjectivity of animals and the possibility of intersubjective interaction between species.

David Hume's moral theory is distinguished from the prevailing modern alternatives—utilitarianism and deontology—primarily by two features: (1) Morality is grounded in feelings, not reason; although reason has its role to play in ethics, it is part of the supporting cast. And (2) altruism is as primitive as egoism; it is not reducible either to enlightened self-interest or to duty.

A pertinent contrast to Hume's understanding of ethics is afforded by Peter Singer. In *Animal Liberation* he heaped scorn on "sentimental appeals for sympathy" toward animals and avowed that his animal welfare ethic was grounded exclusively in "basic moral principles which we all accept; and the application of these principles to victims... is demanded by reason, not emotion."[9] Singer follows the usual theoretical approach of normal modern moral philosophy— elegantly described by Kenneth Goodpaster—which has been to generalize egoism.[10] Baldly stated, it comes to this: I insist upon moral consideration from others or moral rights for myself. My entitlement to moral standing or moral rights may be plausibly defended by appeal to a psychological characteristic or capacity possessed by me which is arguably relevant to ethical treatment. But then "others" are entitled to equal moral consideration to the extent that they possess, in equal measure, the same psychologocal characteristic. I may not love others (in this connection, Singer wants us to know that he keeps no pets) or sympathize with them; indeed I may be entirely indifferent to their concerns or even actively dislike them. Still, I am compelled by the logic of my own moral claim upon others to grudgingly grant their similar claims upon me.

Hume took a different course. He argued that both our moral judgments and our actions are rooted in altruistic feelings or sentiments that are very often opposed to "self-love." Writes Hume, "So far from thinking that men have no affection for anything beyond themselves, I am of opinion that tho' it be rare to meet with one, who loves any single person better than himself; yet 'tis rare to meet with one, in whom all the kind affections, taken together, do not over-balance all the selfish."[11] According to Hume, these kind affections are the soil in which our morals are rooted and from which they take their nourishment.

Aldo Leopold, in "The Land Ethic" of *A Sand County Almanac*, evidently patterned his own concept of an "ethical sequence" on Charles Darwin's discussion of the evolution of ethics in *The Descent of Man*, and Darwin cites both Hume's *Treatise* and Adam Smith's *Theory of the Moral Sentiments* as the philosophical antecedents of his own "natural history" of ethics. I have argued in a variety of venues and in considerable detail that, therefore, Hume's moral theory is the historical ancestor of Aldo Leopold's land ethic, the modern ethic of choice of the environmental movement and of many contemporary environmental philosophers.[12] What's more, the moral fulcrum of the Leopold land ethic is the ecological concept of the "biotic community."

Mary Midgley's suggested animal welfare ethic and Aldo Leopold's seminal environmental ethic thus share a common, fundamentally Humean understanding of ethics as grounded in altruistic feelings. And they share a common ethical bridge between the human and nonhuman domains in the concept of community—Midgley's "mixed community" and Leopold's "biotic community." Combining these two conceptions of a metahuman moral community we have the basis of a unified animal-environmental ethical theory.

Hume regarded the social feelings upon which the edifice of ethics is erected to be a brute fact of human nature. Darwin explained how we came to have such feelings, as he explained so many other curious natural facts, by appeal to the evolutionary principle of natural selection.

Darwin's biosocial reduction of Hume's moral theory is particularly ingenious since, at first glance, altruism seems, from an evolutionary point of view, anomalous and paradoxical. Given the ceaseless struggle for the limited means to life lying at the heart of Darwin's conception of nature, concern for others and deferential behavior would appear to be maladaptive tendencies quickly eliminated from a gene pool, should they ever chance to emerge. Or so it would seem—until we consider the survival-reproductive advantages of social membership. Concern for others and self-restraint are necessary for social amalgamation and integration, Darwin argued. "Ethical" behavior is, in effect, the dues an individual pays to join a social group; and the survival advantages of group membership to individuals more than compensate them for the personal sacrifices required by morality. Since most animals, including most human beings, are not sufficiently intelligent to make a benefit-cost analysis of their social actions, we are outfitted, Darwin theorized, with "social instincts" impelling us toward socially conducive moral behavior.

What is right and what is wrong, Darwin suggests, reflects, more or less, the specific organizational structure of society—since ethics have evolved to facilitate social cohesion. The "ethics" of a hierarchically structured pack of wolves, for example, require celibacy of most of its members. The ethics of apolitical and egalitarian human tribal societies require members periodically to redistribute their wealth. Who is and who is not an appropriate beneficiary of one's moral sympathies, similarly, reflects the *perceived* boundaries of social membership. In our dealings with those whom we regard as members, the rules apply; in our dealings with those whom we regard as outsiders, we do as we please.

Midgely's marvelous insight is that, however exclusive of other human beings the perceived boundaries of historical human societies may have been, they all, nevertheless, have included some animals— aboriginally man's hunting partner, the dog; and, after the Neolithic Revolution, a variety of herd, farm, and work animals: everything from the cow and pig to the Asian elephant and water buffalo. Consonant with my analysis in "A Triangular Affair," Midgley suggests therefore that a big part of the immorality of the treatment of animals in the current industrial phase of human civilization is that we have broken trust with erstwhile fellow members of our traditionally mixed communities. Animals have been depersonalized and mechanized and that goes a long way toward explaining the moral revulsion we all feel toward the factory farm and animal research laboratory.

How we ought and ought not treat one another (including animals) is determined, according to the logic of biosocial moral theory, by the nature and organization of communities. Even to those deeply sympathetic to the plight of animals there is something deeply amiss in the concept of *equal* moral consideration or *equal* moral rights for animals, required by the logic of extending the prevailing modern moral paradigms, just as there is something deeply amiss in the idea of requiring equal consideration for all human beings regardless of social relationship.

Peter Singer, once again, provides a revealing example of the latter as well as of the former. He argues that he has failed in his duty because he does not donate the greatest portion of his modest income to help alleviate the suffering of starving people living halfway around the world, *even though* to do so would impoverish not only himself, but his own children.[13] Suffering is suffering, no matter whose it may be, and it is the duty of a moral agent to be impartial in weighing the suffering of one against the suffering of another. Since the starving suffer more from his withholding money from them than his children would suffer were he to impoverish them short of starvation, Singer concludes that therefore he should give the greater portion of his income to the starving.

From Midgley's biosocial point of view, we are members of nested communities each of which has a different structure and therefore different moral requirements. At the center is the immediate family. I have a duty not only to feed, clothe, and shelter my own children, I also have a duty to bestow affection on them. But to bestow a similar affection on the neighbors' kids is not only not my duty, it would be considered anything from odd to criminal were I to behave so. Similarly, I have obligations to my neighbors which I do not have to my less proximate fellow citizens—to watch their houses while they are on vacation, for example, or to go to the grocery for them when they are sick or disabled. I have obligations to my fellow citizens which I do not have toward human beings in general *and* I have obligations to human beings in general which I do not have toward animals in general.

These subtly shaded social-moral relationships are complex and overlapping. Pets, for example, are—properly so, Midgley argues—surrogate family members and merit treatment not owed either to less intimately related animals, for example to barnyard animals, *or*, for that matter, to less intimately related human beings.

Barnyard animals, over hundreds of generations, have been genetically engineered (by the old-fashioned method of selective breeding) to play certain roles in the mixed community. To condemn the morality of these roles—as we rightly condemn human slavery and penury—is to condemn the very being of these creatures. The animal welfare ethic of the mixed community, thus, would not censure using draft animals for work or even slaughtering meat animals for food so long as the keeping and using of such animals was not in violation—as factory farming clearly is—of a kind of evolved and unspoken social contract between man and beast.

But it is not my intention here to attempt to detail our duties to the various classes of the animal members of mixed communities.

Rather, I wish to argue that whatever our various duties to various kinds of domestic animals may, from this point of view, turn out to be, they differ in a general and profound way from our duties toward the wild animal members of the biotic community.

One of the principal frustrations with the familiar utilitarian and deontological approaches to animal liberation that I have experienced, as an environmental ethicist, is the absence of a well-grounded distinction between our proper ethical relations with, on the one hand, domestic and, on the other, wild animals. According to the conventional approach, cattle and antelope, pigs and porcupines, bears and battery hens are entitled to equal moral consideration and/or equal rights.

The Midgley-Leopold biosocial moral theory, by contrast, clearly provides the missing distinction. Domestic animals are members of the mixed community and ought to enjoy, therefore, all the rights and privileges, whatever they may turn out to be, attendant upon that membership. Wild animals are, by definition, not members of the mixed community and therefore should not lie on the same spectrum of graded moral standing as family members, neighbors, fellow citizens, fellow human beings, pets, and other domestic animals.

Wild animals, rather, are members of the biotic community. The structure of the biotic community is described by ecology. The duties and obligations of a biotic community ethic or "land ethic," as Leopold called it, may, accordingly, be derived from an ecological description of nature—just as our duties and obligations to members of the mixed community can be derived from a description of the mixed community.

Most generally and abstractly described, the ecosystem is, to quote Leopold, "a fountain of energy flowing through a circuit of soils, plants, and animals."[14] The currency, in other words, of the economy of nature is solar energy captured upon incidence by green plants and thereafter transferred from animal organism to animal organism— not from hand to hand, like coined money, but, so to speak, from stomach to stomach. The most fundamental fact of life in the biotic community is eating... *and being eaten.* Each species is adapted to a trophic niche; each is a link in a food chain, and a knot in a food web. Whatever moral entitlements a being may have as a member of the biotic community, *not* among them is the right to life. Rather, each being should be respected and left alone to pursue its modus vivendi— even if its way of life causes harm to other beings, including other sentient beings. The integrity, stability, and beauty of the biotic community depend upon *all* members, in their appropriate numbers, functioning in their co-evolved life ways.

Among the most disturbing implications drawn from conventional indiscriminate animal liberation/rights theory is that, were it possible for us to do so, we ought to protect innocent vegetarian animals from their carnivorous predators.[15] Nothing could be more contrary to the ethics of the biotic community than this suggestion. Not only would the (humane) eradication of predators destroy the community, it would destroy the species which are the intended beneficiaries of this misplaced morality. Many prey species depend upon predators to optimize their populations. And, at a deeper level, we must remember that the alertness, speed, grace, and all the other qualities we most admire in herbivorous animals—all the qualities, indeed, which make them subjects-of-a-life and thus worthy of moral consideration and/or rights—were evolved in direct response to their carnivorous symbionts.[16]

The Humean biosocial moral theory differently applied to larger-than-human communities by Midgley and Leopold has, unlike the more familiar approach of generalizing egoism, historically provided for a holistic as well as an individualistic moral orientation. We care, in other words, for our communities per se, over and above their individual members—for our families per se, for our country, and for mankind. As Midgley might say, *they* "matter" to us as well. Hence, according to Hume," we must renounce the theory which accounts for every moral sentiment by the principle of self-love. We must adopt a more *publick affection* and allow that the interests of society are not, *even on their own account,* entirely indifferent to us."[17]

Darwin's holism is even more pronounced:

> We have now seen that actions are regarded by savages, and were probably so regarded by primeval man, as good or bad, solely as they obviously affect the welfare of the tribe—not that of the species, nor that of the individual member of the tribe. This conclusion agrees well with the belief that the so-called moral sense is aboriginally derived from social instincts, for both relate exclusively to the community.[18]

And the holistic dimension of Aldo Leopold's land ethic all but overwhelms the individualistic. Leopold provides only "respect" for individual members of the biotic community, but "biotic rights" for species and, in the last analysis, "the integrity, beauty, and stability of the biotic community" is the measure of right and wrong actions affecting the environment.

The hyperholism of the land ethic is also itself a function of an ecological description of the biotic community. But since the biosocial moral paradigm provides for various coexisting, cooperating, and competing ethics—each corresponding to our nested overlapping community entanglements—our holistic environmental obligations are not preemptive. We are still subject to all the other more particular and individually oriented duties to the members of our various more circumscribed and intimate communities. And since they are closer to home, they come first. In general, obligations to family come before obligations to more remotely related fellow humans. For example, *pace* Singer, one should not impoverish one's own children just short of starvation in order to aid actually starving people on another continent. But neither should one promote or even acquiesce in human starvation, no matter how distant, to achieve environmental goals— as some overzealous environmental activists have actually urged. Similarly, one should not allow a wild predator to help herself to one's free-range chickens, members of one's immediate mixed community. But neither should one interfere, other things being equal, in the interaction of the wild members of the biotic community.

So the acknowledgment of a holistic environmental ethic does not entail that we abrogate our familiar moral obligations to family members, to fellow citizens, to all mankind, *nor* to fellow members, individually, of the mixed community, that is, to domesticate animals. On the other hand, the outer orbits of our various moral spheres exert a gravitational tug on the inner ones. One may well deprive one's children of a trip to Disneyland or give them fewer toys at Christmas in order to aid starving people on another continent. Similarly, one may well make certain sacrifices oneself or impose certain restrictions on the animal members of one's mixed community for the sake of ecological integrity. Dairy cattle, for example, can be very destructive of certain plant communities and should be fenced out of them when other pasture or fodder is available—despite their own preferences and the economic interests of dairy farmers.

Animal liberation and environmental ethics may thus be united under a common theoretical umbrella—even though, as with all the laminated layers of our social-ethical accretions, they may occasionally come into conflict. But since they may be embraced by a common theoretical structure, we are provided a means, in principle, to assign priorities and relative weights and thus to resolve such conflicts in a systematic way.

Notes

1. J. Baird Callicott, "Animal Liberation: A Triangular Affair," *Environmental Ethics* 2 (1980): 311-38. Chapter 2, this volume.

2. Mary Anne Warren, "The Rights of the Nonhuman World" in Robert Elliot and Arran Gare, *Environmental Philosophy: A Collection of Readings* (University Park: The Pennsylvania State University Press, 1983), pp. 109-31.

3. Ibid., pp. 130-31.

4. Ibid., p. 131.

5. Tom Regan, *The Case for Animal Rights* (Berkeley: University of California Press, 1983), pp. 362-63. For a discussion see my review in *Environmental Ethics* 7 (1985): 365-72.

6. Mark Sagoff, "Animal Liberation and Environmental Ethics: Bad Marriage, Quick Divorce," *Osgoode Hall Law Journal* 22 (1984): 306.

7. Mary Midgley, *Animals and Why They Matter* (Athens: University of Georgia Press, 1983), p. 112.

8. Ibid., pp. 130, 131.

9. Peter Singer, *Animal Liberation: A New Ethics for Our Treatment of Animals* (New York: Avon Books, 1977), pp. xi-xiii. Sympathy has recently been defended as an appropriate foundation for animal welfare ethics by John A. Fischer, "Taking Sympathy Seriously," *Environmental Ethics* 9 (1987): 197-215.

10. Kenneth Goodpaster, "From Egoism to Environmentalism" in K. Goodpaster and K. Sayre, eds., *Ethics and Problems of the 21st Century* (Notre Dame: Notre Dame University Press, 1979), 21-35.

11. David Hume, *A Treatise of Human Nature* (Oxford: The Clarendon Press, 1969), p. 487.

12. My most comprehensive statement to date is "The Conceptual Foundations of the Land Ethic," in J. Barid Callicott, ed., *Companion to A Sand County Almanac: Interpretive and Critical Essays* (Madison: University of Wisconsin Press, 1987), 186-217.

13. Peter Singer, *The Expanding Circle: Ethics and Sociobiology* (New York: Farrar, Straus, and Giroux, 1982).

14. Aldo Leopold, *A Sand County Almanac* (New York: Oxford University Press, 1949), p. 216.

15. Peter Singer toys with this idea in *Animal Liberation:* "It must be

admitted that the existence of carnivorous animals does pose one problem for the ethics of Animal Liberation, and that is whether we should do anything about it. Assuming that humans could eliminate carnivorous species from the earth, and that the total amount of suffering among animals in the world were thereby reduced, should we do it?" (p. 238). Steve Sapontzis in "Predation," *Ethics and Animals* 5 (1984) concludes that "where we can prevent predation without occasioning as much or more suffering than we would prevent, we are obligated to do so by the principle that we are obligated to alleviate avoidable animal suffering" (p. 36). I argue in "The Search for an Environmental Ethic," in Tom Regan, ed. *Matters of Life and Death,* 2nd Edition (New York: Random House, 1986), pp. 381-423, that both Singerian animal liberation and Reganic animal rights imply the ecological nightmare of a policy of predator extermination.

16. See Holmes Rolson III, "Beauty and the Beast: Aesthetic Experience of Wildlife" in D. J. Decker and G. R. Goff, eds., *Valuing Wildlife: Economic and Social Perspectives* (Boulder: Westview Press, 1987), pp. 187-96.

17. David Hume, *An Enquiry Concerning the Principles of Morals* (Oxford: The Clarendon Press, 1777), p. 219, emphasis added.

18. Charles Darwin, *The Descent of Man and Selection in Relation to Sex* (New York: J. A. Hill and Company, 1904), p. 120.

Index

Abbey, Edward, 50, 66
ACLU, 26
Aesthetics, 155, 159-160, 167-169, 235, 236
Ageism, 121
American Association for the Advancement of Science, 182
Animal liberation, ix-xv, 14-24, 28, 37-40, 46, 47-59, 61, 63, 79, 118-119, 143-144, 151-152, 174, 178-179, 186-196, 185-206, 249-259; animal rights and, xii-xv, 61, 63, 79, 118-119, 151-152, 174, 186-196, 201-206, 251; blacks and, 17-19, 21-24, 28; Darwinism and, 46; deontological, 256; domesticity and, xx-xxi, xxiv, 52-59; emotion and, 23; environmental ethics and, ix-xxiv, 37-40, 151-152, 249-259; experimentation and, x, 21-22, 47; extraterrestrial life and, xviii-xix, 143-144, 177; farming and, x, 22, 39, 47; history of, 151-152; holism and, 47-52; the land ethic and, ix-xxiv, 37-40, 42-44, 49, 50, 52, 54, 55, 82, 142-143, 151-152, 174, 177, 186, 244, 245; marginal persons and, xiv, 63-64; slavery and, 53-54, 256; speciesism and, 20-21, 38,

41, 62, 63, 82, 121-135, 224-225; suffering and, x, xix, 1, 13-24, 34, 41, 42, 45, 58, 79-81, 82-84, 90, 93, 144, 152-153, 157, 180, 187-191, 256; sympathy and, xx-xxi, 227-228, 243, 245; tyranny and, x, 22-23; utilitarian, xi, 256; vegetarianism and, 23-24, 39, 57-59, 62, 79-81, 82, 199-200; women and, 15-19, 28, 38
Animals: anthropomorphism and, 214-215, 239, 243, 245, 248; behaviorism and, 212-215, 222, 252; children and, 218-221, 223; domestic, xx, xxiv, 52-59, 214-217; as human artifacts, 52, 54, 58-59, 228; humans and, 6-9, 15, 133-135, 211, 243, 245-246; imprinting and, 129, 217; Kantian dichotomy and, 211; machines and, 12-13, 25, 58-59, 120, 211-212; mixed community and, xx-xxi, 211-225, 252-259; natural bonds and, 125-281, 132-133; neoteny and, 219-221; personhood and, 24-28, 38, 85, 87-89, 213, 216; as pets, 215, 256; savagery and, 222-225; slavery and, 53-54, 213, 256; species barrier and, 211-225, 252-253; suffering and, x, xix, 13-24, 34, 41, 42, 45,

263

the organic analogy and, 45–47,
65–66; pain and, 55–56, 68, 98,
152, 159, 180; rights and the, 39,
54, 59, 87, 185, 201–206; sympathy
and, 227–228; 236–237, 244, 245,
246; vegetarianism and, 57
Langerak, Edward A., 209
Lascars, 124
Leopold, Aldo, xiii, xv, xvi, xxi, xxv,
9, 34, 37, 38, 39, 40, 43, 46, 49, 51,
52, 54, 57, 58, 61, 62, 65, 67, 69,
82, 86, 94, 141–142, 149, 159, 181,
185, 186, 201, 206, 209, 244, 254,
257, 258
Levin, Michael E., 63
Lewis, 153, 154–155
Lewis, C. S., 130
Lilly, John C., 208
Linnaeus, 159
Linzey, Andrew, 63
Lions, 129, 233, 235, 242
Liverpool Philosophical Society, 155
Locke, John, 30, 35, 43
Loizos, Caroline, 215
Long expedition, 156
Lorenz, Konrad, 136
Lynx, 43

McCloskey, H. J., 63, 93, 147, 194, 208
Macklin, Ruth, 76, 92
Malebranche, Nicolas, 12
Mallards, 50
Mammals, x, 31, 200
Manwell, Lisa, 155
Marc, Franc, 227
Marshall, Thurgood, 26
Martin, John N., 74, 92
Masai, 134
Mathematical sense, 8
Mau-Mau movement, 134
Maximilian of New-Wied, Prince,
157, 179
Mead, Margaret, 208–209
Mech, L. David, 92
Midgley, Mary, xviii, xix, xx, xxi,
xxvi, 121–136, 211–225, 239, 248,

252–253, 254, 255, 256, 257, 258,
260
Mill, John Stuart, 41, 51, 55, 186
Miller, Henry, 26
Mineral King Valley, 25, 28, 76, 86,
88, 94
Misanthropy, 49–50
Missouri River, 154–157
Mixed community, xx–xxi, 211–225,
254–259
Mollusks, 200
Monkeys, 111
Montaigne, 234
Moore, G. E., 43
Moral agents, 1–4, 9, 11–12, 22, 23,
26, 29, 32, 41, 45, 97, 99, 104,
112–113, 194; the duty of self-
preservation and, 45
Moral attitudes (*see* Respect for
Nature)
Moral characteristics: autonomy,
105, 111, 194–198; belief and, 233,
241–243; desires, 32, 233; dignity,
105; deliberation, 112; dispositions, 101; freedom to act, 2–4,
5–6, 16, 32, 112; judgment, 112;
having interests, 6, 11–12, 15, 16,
18, 28, 37, 40, 45, 77–78, 81, 82,
84–89, 98, 110, 119; individuality,
1, 26, 45, 77–80, 84, 86–89,
109–110, 152; intention, 2–4, 6, 9,
16, 32, 242; intelligence, 19, 32,
127, 187, 221–222; linguistic abilities, 40, 240–242; loyalty, 132;
moral agents and, 2–3, 4, 20, 23,
26, 29, 32, 41, 45, 104, 112–113,
194–195; moral entities and, 2–3,
4, 32, 33; natural characteristics
versus, 9, 29; physical capability,
3–4, 16, 32; practical reason, 112;
rationality, 19, 32, 41; respect for
nature, 95–119; sentience, 13–24,
31, 32, 41, 63, 82, 91, 98, 144,
187–191, 198, 201, 211; skin color,
18; self-awareness, 19, 20, 40, 196;
self-consciousness, xv, 2–4, 9, 16,

270 *Index*

16, 28, 29, 33, 195
Redwoods, 98
Religious feeling, 5
Regan, Tom, ix, x, xi, xiv, xv, xvii,
xxiv, 61, 62, 63, 68, 149, 187, 206,
207, 208, 209, 251, 253, 260
Reindeer, 211, 213
Reptiles, 31
Respect for nature, xvii–xviii,
95–119; 125; ascribing, 103; belief
and, 103–104, 118; biocentric outlook and, 104–106, 111, 117,
118–119; Cartesian dualism and,
115–116; disinterest and,
100–102; dispositions and,
101–102; ecological outlook and,
115–116; egalitarian outlook and,
113–114; as an end, 101–102;
feelings and, 101; Great Chain of
Being and, 115–117; Greek humanism and, 115–116; human
dignity, 105; human superiority
and, 111–118, 120, 196; individual
organisms and, 97, 109–110, 118;
inherent value and, x, xvii–xviii,
inherent worth and, xvii, 95,
97–100, 102, 103, 113, 114, 118,
120; interests and, 100, 183; intrinsic value and, 99, 102, 113;
Judeo-Christian outlook and,
115–116; Kant and, 105; legal
rights and, 119; love and, 101;
merit and, 112–114, 117, 118, 120;
moral consideration and, 99, 102;
rights and, 118–119; rule of duty
and, 102, 104; species impartiality
and, 118; standards of character
and, 104; teleology and, 105,
109–110, 118; as ultimate commitment, 100; as an ultimate moral
attitude, 100, 104, 119; universal
law and, 101
Rights (*see also* Good and Value):
abortion and, 208; animal, 12–13,
13–24, 32, 127, 143–145, 151–152,
159, 185–206, 249; animal liberation and, xii–xv, 61, 63, 79,
118–119, 151–152, 185–206; art
objects and, 172; assigned, 8,
12–13, 24, 26, 34, 92, 182–183,
197–198; autonomy and, 194–196;
basic, 1, 190, 208, 209; biotic, xiii,
xv, 39, 258; of blacks, 17, 18, 19,
28; of children, 196–198; climax
state and, 10–11; contractual
argument for, 24–28; of corporations, 24, 26, 86–87; deontological,
xvi, 78; desires and, 192, duties
and, 1–6, 7; divinely ordained, 6,
7; of dogs 15–16; dynamic equilibrium and, 10–11; ecological argument for, 9–12, 27; of ecosystems,
xii, 9–12, 89, 160; emotion and,
xxii, 5, 23; of environmental collectives, 87–89; to equality, 38,
195–196; to exist, 9–12, 85; extrinsic, 7, 8; fairness and, 85; of
foetuses, 208; of forests, 93; to
freedom, 191–192; human, 20, 24,
26–27, 85, 87–88, 96, 114, 127,
146, 191–198, 249; identical, 201;
individuals and, 1, 26, 45, 77–82,
84–85, 86–89, 93, 109–110,
118–119, 152, 201, 205, 251; of
infants, 20, 196–198, 208; inherent
worth and, x, xvii, 95–119; interests and, xii, 6, 11–12, 15, 16, 18,
28, 37, 40, 45, 77–80, 81–82, 83,
84–89, 110, 119, 183, 194, 198,
204–205; intrinsic, xv, xix–xx, 7,
13, 17, 22, 64, 182–183; intrinsic
possession of, 2, 6, 8; intrinsic
value and, xix–xx, 182–183,
202–206; the land ethic and, xiii,
xv, xvi, 39, 54, 59, 87, 185, 201–206;
legal, xii, 6–8, 24–28, 62, 76, 85,
87–88, 119, 153, 186, 194; of legal
persons, 24–28, 85; to liberty, 6,
38, 191, 195, 208; to life, 1, 6, 13,
20, 34, 39, 192–193, 195, 198, 199,
208; of mammals, x, 81; medicine
and, 76; men's, 16; mere existence

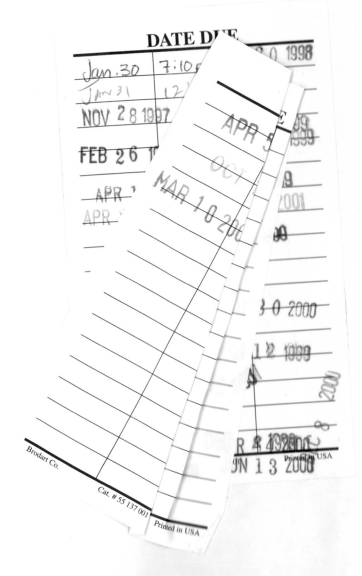

DATE DUE

Jan. 30	7:10
Jan 31	12
NOV 2 8 1997	
FEB 2 6 1	
APR	
APR	

3 0 1998

APR 5 1999

OCT 9

MAR 1 0 2001

3 0 2000

1 2 1999

2000

JN 1 3 2000

MAR 1 0 200

APR